THE
WORLD
OF
ISAAC
NEWTON

Above: 'Worthies of Britain' (*Sir Isaac Newton; Edmond Halley; Nicholas Saunderson; John Flamsteed*), by John Bowles (died 1784), given to the National Portrait Gallery, London in 1916.

Half title page: Sir Isaac Newton in his role as President of the Royal Society. Wood engraving by J. Quartley after (J.M.L.R.), 1883.

THE
WORLD
OF
ISAAC
NEWTON

TONI MOUNT

AMBERLEY

This book is for Isaac Albert.
A small boy with a great name to live up to.

First published 2020

Amberley Publishing
The Hill, Stroud
Gloucestershire, GL5 4EP

www.amberley-books.com

Copyright © Toni Mount, 2020

The right of Toni Mount to be identified as
the Author of this work has been asserted in
accordance with the Copyright, Designs and
Patents Act 1988.

ISBN 978 1 4456 8318 8 (hardback)
ISBN 978 1 4456 8319 5 (ebook)

British Library Cataloguing in Publication Data.
A catalogue record for this book is available
from the British Library.

Typesetting by Aura Technology and Software
Services, India. Printed in the UK.

CONTENTS

Contents

ACKNOWLEDGEMENTS

I owe especial thanks to Sandy Paul, Sub-Librarian at the Wren Library, Trinity College, Cambridge, for permitting my free use of any of their images, in exchange for a copy of this book. I hope they are not disappointed.

Also to Lincolnshire Archives who hunted down the will of Isaac Newton senior for me, the document having been wrongly filed for so long. It is now available to view upon request.

To Su Orrey at King's School, Grantham, for the fascinating personal guided tour and photo opportunities, which were inspiring.

A particularly big 'thank you' is owed to the Church Warden of St John the Baptist's Church at Colsterworth, Lincolnshire, Simon Jowitt, for his insightful knowledge of all things Newtonian concerning the church and the village.

To Rob Cottrell for the extra info on Edmund Halley.

To Glenn Mount for being my chauffeur, photographer, IT consultant and number one supporter.

Thank you everyone.

INTRODUCTION

This book, *The World of Isaac Newton,* is not intended as an academic science treatise but as a popular work covering a number of disciplines, including biography, political and social history, as well as science and mathematics. Isaac Newton is, obviously, famous for his experiments with light, gravity and falling apples but the period of history into which he was born was turbulent, vibrant and on the cusp of industrialisation. These were exciting and frightening times. Newton may have preferred the quiet life of a Cambridge scholar for many years but the world beyond affected every aspect of his life.

In the century before Newton's birth, the world was already moving away from the old medieval ideas. The New World of the Americas had been discovered, rewriting the ancient geographies of the Greeks and Romans, which had served well enough for a thousand years. Exploring this expanded globe required new methods of navigation, maps and magnetic compasses, all of which had to be revised and made more accurate and sophisticated. Advances in mathematics introduced new conventions, such as the plus, minus and equals symbols, simplifying the writing of equations. Newton would reap the benefits and go on to expand the entire field of calculation.

Born at the outbreak of the English Civil War, childbirth was a most dangerous time for both mother and baby in an age before hygiene was considered necessary and female anatomy was little understood. No wonder the underweight infant Isaac was not expected to survive but, against the odds, he did. Newton's childhood was spent under a Puritan regime. During his time at Grantham Grammar School he lodged with William Clarke, a strict Puritan and a skilled apothecary. Clarke's influence affected Newton greatly for the rest of his days. The Puritan regime came to an end, replaced by a pleasure-loving monarchy but Newton maintained a puritanical lifestyle and an interest in laboratory experimentation, inspired by Clarke, until the end of his life. The school curriculum, which at first bored Newton and then drove him to improve his methods of study, will be considered in this book, as will many aspects of religion – a matter of daily significance in the period we are discussing.

This book will set Newton in the world of his philosophical acquaintances, peers and, in particular, his fellows at the Royal Society, a group which became so significant in his life. He acquired powerful friends and patrons but through his tendency to take offence and to offend others, he had enemies too, who would thwart his efforts if they could. Edmund Halley proved to be a good friend and the Earl of Halifax a fine patron. Robert Hooke became a life-long opponent and John Flamsteed's friendship turned to enmity.

There were foreign influences as well, not only in scientific circles but in methods of travel, fashion and food. The Dutch figure significantly as participants in the philosophical world, in wars as sea, as monarchs and even as the originators of that eighteenth-century curse – gin. A new coffeehouse culture was developing, new foodstuffs becoming popular: Newton may not have cared for either but his associates certainly did.

That English preoccupation, the weather, affected everyone and the advent of the 'Little Ice Age' made winter a particularly difficult time. Frost Fairs were set up on the frozen River Thames to enliven the gloom of long winters. Health issues were on the agenda for rich and poor alike, from plague to smallpox, from over-enthusiastic physicians to experimental self-medication. The royal family suffered from both ill-health and the misadministration of medicine as much as any of their subjects. Health problems also played a part in the downfall of the Stuart dynasty, bringing the Hanoverian kings to the throne of Great Britain. Just a few people, such as Samuel Pepys, could celebrate the successes of surgery.

As well as the everyday things of life in the period, we shall consider the trials and tribulations of the unfortunate dynasty of Stuart kings and queens, since their personalities influenced history and, here again, religion was key, inspiring war and witch-hunts, rebellion and abdication.

During Newton's life at Cambridge, the Trinity College Library was rebuilt to a design by Christopher Wren, making more books available for study. The Lucasian professorship was set up, Newton's mentor and namesake, Isaac Barrow, being the first appointee to the post.

In his later years, his work at the Royal Mint became pivotal for Newton, taking him from the quiet life of Cambridge and into the seamier side of London: the world of counterfeiters and crooks. His own financial dealings were not always as successful as might be expected of a genius with figures and make interesting reading. Meanwhile, his knowledge of alchemy and his organisational skills enabled him to undertake the vast project of re-minting all the coins of the realm and, in this, he was successful.

His other preoccupation was the study of ancient religions and the origins of Christianity: a topic that could have landed him in deep trouble with the Church authorities, had they known of his unorthodox beliefs. Secrecy was always Newton's watchword.

This book will conclude by considering the continuing advances being made and explored in our own time as a result of Newton's scientific work. As I write (July 2019), the fiftieth anniversary of the first Moon landing is being celebrated, a timely reminder that without Newtonian mathematics, such adventures would not be possible. Space exploration, micro-surgery and the world of Artificial Intelligence: all these and far more are derived from Newton's legacy, the wonders of physics and mathematics that he strived to consolidate in a coherent, measurable form. How much we owe to one man's thought processes is more than he could ever have imagined.

Chapter 1

1540–1640: LIFE AND SCIENCE BEFORE NEWTON

The century before Isaac Newton's birth in 1642 was a dramatic one. In the 1540s, England's Reformation changed the religious life of the community beyond recognition. Henry VIII had broken the kingdom's allegiance to the Church of Rome, severing the last vestige of Catholic papal authority from the new Protestant Church of England in 1536. Yet the break was just the beginning. The real Reformation required a swathe of new ideas to be shared and discussed, changes made to Church liturgy, ceremony and worship. Clerics had difficulty agreeing among themselves precisely what changes should be implemented and, therefore, the new Church of England was never going to be an homogenous entity, as the Roman Catholic Church was and remained. This fact proved to have terrible consequences in Newton's early life.

However, this opening up of new ideas in religion led to a widening of other horizons – quite literally. No longer shackled to medieval Catholic traditions of learning, studying Aristotle, Ptolemy, Galen and other Classical thinkers, the Tudors dared to contemplate the possibilities of things existing which were previously unknown to the ancients. The discovery and exploration of the Americas, a void on the world map of the Greeks and Romans, had revealed new species of fauna and flora, unimagined landscapes and unique indigenous peoples. It was swiftly becoming apparent that Classical texts were inadequate for sixteenth-century scholars. Novel methods of learning were required and came to include the radical innovation of experimentation.

To the Tudors and Stuarts, 'science' was simply another word for 'knowledge'. It could apply to astronomy or medicine but it made equal sense to refer to the science of music or military tactics. Whatever the case, no Tudor scholar would have called himself a 'scientist' since this word was first coined by a Cambridge professor, William Whewell, in 1834 and even then it took a while to catch on. A Tudor gentleman, studying the heavens or the plants in his garden or any aspect of Nature would have described himself as a 'natural philosopher', as did others with similar interests well into the nineteenth century. Isaac Newton was a natural philosopher and it is, perhaps, a more appropriate description of him, since not all aspects of his studies could qualify for our modern definition of 'science'.

These days, it often seems that modern science and religion are mutually exclusive and belief in one makes it difficult to believe the other. However, in the sixteenth and seventeenth centuries, natural philosophy was seen as a supporter of theology, the term used was 'the handmaid of religion'. For centuries, mankind had two 'books' of knowledge to explain the universe and his place in it. One was the Bible, in which God had dictated all the necessary information in words. The other was Nature, God's own creation in which practical examples of all that theological information could be found. A man who studied both 'books' and interpreted them correctly would eventually understand God's ultimate purpose for mankind and the secrets of the universe. It seems we still have a long way to go on both but Isaac Newton assiduously studied those 'books' in his quest for understanding.

So, how would Newton's forebears have envisioned their world? Not flat, for a start. The Flat Earth Society was founded in 1956 by Samuel Shenton of Dover, Kent, in England. His idea had already been disproved by photographs taken from 100 miles above the Earth in 1947, showing the curve of the planet from every angle, proving it must be a sphere. The iconic blue planet photograph, taken from Apollo 17 in 1972, left no doubt for even the most hard-line flat-earthers.[1] Christopher Columbus knew the world was round, else he would never have dared think about reaching China and the East Indies by sailing west – seemingly, in the wrong direction – in 1492. Unfortunately for the intrepid explorer, he did not know the American continent would bar his passage. Landlubbers might have doubted it was possible but sailors had seen for themselves the curve of the horizon that was visible at sea: a sure clue that the Earth was shaped like a ball, not a dinner plate.

Besides, God had described it so in the Bible. In *Isaiah* 40:22, the 'circle of the earth' is mentioned.[2] Admittedly, a circle can be flat but scholars of ancient Hebrew in the sixteenth century studied the Old Testament in its original language, and here the word *khûg* was used – the Hebrew word for 'sphere'. We know that scholars understood this because their Latin translations use words such as *sphaera* and *globus*.[3] They also knew from reading the *Book of Job* 26:7 that God 'hangs the Earth on nothing'. This must have been a difficult concept, to imagine a free-floating, unsupported world, but theologians and natural philosophers seem to have accepted such a sophisticated idea.

Christopher Columbus was familiar with previous thoughts on world geography from Claudius Ptolemy's maps drawn *c.*150 AD. These were made for the benefit of the Roman Empire and apart from showing Asia far larger than it is, they were surprisingly accurate for Europe, North Africa and the Middle East. Ptolemy's *Geographia* had been lost for centuries but came to light for western scholars around the year 1400 and was assumed to be *the* infallible source of knowledge about the world. It was soon a bestseller, running to more than forty editions within a century.[4] It was probably the apparent great expanse of Asia in Ptolemy's maps that led Columbus to think the Far East might be more easily reached by sailing west.

However, early in the fifteenth century, explorers were already proving Ptolemy's information wrong. For example, the classical geographer had stated that life was impossible close to the equator because the heat of the sun there would cause men's blood to boil. Yet the Portuguese navigator, Bartholomew Diaz, had crossed the equator on the West African coast and sailed around the southern point of Africa in 1488. He not only survived to tell of it but reported that native populations thrived there.

When Columbus landed on the Caribbean island of San Salvador in the Bahamas, it is no wonder he called the locals 'Indians', thinking he had somehow missed Japan and China, so this must be India, according to Ptolemy's map. But, of course, the Roman cartographer had no idea that the continent of America existed – his work was far from infallible after all. Clearly, the maps would have to be redrawn and Martin Waldseemüller constructed one of the first to include the east coast of America in 1507.[5]

A few years later, Gerard Mercator (1512–94), a Flemish-born German working in the Netherlands, became famous for his vast knowledge of geography, his detailed atlases, globes and navigational maps for mariners – all produced without ever leaving home. Instead, he used his huge library of over 1,000 books and corresponded in six different languages with merchants, scholars and seamen who travelled across the world. In 1541, he produced a marvellous globe, showing the world as it was then known, with quite a degree of detail for the eastern coast of America but the western coast remained vague, guesswork for the most part.

In 1547, the young English scholar, John Dee, visited Mercator. They got along well together, sharing their fascination for maps and instruments and remained fervent correspondents for decades to come, until Mercator's death. Dee spent time with Mercator during his three years of study at Louvain University and took assorted maps, globes and astronomical instruments back to England when he left. This was not a one-way trade: in return, Dee sent Mercator copies of the latest English texts on all sorts of subjects that might prove of interest, and most importantly any new geographical knowledge discovered as a result of English exploration around the world. Incidentally, it was Dee who rewrote the works of Euclid to make them more accessible. Dee also linked the study of mathematics to music, painting and even medicine, believing everything could be explained in numerical equations – an idea Newton would take to heart.

Perhaps the most significant contribution to the changing concept of the world would have been Sir Francis Drake's logbook and reports of his circumnavigation of the globe in 1577–80. However, despite proving, once and for all, that the Earth was a sphere, for political reasons Drake said very little about his voyage that was made public. This was mainly because he had been harassing Spanish territory in the New World and waylaying their treasure-laden galleons at sea – so the less said about that, the better. Also, it is now believed that Drake explored the Pacific coast of America, perhaps as far north as Alaska, and the English had no intention of revealing their knowledge and discovery of these places to others, especially not the Spaniards who were the enemy at the time.

Interestingly, in the seventeenth century, when the English began to colonise the eastern seaboard of North America, they actually laid claim to the entire expanse of the continent, from 'sea to shining sea', as they put it. This was done on the grounds that Drake had landed in California, most likely in what became San Francisco Bay, on 15 June 1579, naming the land *Nova Albion*, (New England in Latin and predating New England on the eastern seaboard of North America) claiming it in the name of Queen Elizabeth and planting the English flag there.[6]

So the view of the world had expanded vastly since the medieval period, to encompass not only the southern extent of the African continent but the whole New World of the Americas. However, the situation of the world within the universe had changed as well owing to another new concept that must have been even more difficult to comprehend.

A New Universe

The Roman Catholic faith taught that the Earth was created by God and set at the centre of a universe consisting of a series of concentric crystal spheres – like the layers of an onion – purely for the benefit of mankind. Rocks, plants and animals were all servants of man. Everything either had an obvious use – domestic animals, crops and medicinal plants for example – or was believed to hold a moral lesson to be learned for the betterment of mankind. Such things as devious, poisonous snakes served as examples of immoral behaviour to be avoided by man, and biting insects, such as annoying fleas, were humbling reminders that flesh was mortal. The planets and stars served man by foretelling the future – for those trained to read them. In fact, the word 'disaster' comes from the Latin *dis astra*, meaning 'against the stars' and therefore an event not foretold.[7] Catholics also believed that whenever He wished, God could intervene in everyday life and perform miracles. Opposed to this, Protestantism declared the Age of Miracles ended long ago and that God was allowing mankind to continue on its chosen path, heading for an imminent apocalypse. Yet Protestants and Catholics did agree that studying Nature was the way to understand God's creation, as the Bible explained in Psalm 19: 'The heavens declare the glory of God and the firmament sheweth his handywork.'

With conflicting doctrines as a backdrop, a revolutionary new concept would upset the traditional view of the cosmos. Surprisingly, the radical idea that the Sun, rather than the Earth, might be at the centre of the universe, was first proposed by a Catholic theologian and astronomer, Nicolaus Copernicus (1473–1543). Copernicus had struggled with the traditional system of an Earth-centred universe, worked out by Ptolemy, convinced it was too clumsy to be a true representation of God's creation. He tried to simplify the matter and a Sun-centred universe solved some problems, though not all. He also wondered at the arrogance of man in believing himself to be at the centre of everything: 'For who would place this lamp [the Sun] of a very beautiful temple in another better place than this [at the centre].'

However, Copernicus was a cautious man and stated that his new ideas were merely 'theoretical' and, in case the pope should still take exception to them, he only gave permission for the publication of his writings as he lay on his deathbed in 1543. His book, *De revolutionibus*, was slow to have an effect and probably was not read in the backwater that was England until a few years later. But there were difficulties in believing Copernicus' ideas because, if the Sun sat still at the centre, it must be the Earth that moved. But that seemed absurd and counterintuitive. If it was true, why did not clouds and birds get left behind as the Earth moved on?

Fortunately, a good analogy was used to explain the problem: if you ride in a cart, it seems the world moves past you, but you know it is the cart that is moving. Likewise, if you toss a coin while riding in the cart, it still falls back into your hand, as it would if you were not moving. The coin does not fall behind you. This is the concept of 'inertia' but it was not explained for more than another century, when Isaac Newton worked it out. This explanation may have helped the people of Tudor England to understand how the Earth could be moving but the analogy failed on one point: you can feel the cart moving but you cannot feel the world moving beneath your feet. That still required a leap of faith.

Once the idea of a Sun-centred universe was proposed, other people began to see how it could work. Robert Recorde, a Welsh mathematician in England, read Copernicus' book and gave the theories much thought, noting his favourable conclusions in *The Castle of Knowledge*, published in 1551, agreeing that the new 'heliocentric' universe fitted the calculations more nearly and made more sense. Recorde was the first 'popular science' writer, as we would call him today. Though he knew Greek and Latin, he taught and wrote in English so anyone who was literate could understand his work. In 1542, his text book on arithmetic, *The Grounde of Artes,* first introduced the plus, minus and equals signs (+, -, =) that make the writing of equations so much quicker. In 1551, he published *The Pathway to Knowledge,* the first geometry book in English.

Returning to the analogy of riding in a cart, this could also be used to explain another of Copernicus' astounding ideas: the possibility of an infinite universe, very different from the medieval view of the cosmos. Unlike the apparent daily passage of the Sun across the sky, the other stars were termed 'fixed stars' because they kept to their constant patterns: the constellations, and maintained their positions. Yet, if the Earth was moving, surely the stars should appear to travel past it, displaying what astronomers call 'parallax'. There was only one explanation: just as a tree beside the road would quickly seem to pass by the cart, a distant hill apparently moved by far more slowly. Therefore, since the fixed stars never varied, the only answer was that they were infinitely far away, at an unimaginable distance from the Earth.

Surprisingly, as early as the thirteenth century, astronomers had calculated that the planet Saturn was seventy-three million miles away – a staggering distance to the medieval mind, though wildly inaccurate – and the stars even farther. This in an age when it was believed the universe existed for mankind's benefit alone. Incredibly, medieval philosophers had already argued that an omnipotent

God could have created as many worlds as He wanted, yet He had decided to make just one: Earth.[8] Now Copernicus' universe made the Solar System a tiny part of an endless cosmos and, as he wrote: 'How astonishing if, within the space of twenty-four hours, the vast universe should rotate, rather than its least point [the Earth]!'

By 1580, a Frenchman, Michel de Montaigne, was ridiculing a human-centred cosmos as laughable in that 'a wretched creature that cannot master himself should call himself master and emperor of a universe'. But not everyone agreed with Copernicus. An English astronomer, Thomas Blunderville, writing in 1594, fifty years after Copernicus published his book, referred to the heliocentric view of the universe, 'that the Earth turneth and that the Sun standeth still' as a 'false supposition'.[9] Another Englishman, Thomas Digges, who was a pupil of John Dee and a keen astronomer, had other opinions. When he read Copernicus' *De revolutionibus*, Digges had no doubts that the heliocentric version was correct and he translated the important chapters into English 'so that Englishmen might not be deprived of so noble a theory'. In his book, *A Prognostication Everlasting* (1576), he included a large fold-out diagram with the translation, showing the Earth and other planets orbiting the Sun with the 'fixed stars' scattered to infinity.

It was fortunate for Digges that he lived in Protestant Tudor England since the Italian Giordano Bruno was condemned by the Catholic Church and burned at the stake in Rome in 1600 for agreeing with Copernicus.[10] Students would have to tread warily if they discussed these revolutionary ideas in parts of Europe where the Catholic Church remained powerful. However, in some countries, Denmark for example, such ideas were wholeheartedly encouraged by the authorities and new inventions would add support to Copernicus' theories.

In early November 1572, a new star appeared in the sky. This was something that stunned everyone since it was believed that whereas all things below the Moon changed continuously, everything beyond the Moon was supposedly perfect, constant and unchanging. The creation of a new star would imply that God the Creator was not happy with the heavens as He had made them – impossible! Today, we know this new star was a supernova, an exploding star, but at the time it was an inexplicable phenomenon and caused great concern. Astronomers across Europe wondered if it was a comet: something they understood, but a Danish astronomer, Tycho Brahe, realised this was different and wrote:

> I conclude that this star is not some kind of comet or fiery meteor, but that it is a star shining in the firmament itself – one that has never previously been seen before our time, in any age since the beginning of the world.[11]

Even more disturbing, the star disappeared a few months later, suggesting God had changed His mind again. How could that be?

Then, in 1577, a true comet – known then as the 'Great Comet' – suddenly appeared in the sky. Tycho was fascinated and made comparisons with the 'new star' of a few years earlier, making observations and detailed measurements of both and corresponding with other astronomers across Europe to compare notes. Frederick II, King of Denmark, was impressed with Tycho's work and made him an offer he could not refuse: his own island of Hven, in the channel between Denmark and Sweden, on which to build an observatory to study the heavens and carry out any other scientific investigations undisturbed. Within months, Tycho's castle of Uraniborg (the 'heavenly castle') was taking shape. With his enthusiastic young disciples, he observed the universe, inventing better instruments to aid both astronomers and map-makers, using the printing press to spread information and ideas far and wide. Uraniborg became famous, attracting celebrity visitors. The King of Denmark was not the only royal to visit: King James VI of Scots (later James I of England) went to see Tycho and discuss the science of the day.

Thomas Digges (*c.*1546–95), mentioned above, was the epitome of a Tudor gentleman-philosopher and deserves to be more famous than he is. He was probably born at Wootton in Kent, 7 miles from Dover. His father, Leonard Digges was a wealthy landowner but had become involved in Sir Thomas Wyatt's rebellion against Queen Mary Tudor in 1554. He was fortunate not to be tried for treason so kept a low profile after that, pursuing his hobby of compiling and writing almanacs. An almanac is an annual publication that contains information about the forthcoming year: weather predictions, the best dates for planting crops, sunrise and sunset times, the Moon's phases, dates of eclipses and ocean tide timetables. Leonard preferred to make his own calculations, especially those concerning astronomical data.

Young Thomas was taught mathematics and how to observe the stars by his father.[12] In later years, Thomas wrote that in the 1550s his father was using a 'perspective tube' that could reveal minute details over great distances. Surely, this must have been some kind of telescope? Could the Diggeses, father and son, have used such an instrument to better observe the stars? Perhaps an Englishman invented the telescope half a century before Galileo thought of turning his 'device for seeing things afar off' towards the night sky. There is further evidence that Digges had used 'a kind of looking glass' to 'see things of a marvellous bigness' since William Bourne – co-inventor of the submarine with Cornelius Drebbel – wrote to William Cecil, Queen Elizabeth's secretary, about it. John Dee suggested the military uses that such a device might have decades before Galileo 'marketed' the telescope, persuading the Doge of Venice it would enable him to see his enemies approaching by sea before they could see Venice.[13]

Thomas Digges was also intrigued by maps and charts so may have possessed a printed copy of the *Atlas of the Principal Cities of the World* that was published in 1588. In the sixteenth century, further exploration of the world was rewriting the ideas of global geography: Sir Francis Drake's claiming of America's West Coast in the name of Queen Elizabeth and the first tentative efforts at colonising Virginia on the East Coast. Back in England, few would have known of these ventures into uncharted lands if not for the work of Richard Hakluyt (c.1552–1616), a man from a Herefordshire family, born possibly in London, and sometimes referred to as 'the father of modern geography'.[14]

A New Geography

His father died when Richard was just five and his mother and all the children were cared for by a cousin – also named Richard Hakluyt. The cousin was a lawyer with close connections to London merchants at the forefront of trading ventures, as well as explorers and map-makers of the day. These acquaintances, as well as his cousin's geography lessons, inspired the younger Richard. One lesson in particular ended with a biblical reference: 'They that go down to the sea in ships, that do business in great waters; These see the works of the Lord, and his wonders in the deep.'[15] These were words that the younger Richard never forgot. The lad attended Westminster School, a forward-looking educational institution in Tudor times, and then went to Oxford University, gaining his Master's Degree in 1577. By 1580, he was giving public lectures on geography, using the old, out-dated maps and globes as visual aids and comparing them to the latest, revised versions, showing new lands and recent discoveries.

Hakluyt made a point of getting to know some of England's most daring sea captains and discussing their previous adventures and forthcoming plans for exploration. During Queen Elizabeth's reign, trade with the Far East was the ambition of any merchant who hoped to get rich. Commodities like spices and silks could be sold in Europe and make a fortune but the Portuguese had a monopoly on sailing around Africa while the Spaniards dominated South America. The English were latecomers to such trading ventures and desperate to find a short cut to the Orient, avoiding any Portuguese or Spanish interference either by sailing to the north of Russia or to the north of Canada. These routes – known as the North-East and North-West Passages – had not yet been investigated, mainly because both were ice-locked for much of the year. In fact, no one was certain there were ways through either route, even in high summer, but that did not deter intrepid explorers such as Sir Hugh Willoughby (1495–1554) and Richard Chancellor (*c.*1521–56).

Willoughby and Chancellor's combined expedition to Lapland and Northern Russia in 1553 led to a royal charter being granted to the Muscovy Trading Company in 1555. Willoughby, Chancellor and Sebastian Cabot, another adventurer, were named as having founded the company in 1551. Sadly, Willoughby had already perished during the first Russian voyage but Chancellor made another voyage to Russia and when Tsar Ivan the Terrible heard of the Englishman's arrival, Chancellor was summoned to the tsar's court. As a result, the first Russian ambassador to London met Queen Elizabeth on behalf of Tsar Ivan. However, Chancellor had died during the voyage home. So neither of these two intrepid captains lived to enjoy the fame they deserved and their attempts to find that elusive North-East Passage were unsuccessful.

Despite this, Richard Hakluyt wrote detailed accounts of their expeditions in his vast work: *The Principal Navigations, Voyages, Traffiques and Discoveries of The English Nation, made by Sea or over Land to the most remote and farthest distant Quarters of the Earth at any time within the compass of these 1500 yeeres: Devided into three severall parts, according to the positions of the Regions wherunto they were directed.*[16]

This three-volume book – its title usually abbreviated to *The Principal Navigations* – was published in London in 1589 under licence to the Queen's printer Christopher Barker and became a Tudor bestseller, for those who could afford it. Part I dealt with the lands around the Mediterranean, the West Coast of Africa and as far south as the Cape of Good Hope. Part II covered the New World 'further than ever any Christian hitherto hath pierced', as Hakluyt tells his readers on the title page. The English adventures in 'North-Eastern Europe and Adjacent Countries: The Muscovy Company and the North-Eastern Passage' were also dealt with in Part II.

With the search for the North-East Passage getting explorers no closer to the Far East, the hunt was on for a navigable way through arctic waters north of 'the backside of Canada', as Hakluyt called it – in other words, hoping to reach the Pacific Coast as a shortcut to China. Humphrey Gilbert (c.1539–83) and Martin Frobisher (c.1535–94) both attempted it with Frobisher making three voyages in search of the North-West Passage. All their efforts failed, although a route through does exist using modern ice-breakers or submarines beneath the ice.

In Part III of his book, Hakluyt recommended that anyone who was unemployed in England should sign up to go to Virginia as a colonist and that the prisons should be emptied by sending all the inmates as well, but they would not be given a choice. The Elizabethan government did not take his advice.

As an additional section at the end of his book he added 'The last most renowned English Navigation round about the whole

Globe of the Earth', telling of Sir Francis Drake's incredible circumnavigation achieved in 1577–80. Drake had sailed in a ship barely 100 feet long manned by a crew of seventy-five. It was called *The Pelican* and sailed with four other vessels in his little fleet. Only Drake's ship returned to England after 1,020 days with just fifty-six crewmen remaining, by which time he had renamed it *The Golden Hind*. The secret objective of Drake's voyage was to intercept the valuable cargoes the Spanish were taking from the western coast of South America (the Spanish 'Main') and shipping back to Spain by crossing the narrow strip of land in Central America, known as the Isthmus of Panama, and then sailing home across the Atlantic Ocean. To carry out his objective, Drake first had to risk the perilous waters of Cape Horn to round the southern tip of South America and then sail into the Pacific. This part of the plan was incredibly successful. Drake captured 26 tons of silver, half a ton of gold and thousands of coins and jewels, brought out of Peru and Bolivia by the Spaniards. But having stolen the treasure off the coast of Peru, he dared not sail home by the same route because Spanish ships were waiting to take revenge.

Instead, Drake sailed northwards, up the West Coast of the Americas, to California and then on to present-day Vancouver in Canada. One of Queen Elizabeth's secret instructions to Drake was that he should attempt to discover that elusive North-West Passage from the western end and return to England by that route, so he sailed more than 1,000 miles north to Alaska. He could not find any way through the Canadian arctic so had to sail west instead, towards Japan. His tiny ship crossed the vast Pacific Ocean. Australia and New Zealand were yet undiscovered but Drake made landfall in the Spice Islands of Indonesia where he added tons of valuable cloves to his haul of treasures. The *Golden Hind* then voyaged south-west across the Indian Ocean and back into the Atlantic at the southern tip of Africa, via the Cape of Good Hope. The voyage had taken three years with a considerable loss of life but the queen was so delighted with her share of the plunder – enough to wipe out all England's debts – that she knighted Drake. Sir Francis also earned a nickname from the Spaniards, '*El Draco*', a play upon his surname that meant 'the Dragon'.

Drake's ability to evade the mighty Spanish galleons would again prove useful during the attempted Armada invasion of 1588. The huge galleons were cumbersome and difficult to manoeuvre but could overwhelm the much smaller English ships. Yet improved ship design meant the English could make better use of the weather in their agile little craft. It was also clear that the small vessels were just as capable as the galleons of crossing vast oceans but such intrepid endeavours also needed a better understanding of magnetism and the use of a compass to locate the magnetic north pole.

William Gilbert (1544–1603), although he often signed himself Gilberd, was born into a prosperous family in Colchester, Essex.[17] His house, called 'Tymperleys', is still there in the centre of Colchester and is open to the public. William was educated at Cambridge University, where he received a BA, MA and MD, after which he became a senior fellow. He practised as a physician in London for many years and in 1600 became president of the Royal College of Physicians and served as Queen Elizabeth's doctor.

Gilbert spent much of his income on his hobby of studying rocks, as England's first geologist. He was particularly fascinated by 'lodestones' – a rare form of the mineral magnetite (Fe_3O_4) that occurs naturally as permanent magnets.[18] They attract metallic iron and this 'magic' property was known to many ancient cultures. By the eleventh century AD, the Chinese had discovered that freely suspended, elongated lodestones would tend to hang with their long axes approximately north–south and used them as magnetic compasses. They also discovered that this magical ability could be passed on to a steel needle by stroking it with a lodestone.

Gilbert studied these stones in a more scientific manner, writing about his work and publishing his discoveries in his book *De Magnete* (About Magnets) in 1600. The book soon became the standard text on electrical and magnetic phenomena throughout Europe. In it, Gilbert discussed and disproved the folktales about lodestones – that their effect was reduced if diamonds or garlic were nearby and that they could cure headaches. He replaced such odd ideas with proper physical laws of magnetism: that the north and south poles of a magnet attract each other but like poles repel. He also distinguished between magnetism and static (known as the amber effect), inventing the word 'electricity'. He compared the magnet's polarity to the polarity of the Earth, suggesting that magnetism was the soul of the Earth, and that a perfectly spherical lodestone, aligned with the Earth's poles, would spin on its axis, just as the Earth spins, over a period of 24 hours. Gilbert was adding further weight to Copernicus's theory that the Earth revolves around the Sun. Gilbert also studied inclination and variation in the Earth's magnetic field as possible aids to mariners in finding their location at sea. His work may well have continued to assist navigators but, sadly, Gilbert died in 1603, probably of the plague. Even the queen's physician was not immune to this dread disease.

Studying the Stars

While England was concerned with exploration on a global scale, elsewhere in Europe others were making great advances on the work of Thomas Digges. Galileo Galilei (1564–1642) was born in Pisa in northern Italy, the illegitimate son of a musician and teacher Vincenzo Galilei. His father hoped he would become a physician and Galileo enrolled at the University of Pisa to study medicine but changed his mind, preferring philosophy and mathematics, leaving without gaining a degree. He was intrigued by motion: why did a pendulum swing? Why do objects roll downhill but not up? Likewise, why do things fall down? Do heavy objects fall more swiftly than lighter ones? In essence, he was studying the force of gravity, although the word was not yet used in this context.

Galileo was equally fascinated by the night sky. As he wrote in his book *The Assayer* (1623), 'Philosophy is written in this grand book, the universe, which stands continually open to our gaze.' Stargazing might well be open to all, when the weather permitted, but observing the stars and planets in any detail was impossible without some kind of optical enhancement. In 1608, a Dutch spectacle-maker, Hans Lippershey, applied to patent a device that magnified distant objects threefold. Galileo heard of this instrument, or may even have obtained one, and set about improving it and increasing its magnifying capabilities. With monetary profit in mind, Galileo demonstrated his version of the 'perspicillum', as he called it, to the Doge of Venice, pointing out how it would enable the observer's naked eye to see enemy ships afar off, allowing valuable time to prepare for defence or counter-attack, before the enemy could see him.

The first detailed drawings of the lunar surface were produced by the English astronomer Thomas Harriot (1560–1621), made with the use of a Dutch telescope early in 1609. Mountain ranges, 'seas' and craters revealed a three-dimensional heavenly body, rather than a flattened disc. The Moon was no longer the realm of gods, goddesses and ancient myths but a recognisable – if alien – landscape.

In the autumn of 1609, with his device still further improved, Galileo used it to take a look at the heavens. What he saw came as a shock but confirmed that Copernicus had been correct in thinking that the Earth was by no means at the centre of the universe. As Harriot had observed a few months before, heavenly bodies were not perfect and neither were they unchanging, as the Catholic Church insisted. The Moon was pock-marked with craters and what had been thought to be clouds marring its perfect silvery disc were topographical features as varied and irregular as any on the imperfect Earth. The Milky Way was not just a pale streak in the sky but consisted of thousands of stars.

Observing Jupiter over a number of nights provided the greatest surprise. Galileo noted up to four bright pinpoints of light close to the planet but sometimes they were not all present and their positions changed with respect to the planet and each other. Eventually, he deduced that Jupiter had not one but four moons that disappeared and reappeared as they orbited the planet. In other words, Jupiter was at the centre of their orbits, not the Earth, nor even the Sun. This was a controversial revelation and brought Galileo into conflict with the Catholic Church. His book, *The Starry Messenger,* became the Renaissance equivalent of a bestseller. James I in England received a copy and so did his eldest son, Prince Henry.[19] Within a year, Oxford academics were discussing whether the Moon might be habitable, acknowledging that it was a three-dimensional world, not just a bright light in the heavens put there by God to enable mankind to see his way at night.

Such debate was encouraged in Protestant countries but in Italy it was forbidden by the pope. *The Starry Messenger* was added to the Catholic Church's ever-expanding list of banned texts but, in general, theologians seem to have been unimpressed by Galileo's writings. Perhaps they regarded him as a mere eccentric whom no one would take seriously. However, Galileo – despite lacking any university degree – was teaching at the University in Padua, spreading his controversial ideas among his students. Other astronomers were duplicating his findings and support grew.

Then, in 1632, Galileo published a *Dialogue Concerning the Two Chief World Systems*. The systems in contention were the geocentric version of the universe, supported by the Catholic Church, and Copernicus' heliocentric one. Galileo clearly supported the latter and continued to teach heliocentricity to his students, despite having been ordered by the authority of the Holy Office not to do so as long ago as 1616. The Church was finally forced to act against him. He was tried by the Inquisition in Rome in April 1633 and threatened with physical torture. He was found guilty of heresy. Unlike Giordano Bruno in 1600, he was not condemned to burn at the stake but was kept under house arrest in Florence for the remaining nine years of his life. He died in April 1642, nine months before the birth of Isaac Newton, who would take Galileo's ideas on gravity and motion to an entirely new level.

Mechanical Systems

Towards the end of the sixteenth century, as mechanical constructions became more sophisticated, for example in the increasing accuracy of clocks, philosophers began to envisage the universe as an enormous mechanism created and set in motion by God. This became a popular metaphor for describing the workings of the heavens with stars and planets following their paths as prescribed by God from the beginning.

It was also possible to think of the human body in terms of its mechanical functions, considering it to be a 'microcosm' reflecting the great 'macrocosm' of the universe. The English physician William Harvey (1578–1657) even went so far as to describe man's body as a kingdom in miniature; the heart represented the king ruling all actions within his realm with other bodily parts performing their appropriate functions, like the king's subjects, to keep the whole running smoothly for the benefit of all.[20] Without its heart, the body could not survive. Harvey had studied medicine and anatomy at Gonville and Caius College, Cambridge, and then at Padua University in Italy. Gonville was the first English college to have a charter granting it the bodies of two executed criminals each year for the purpose of dissection. So Harvey already knew more about the construction of the human body than generations of physicians before him, when he went to Padua to complete his studies in 1600. There, he was tutored by the renowned anatomist and medical artist Andreas Versalius.

Harvey, as physician to royalty, never lost his fascination with the mechanics of the body, dissecting anything that came across his work table, from fish and frogs to royal deer and a pet parrot, from executed 'witches' to a man said to be 152 [*sic*] years old and even his own deceased family members. From his detailed studies, particularly the vivisection of injured animals, Harvey discovered a vital aspect of the body's mechanical functions: the circulation of the blood. Historically, it had been believed that blood ebbed and flowed like the tide. Harvey realised the heart was a tireless muscle that worked as a pump, complete with non-return valves just like its industrial counterparts, circulating blood in one direction around the system of arteries and veins. Although the use of such a mechanical analogy was acceptable to many students of medicine and natural philosophy, when he published his discoveries in 1628 in *De Motu Cordis* (The Motion of the Heart), some of his private patients preferred to change doctors, rather than be treated by a 'crack-brained' physician with such outrageous ideas. Medical practice was advancing, if very slowly, alongside other branches of scientific study. Concerning this too-gradual progress of medicine, Francis Bacon (1561–1626) complained in his treatise *The Advancement of Learning* (1605) that most physicians were charlatans and the old-fashioned ways of education was to blame.

The preferred method of learning medicine was to trawl through the writings of the ancient authorities – Hippocrates, Aristotle, Galen and others – rather than for students to observe and investigate diseases and treatments for themselves. This acquisition of knowledge at second hand and the unquestioning acceptance of centuries-old dogma were holding back the advance of new ideas. Not that medicine had been entirely stagnant. As early as 1546, an Italian physician, Girolamo Fracastoro (1478–1553), had suggested that diseases were caused by 'seed-like' entities which not only carried and transmitted infection but could do so at a distance and without those infected necessarily having physical contact. The idea seemed absurd at the time and it would be another three-and-a-half centuries before 'germ-theory' was proven true. But, in the meantime, Bacon realised the deleterious effect of general reliance on ancient knowledge not only applied to medicine but to all branches of natural philosophy.

Bacon proposed a new way of looking at Nature by studying and making close personal observation of a particular phenomenon; proposing a hypothesis to explain it; carrying out experiments to test that hypothesis and then giving consideration to the results of the experiments. If the hypothesis was disproved, it should be adjusted and a new one proposed and tested. If the hypothesis was proven, then knowledge was advanced and the process could move on, either to another phenomenon or, more likely, to the next level of study of the original phenomenon. This became known as the 'empirical' method and remains the basis of scientific research today.

Galileo in Padua – where he was a professor of mathematics at the time William Harvey was a student there – was another proponent of this revolutionary method, yet Bacon criticised Galileo for abandoning ideas as soon as he had satisfied himself with a couple of experiments in any given field. Perhaps Galileo had so many ideas in his fertile imagination, he failed to persevere with any single one to its ultimate conclusion and Bacon viewed this as a grave fault. He preferred to consider individual genius of less merit than an in-depth course of experimentation – hopefully, funded by the Crown – that would eventually lead to mankind's complete understanding and, therefore, dominance over every aspect of Nature.

Bacon was a Londoner and attended Trinity College, Cambridge, from 1573, when he was just twelve years old. He studied law and became an astute politician. Queen Elizabeth brought him onto her Privy Council in 1596. The queen's death in 1603 did not hamper Bacon's career in the least and he continued to serve her successor, James I, who knighted him in 1606. His rise at court continued, reaching the distinction of Lord Chancellor in 1618, Baron Verulam the same year, and Viscount St Albans in 1621. More of a thinker than an experimenter who got his hands dirty, despite his writings, it is said that he died of pneumonia after burying a chicken carcass in the snow, hoping to prove that the cold helped preserve the body. Now an everyday fact of life, with frozen peas and fish available from the freezer, at the time this was a revolutionary idea. At Bacon's funeral in St Albans, dozens of philosophers of the day came to eulogise him, even though he died in debt and in disgrace, Parliament having found him guilty on twenty-three counts of bribery and corruption in 1621 and expelling him from office.

René Descartes (1596–1650) was a Frenchmen trained as a lawyer but also interested in natural philosophy. He carried out the dissection of live specimens, proving to his own satisfaction that Harvey was correct about the heart's function as a pump. However, another intention of his experiments with live animals was to determine that they did not have souls. With this in mind, Descartes viewed living bodies as mechanical instruments – like Harvey – but theorised that in the case of man, possession of a soul made him unique and capable of feeling pain. Without souls, animals were just living machines, lacking any awareness of self. Determined to make the point, he nailed his wife's pet dog to the table and dissected it, claiming that the animal's reaction to extreme pain was simply an unfeeling mechanical one, since a soul was necessary for suffering to be experienced. Man, having a soul, therefore had self-awareness and was able to think, reason and doubt. In his *Discours de la Méthode* (1637), he stated that all knowledge should be doubted because perception and reasoning could be deceptive. The only certainty, he claimed, was man's ability to doubt everything. This philosophy is frequently summed up in Descartes' famous axiom: *Cogito ergo sum* – 'I think, therefore I am.' Despite his questioning of absolutely all things, nonetheless, he did conclude one certainty: the existence of God.[21]

Mathematics as the Key

Descartes was equally interested in mathematics, combining algebra and geometry. He was the first to use *x*, *y* and *z* to represent unknowns in algebraic equations and invented the concept of graphs as a means of expressing these equations, using *x* and *y* axes to plot co-ordinates – a system that still bears his name: Cartesian geometry. Descartes was also an avid proponent of the universe as a perfect mechanical device, wound up like a clock and set in motion by God but then left to run without further divine interference. He was a Roman Catholic by faith and the idea that God no longer intervened in the continued functioning of His creation – i.e. would no longer perform miracles – was contrary to Church doctrine. Fearing difficulties if he remained in Catholic France, Descartes spent most of his productive years in the Protestant Netherlands.

His concept of the universe involved the reasoning that Nature could not permit the existence of a vacuum; every space had to be filled with matter. He termed matter to be undifferentiated 'brute stuff' swirling in vortices throughout the entire universe. This particular theory caused headaches for contemporary experimenters such as Robert Boyle who were determined to create a vacuum, if such a thing could possibly exist.

Descartes had a theory concerning the formation of colours, believing colour was produced by revolving spheres of pristine white light. He also determined that the force of motion could be calculated as mass x velocity – i.e. momentum. In decades to come, Isaac Newton would be equally fascinated by these subjects and pursue his ideas and theories with alacrity. His review and refinement and, indeed, rejection of some of Descartes' work would advance science significantly.

The State of England

When James I died in 1625, he was succeeded by his son Charles. Until 1612, Charles had not been destined to rule but, in that year, his elder brother Henry, Prince of Wales, died unexpectedly, leaving Charles as their father's heir. Henry had been educated and prepared to fulfil his destiny as King of England, Scotland

and Ireland and raised as a Church of England Protestant. He was good with people, clever, tall, athletic and expected to become an exceptionally fine monarch as Henry IX. It was not to be; so much promise came to nothing. Charles was diminutive, suffered rickets as a child and lacked any empathy with his subjects. He had been raised in his mother's covertly Catholic household and was probably spoilt as a sickly youngster with few expectations of greatness. Having the prospect of a crown thrust upon him seems to have figuratively gone to his head.

Self-obsessed and convinced that he ruled by Divine Right as God's chosen, King Charles spent a fortune on display, acquiring a vast art collection, having his portrait painted innumerable times, often by Van Dyke. He even had the public admitted to the palace one day a week, to file past and watch him dine off gold plate, while musicians played and a trumpet sounded every time he took a bite. His love of ceremony and lavish artefacts spilled over into his religious observance, probably influenced by his mother's preference for Catholicism.

Whereas Charles's father, James, had been raised in the Scottish Presbyterian Church and happily converted to the Church of England's softer attitudes to worship, Charles I wanted all the frills of Catholicism while remaining Head of the Church of England. Gorgeous clerical robes, genuflection during Holy Communion and the altar to be kept apart from the congregation: the English Church had abolished these things. Charles reinstated them and then determined that such matters must be consistent throughout his realm – Presbyterian Scotland included. Strapped for cash because of his reckless expenditure on finery and the requirements of a kingly lifestyle, with no understanding of his subjects' attitudes and opinions on either religion or monarchy, it all came together as a sure recipe for trouble.

This was the England into which Isaac Newton was born on Christmas Day 1642, according to the old style Julian calendar of the day.

Chapter 2

THE 1640s: A GENIUS IS BORN

Isaac Newton was born when England still used the old Julian calendar and, even more confusing for us in the twenty-first century, dated the year as beginning on Lady Day, 25 March. This means that although the baby arrived on 25 December 1642, the parish records of St John the Baptist Church, Colsterworth, in Lincolnshire, show that Isaac, son of Isaac and Hannah Newton, was baptised on 1 January 1642. Of course, by modern reckoning, that was January 1643.

Little Isaac was born at Woolsthorpe Manor in Lincolnshire. The original house was built in the reign of Elizabeth I and Robert Newton, a successful yeoman farmer who had profited from his sheep and already owned land nearby, bought Woolsthorpe in 1623. It was a comfortable though not particularly grand house but it came with the title of Lord of the Manor, raising Robert's status from 'yeoman' to 'gentleman' and giving the Newtons their own private pew in the church at Colsterworth. Robert improved the house and presented it to his son Isaac in 1639. When Isaac wed Hannah Ayscough in April 1642, their status was improved further since her father, James Ayscough and mother, Margery Blythe, both came of local gentry stock.

Isaac junior was the couple's first and only child and his birth seems to have been a month or two premature. Whatever the case, his mother was not prepared for his arrival, perhaps because she had recently been widowed. His father had died the previous autumn although the baptismal entry does not mention that Isaac senior was deceased. However, lower down on the same page of the register under 'Buried', the funeral of Isaac's father is noted down as having occurred on 6 October 1642.

It was a time of great upheaval and not only for the Newton family. The country was in the preliminary throes of the English Civil War. Charles I had unfurled the royal standard, declaring war against his own Parliament, at Nottingham on 22 August 1642. The first major engagement of that long conflict was contested at Edgehill, near Kineton in Warwickshire, on 23 October, less than 70 miles from Colsterworth.

Isaac Newton senior made his will on 1 October, describing himself as a yeoman of Woolsthorpe in the parish of Colsterworth, and stated in the traditional wording of the introduction that although he is 'of good and perfect memory' he is 'sick of body'.[1] In the will, he makes generous bequests to daughters of relatives and acquaintances: Thomas Cristian's daughter Elizabeth is to have £5, as is John Cooke's daughter Isabell. Cooke's other children share £4 equally between them. His niece Ann Newton, daughter of his brother Richard, is to have £7 and old Uncle Richard Newton just £1. The poor of the parish are to receive £2, and 10 shillings is left for repairs to the bridge between Colsterworth and Woolsthorpe. Everything else is given to his 'loveinge' wife whom he also makes his executrix under the supervision of her father James Ayscough and her brother William Ayscough, parson of nearby Burton Coggles, though he does not mention Hannah by name. He was unable to sign his name but made his mark – a very shaky capital 'I' – and set his seal to it in red wax. James Ayscough witnessed the document, signing his name boldly, along with two others, William Venton and Edward Foster. These last two also signed the inventory drawn up a week later, on 13 October, to accompany the will, along with Richard Newton and Henry Whittle who, like Isaac senior, could only make their marks by putting the capital letter of their forename in each case.[2] From this we can see that illiteracy was not uncommon among the Newton family and their neighbours.

Despite a lack of penmanship, the inventory of Isaac senior's goods and chattels, all of which he bequeathed to Hannah, demonstrates that he was far better off than the average yeoman. 'Eleven score and fourteen sheep' (234) were a major item worth £80. Unfortunately, the inventory has been damaged and some items are hard to make out but it includes oxen and calves, horses and foals, hogs and barns full of corn, oats and farming equipment such as harrows, ploughs and carts. Some entries, particularly regarding household goods, are frustratingly imprecise, using phrases such as 'brewing vessels and other things', 'goods in the dairy' and 'chests with other implements'. At least the linen is itemised: ten pairs of flaxen (linen) sheets, five pairs of hempen sheets, three dozen napkins, five pairs of pillowbears (cases or slips), five towels and six tablecloths. There were brass and pewter items – bowls, dishes and cups, presumably – and there was coal and firewood ready for the winter. In all, the sum total of goods came to £459 12s 4d.

No details of what ailed Isaac Newton senior are known but he was only thirty-six years old when he died, leaving Hannah quite an affluent widow. But, if he had lived, it is worth considering with which side, king or parliament, would the Newton family have sympathised at this time of civil war?

Taking Sides

This was a dilemma facing families across England during the first year of war. Edgehill did not result in outright victory for either side but people of note were present and one important death occurred when the king's personal standard bearer Sir Edmund Verney of Oxfordshire was cut down, banner still in hand. The Verney family was among those with divided loyalties: Sir Edmund's eldest son, Ralph, was a London lawyer and sided with Parliament, as did a majority of Londoners. The rest of the Verneys, at home in Oxfordshire, supported the king. Yet otherwise, Ralph and his siblings remained on good terms, helping each other out whenever the tide of war afflicted the fortunes of each side in turn.

Also at Edgehill was William Harvey, the king's physician, but Sir Edmund would have been beyond his help. The tale was told by Harvey himself that, while the battle raged, he sheltered under a hedge with the king's sons – lads as yet too young to fight – in his care. Apparently he told them stories to distract their attention from the carnage on the other side of the hedge until 'a Bullet of a great Gun grazed on the ground nearby', forcing him to find a safer refuge for his royal charges.[3] Staunchly Royalist, Harvey described the Roundhead Parliamentarians as a 'pack of Anabaptists, fanatics, robbers and murderers'. How disturbing it must have been for the man who likened the heart to the king in ruling the body to learn that the opposing Puritans preferred the analogy of the heart being like Parliament, in diligently and steadily governing the workings of the whole.

During the turbulent times of the English Civil War, gentlemen farmers, like the Newtons, often had little option but to take sides in the conflict. Royalist or Parliamentarian: the choice might be a matter of religion, ideology or loyalty but, for lesser people it often came down to survival. If your neighbours chose to support the king and you elected otherwise, or even attempted to remain neutral, your land, property and possessions might become fair game and seized as spoils of war.

We know nothing of the sympathies of the Newtons or the Ayscoughs – Isaac's maternal grandparents – despite the fact that Lincolnshire was at the heart of events during the first year of the Civil War. The county was situated between the Parliamentarian Eastern Association, consisting of Essex, Hertfordshire, Cambridgeshire, Norfolk and Suffolk, and the Royalist counties of Oxfordshire to the south – King Charles had removed his court from London, which was under Parliament's control, to Oxford – and Yorkshire to the north. This meant Lincolnshire was the scene of a number of battles and skirmishes.

The war came closest to Newton's home at Woolsthorpe Manor during the spring of 1643. In March, a Royalist force under Sir Charles Cavendish and Sir John Henderson made a surprise attack on nearby Grantham and took the town before marching on to Boston. Since the Royalists neglected to garrison Grantham, in May, Francis, Lord Willoughby of Parham was able to occupy the town for the Parliamentarians. Two days later, on 13 May,

Cavendish surprised Willoughby's troops as they quartered in the village of Belton close by, killing seventy men and taking forty prisoners. Later that day, Cavendish attacked again but was driven to retreat from the field by a new cavalry commander in his first action: a gentleman farmer, like the Newtons. His name was Oliver Cromwell.[4]

On 11 October 1643, at the little-known Battle of Winceby, to the east of Lincoln, a short but decisively victorious action by Cromwell and Sir Thomas Fairfax of Hull brought the whole county within Parliament's sphere of influence, where it would remain for the rest of the war and into the Commonwealth and Protectorate periods, until the Restoration of Charles II in 1660. It was almost a year since the Battle of Edgehill and regardless of which side the family may have wished to support, Lincolnshire was now under the dominion of a Puritan Parliament. But how had matters come to such a head?

Religious Causes of War

As we saw in the previous chapter, when his elder brother Henry died suddenly in 1612, possibly of typhoid, young Charles Stuart, entirely unsuited and untrained for kingship, became his father's heir. The accession of Charles I in 1625 brought chaos to the religious situation. The king used his supremacy over the Anglican Church, as one bishop wrote,

> ... to promote his own idiosyncratic style of sacramental Kingship which was a very weird aberration from the reformed Church of England. The king even questions the parliamentary basis of the Reformation Church and unsettles to a great extent the agreed acceptance of Anglicanism.

Having wed a Roman Catholic princess, Henrietta-Maria of France, who continued to practise her religion openly with her husband's approval, Charles also had another co-conspirator in the undermining of the Church of England: William Laud.

Laud's flamboyant style of religious service first attracted the attention of the courtier, George Villiers, Duke of Buckingham, and he became the duke's religious adviser. When his master became the new king's favourite, Laud's influence rose rapidly. In September 1626, he became Dean of the Chapel Royal and immediately changed the services to acts of ceremonial worship, rather than preaching, much to King Charles's pleasure. In July 1628 Laud was installed as Bishop of London and dramatically changed church politics. He was almost sixty years old when he became Archbishop of Canterbury and was not prepared to compromise. He wanted uniformity in the Church of England with no alternative sects to be permitted, whether Catholic, Puritan, Presbyterian or any other. More than that, the official form of Anglicanism was to be High Church with ministers wearing gorgeous vestments, the use of incense and a great deal of veneration on bended knee – all bordering on the dreaded Catholic rituals: an anathema to the Puritans who were well represented in Parliament.

Charles and Laud tried to enforce uniformity on the established churches of the king's realms, including Scotland and Ireland, all to use the High Church Anglican form of worship and the English *Book of Common Prayer,* which was imposed on Scottish kirks in 1637. This was not appreciated by the Presbyterian Scots. The first time the prayer book was used in the High Kirk of St Giles in Edinburgh on Sunday 23 July 1637, when James Hannay, the dean, began to read the Collects from it, Jenny Geddes, a market-trader, threw her stool straight at the minister's head, shouting: *De'il gie ye colic, the wame o' ye, fause thief: daur ye say Mass in my lug?* She meant: 'Devil cause you colic in your stomach, false thief: dare you say Mass in my ear?' Compared to the Scottish dialect, the English of the prayer book was as incomprehensible as a foreign language and the stool-throwing led to the congregation shouting abuse and throwing Bibles, stools, sticks and stones. Serious rioting followed on the streets of Edinburgh and spread to other towns and cities in Scotland. Meanwhile, the Provost and magistrates were forced to negotiate with the Edinburgh mob.

When the king's attempts to control the situation from London failed, in July 1638 he told his English Privy Council that force would be needed. With problems raising funds, Charles gathered a poorly trained English force of about 20,000 men in the early summer of 1639 and marched towards Berwick-upon-Tweed, just on the English side of the border. The Scottish army of 12,000 men, led by General Alexander Leslie, was encamped a few miles away on the other side of the border. However, since neither army wanted to fight, a settlement was reached, the king agreeing that all disputes should be referred to the Parliament of Scotland. When it met, the Scottish Parliament promptly re-abolished all bishops – posts the Scottish Kirk had done away with in the previous century that had been reinstated at Charles's and Laud's insistence – and declared itself free from royal control.

In retaliation, Charles spread rumours that the Scots were intriguing with France – a ploy certain to cause the English to readily rally to his standard. But to pay and equip a decent army, he needed money that only the Parliament at Westminster could grant. So Charles summoned the English Parliament – having fallen out with the last one eleven years before; he had ruled without ever since. In April 1640, Parliament convened but was more interested in demanding its long list of grievances, mounted up over the previous decade, be dealt with first. Charles wanted cash, nothing more, and since the Members of Parliament were not willing to consider the matter until their complaints were answered, he promptly dissolved Parliament again.

Meanwhile, the Scots crossed the River Tweed, taking the English counties of Northumberland and Durham as Charles's ill-equipped army retreated before them. He was forced to leave the counties in Scots hands as a guarantee that he would pay the Scots' expenses when he signed the Treaty of Ripon in October 1640. Now in dire straits, the penniless king had no choice but to summon another English Parliament to grant him the money to make that payment. This Long Parliament, as it became known, would exist until 1648. It agreed to grant money to the king but it would cost him dear: his chief supporters, including Archbishop Laud, were impeached by Parliament, imprisoned in the Tower of London, tried and, eventually executed, Charles being forced to sign their death warrants. Throughout history, the impeachment of a king's 'evil advisers' was the only safe way of criticising the monarch without the risk of committing treason, but Parliament was reaching its limits on that score.

Unpopular with his English Parliament and now hoping to win Scottish support, Charles went to Scotland in the autumn of 1641, accepting all the decisions of the recent Scottish Parliament, including confirming their right to challenge the actions of his ministers. He had now withdrawn all the causes of the original dispute. But within a year, these troubles, known as the Bishops' Wars, combined with his disputes with the English Parliament, would lead to civil war in Charles's other two kingdoms, first in Ireland, then in England. The Scottish problems were a prelude to the English Civil War of 1642–49.

In 1641, public criticism of Laud's changes to Church liturgy was reflected in the theatre when the playwright Richard Overton wrote a satire, *A New Play called Canterbury His Change of Diet.*⁵ Canterbury meant, of course, Archbishop Laud and the play opens with the churchman sitting down to a feast. Wholesome English meats from the shambles (butchers) are not good enough; he demands 'the rarest dainties, dressed after the Italian fashion'. The reference is to Laud's reintroduction of Roman Catholic ceremony and embellished vestments to the plain, straightforward services of the Church of England. By the fourth act, Canterbury, now openly Catholic, is in a cage with his Jesuit confessor, like a magpie and a crow. When asked by 'the king' what song they sing, the jester replies 'nine notes' – a reference to the Catholic recitation of the *Novena,* the nine 'Hail Marys' that preceded the Lord's Prayer in working through the rosary.

Despite the fact that these anti-Catholic sentiments must have had some appeal to the Puritans in Parliament, the *Journal of the House of Lords* – the Upper House of Parliament – recorded an order for stage plays to cease, dated 2 September 1642, just a few weeks after King Charles declared war. It stated that:

> as ... spectacles of pleasure, too commonly expressing lascivious mirth and levity ... public stage plays shall cease and be forborn; instead of which are recommended ... considerations of repentance, reconciliation and peace with God.⁶

Thus began the regime of Puritan rule under which young Isaac Newton would be raised. In essence, it seems to almost to have had an eleventh Commandment: Thou shalt not enjoy thyself.

Childbirth in Seventeenth-century England

As we saw at the beginning of this chapter, Isaac junior was born prematurely on Christmas Day 1642. So what could the young widow, Hannah Newton, expect to happen to her when she went into labour on Christmas Eve? Her mother, Margery Ayscough, travelled the few miles from Market Overton to take charge, for childbirth was still a women-only event, as it had been since medieval times. Female friends and neighbours would be summoned and among their number were two local women who were paid a few pence for their services and may have been the village midwives.

Most medieval religious rituals regarding childbirth had been swept away by the Reformation of the previous century: holy relics, amulets and such like. Yet childbirth retained many old customs and superstitions because otherwise it was a situation beyond any woman's control. One tradition was to throw open doors, windows, chests and drawers, loosen belts and untie laces, supposedly to show the reluctant womb what it was supposed to do to allow the child to burst forth. The fear and sense of helplessness, especially for a first-time mother like Hannah, would make her desperate for moral support and reassurance of any kind. This was still a time when tables of mortality recorded a high death rate among mothers and babies during labour and in the days following delivery. Estimates for seventeenth-century England suggest one in forty births resulted in the mother's death and only one-fifth of infants lived to reach their fifth birthday.

These startling figures actually skew the statistics for the average life span for the period; so many infant deaths bringing down the average age at death considerably. Thirty-five years was the norm but those who survived to adulthood and avoided the dangers of battle, childbirth and disease could quite likely enjoy their biblical three-score-years-and-ten, i.e. seventy years, as Isaac himself would prove. However, many were less fortunate.

A decade after Newton's birth, the poet John Milton lost his first wife, Mary, three days after she gave birth to their fourth child. Four years later, his second wife, Katherine, died of a 'consumption' – probably an infection – contracted during her first confinement.[7] The child, a daughter, also died. Grief-stricken, Milton wrote a sonnet: *Me thought I saw my late espousèd saint* (Number 23). It continues:

> Her face was veiled, yet to my fancied sight,
> Love, sweetness, goodness in her person shined
> So clear, as in no face with more delight.
> But O as to embrace me she inclined,
> I waked, she fled, and day brought back my night.

Despite her early confinement, Hannah Newton survived the rigours of childbirth but the premature baby did not look likely to live. The story of his birth was told by Newton to his niece's husband, John Conduitt, in later years. Apparently, he was small enough to fit into a quart pot and so weak that his neck had to be supported by a bolster to keep his head on his shoulders. (In fact, all new-borns require full head support, so this was not a sign of undue weakness but Newton would likely have been completely unfamiliar with tiny babies.) The tale continues that two women were sent across the fields from Woolsthorpe very early on Christmas morning – Isaac having been born around 2 a.m. – to Lady Jane Pakenham, wife of Sir Clement Pakenham at North Witham, to ask for medicines for Hannah and clothes, probably swaddling bands, for the baby. Having fetched what was required, the two women did not hurry back to the manor, so certain were they the baby would be dead before they arrived. Of course, he still lived.

It has been suggested though, that this story was fabricated by Newton to support the idea that his mother was unprepared for his premature birth and dispel any notion of his conception having been prior to his parents' marriage. They were wed the previous April without any record of the exact date, so the earliest a full-term child could arrive was January 1643. In fact, it was not unusual in those days for a betrothed couple to pre-empt the wedding. As the whole point of marriage was to beget heirs, it was thought wise to test whether the couple was compatible and conception likely to result. No stigma attached to the child so long as the parents were wed before it was born, even if only by a few days. However, it seems Newton was most concerned that there should not be the remotest chance of any stain to tarnish his spotless reputation on that account; in 1705, at the time of his knighthood, he informed the College of Heralds his mother and father were married in 1639, three years before his birth. Whether this was a genuine error or an intended piece of misdirection, it is hard to imagine the great mathematician making any mistake when it came to basic numbers.

Regardless of Newton's concerns for his parents' marital status at the time of his conception and his father's death just a few months later, medical ideas at the time are intriguing. In 1651, Nicholas Culpeper (1616–52) published a book entitled *A Directory for Midwives – A Guide for Women in Their Conception, Bearing and Suckling their Children,* a work that contained the current beliefs and attitudes towards childbirth. Culpeper described himself as a 'Gentleman Student in Physick and Astrology' and a student he ever remained, never qualifying in any field. That said, he certainly knew about herbal medicine and his most famous publication, *Culpeper's Herbal,* can still be found in print today. He fell out with the London College of Physicians, partly because he never bothered to qualify as a physician, yet openly practised medicine and was, therefore, deemed a quack and a charlatan, but also because he had the temerity to translate the college's Latin *Pharmacopaea* into English, so any layman might read it. A pharmacopaea contains the recipes for all approved medicines. Such books still exist today and any new medicine must pass the strictest testing in order to be included in the relevant national and international pharmacopaeae before it can be administered to patients. Culpeper not only made it possible for unqualified people to make their own herbal remedies, following the official recipes, denying profitable business to the physicians, he criticised some of their concoctions, 'improved' on others and added some of his own. Much to the annoyance of the college, his books became very popular and attempts were made to prosecute him.

The public must have found his writings – in English – to be a tonic compared to the stuffy attitudes of 'proper' physicians, so when his book for midwives was published, it, too, became a 'bestseller', remaining in print until 1777. Culpeper had a personal interest in attempting to improve the situation for mothers-to-be and new mothers, stating in his preface that 'having buried many of my children young caused me to fix my thoughts intently on this business.' Sadly, he and his wife had seven children, losing six of them as infants. His *Guide for Women* contained the current thinking on conception:

> The reason why a male is conceived, sometimes a female, is the strength of the seed. If the man's seed be strongest, a male is conceived; if the woman's, a female... and that is the reason why weakly men get most girls, if they get any children at all.[8]

Of the sexual act itself, Culpeper says neither party should be drunk, nor hungry, and the man should 'go to the school of Mars before going to the school of Venus'. In other words, martial pursuits should come before marital ones, before 'taking counsel of the under sheet', as he coyly puts it.

Once the woman realised she was pregnant – tender nipples and enlarged breasts are the main signs, according to Culpeper – she should eat tender meats, particularly hens' meat, quinces to strengthen the child, almonds with honey, sweet apples and grapes but nothing bitter or salty, no garlic, onions, olives, mustard, fennel, pepper and other spices, until the final months when cinnamon is good. Summer fruits, such as strawberries and cherries, and pulses, such as beans and peas, are unsuitable too. He advised drinking moderately of clear (white) wine, not too much exercise, dancing or riding in a coach that may shake her about. After her fourth month, wearing a cloth dipped in oils of almonds, jasmine and lilies on her belly prevents stretch marks, or 'clefts and wrinkles', as he referred to them. Bathing once a week was prescribed towards the end of pregnancy to 'loosen the privy parts'. Culpeper followed the age-old idea that a pregnant woman must avoid anger, sorrow, fear and even an excess of laughter.[9]

Unfortunately, Hannah Newton must have been exposed to certain of these emotions when her husband died. Sorrow for certain, as well as anger and fear for her own future and that of the child she carried, would all be common aspects of grief and bereavement. Therefore, the omens for the baby's birth, by Culpeper's reckoning, were not propitious and the fact that the father may have been already somewhat weakened by illness at the time of its conception must have made it seem likely to be a female.

Eventually, 'the womb... sends it [the baby] forth with great straining and this is called travel', Culpeper said, though 'travail' was the more usual spelling. He continued:

> Though child-bearing since Eve's sin is ordained to be painful as punishment thereof, yet sometimes it is more painful than ordinary... Let her [the mother] avoid great noises and sadness [when] she should be praising God for her delivery.[10]

Thus a man who, like most others of the time, had probably no idea what went on during a woman's labour, described the process of giving birth.

In the event, whatever Hannah Newton's experience of childbirth, whether premature or full term, matters turned to advantage: any child born on Christmas Day was considered especially blessed and, better yet, if it was a boy. Also, a posthumous child was believed to receive more than its share of good luck in later life, perhaps as compensation for an unfortunate beginning.[11] Newton certainly seems to have believed he was special, eventually regarding himself as one of God's miracles; literally, as God's gift to mankind. Humility was never among his virtues. The baby was baptised in the church of St John the Baptist, Colsterworth, on 1 January and given his deceased father's name.

The font in the church today stands on the same pedestal as it did at the time of Newton's christening but the font itself is of a later date. There is a story that the original font basin is still there, buried beneath the pedestal, having been 'saved' from destruction when it proved 'too popish' in design for Puritan tastes. The church also contains the Newton family chapel where both Isaac's parents were buried. Sadly, at present, their grave lies under the organ but the parish is hoping to restore the chapel, remove the organ to another position and reveal the grave. Other connections to the family include the Newtons' special pew as lords of manor which is on the left hand side of the nave, near the pulpit. A sundial, carved by Isaac at Woolsthorpe manor, was removed from the house long ago but can still be viewed in the church. A final point of interest in St John's Church is a 'daisy wheel' witch mark, carved on a window ledge and there are other such marks at Woolsthorpe also, so the parish must have had some serious concerns about witchcraft.[12]

Hannah would have swaddled her baby for the first few weeks at least. Binding the limbs was believed to ensure they grew straight at a time when rickets was common in children – King Charles having suffered from it. However, it is possible that swaddling actually contributed to the problem, since sunshine on the skin enables the body to produce the vitamin D vital for strong bone growth and a baby wrapped tightly from head to foot would be denied the sunlight. Another contributing factor to rickets is a lack of calcium and phosphate in the diet. Human breast milk is perfectly evolved for the infant's needs but being born premature – if that was indeed the case – Hannah may not have had sufficient milk to suckle her baby herself. In which case, a wet nurse was the best solution, rather than goats', sheep or cows' milk, the usual alternatives, which lack certain constituents required for human babies. I have found no information as to whether the child was suckled by his mother or not but neither is there any suggestion that young Isaac was anything other than a healthy, straight-limbed child.

His physical wellbeing may have been good but his emotional health could have been quite another matter. When he was just three years old, Hannah married again. Her second husband was three decades her elder, the Reverend Barnabas Smith, rector of North Witham just over a mile from Woolsthorpe. The wooing was hardly romantic: a servant delivered a matrimonial-cum-business proposal from Smith for Hannah and her family to consider.[13] He was in his sixties and had no children by his recently deceased wife but he was independently wealthy. It may be that Hannah foresaw a brief and childless marriage with the old man and a widowhood of comfortable affluence after that. Whatever the case, with the Ayscoughs' blessings, Hannah moved to the rectory at North Witham but her little son was not included in the marriage deal. Isaac was to remain at Woolsthorpe in the care of his grandmother, Margery Ayscough. At least Barnabas Smith saw to it that his stepson's home was in good repair and gave him an extra small piece of land to inherit when he was twenty-one at Hannah's insistence but otherwise, it seems the rector wanted as little to do with his wife's child as possible.

Early Education

James Ayscough, Isaac's grandfather, is not mentioned in the arrangements for the boy's care so, it would seem, he was raised by his grandmother, Margery. Affection appears to have been in short supply in his upbringing. He must have missed his mother and the manor was isolated, so friends and playmates of his own age simply were not around. His childhood was lonely and his recreations solitary ones. This situation led to him becoming insecure, antisocial and secretive in adulthood, also self-reliant and obsessive. But there was probably one huge advantage to growing up in his grandmother's care: she was educated. If Isaac had been raised by his parents and surrounded by siblings, whatever his temperament, he would probably have filled his father's role eventually as an unlettered, if prosperous, yeoman farmer; never gone to Cambridge and science would have fallen behind by a century or more without his achievements.

We do not know much about young Newton's earliest education but it may have been his grandmother who taught him his alphabet and how to read and write. He also attended dame schools at Stoke Rochford and Skillington. Dame schools – or 'petty' schools – were run by women who charged a fee to teach children how to read and recite the Lord's Prayer, the Creed and the catechism which, in the 1650s, would have been the basic tenets of the Puritan faith, with emphasis on the Ten Commandments as the foundation for godly living.

Some guide as to the cost of such schooling can be found in the Churchwarden's Accounts of 1653 for Darlington, County Durham, showing payments made by the parish:

To Edward Holmes, a poor scholar for half a year's teaching	35 pence
To Dame Seamer for teaching one boy for a year	4 shillings
To Ralph Hall for three lads' learning for three months	4 shillings
To Roger Jewet for learning [sic] a boy for three months	1 shilling
To Master Swinburne for learning [sic] John Wilson's children and Giles' daughter's child	7 shillings.[14]

In 1642, Samuel Harmer had noted that people in many parishes were complaining about the authorities' attempts to force them to send their children to dame schools to learn to read. For one thing, it cost them money, if they could afford it; for another, while at school the children were not contributing to the family income, and thirdly, poorer parents were having to claim off the parish, as evident in the Darlington accounts above. Of interest is the payment to Edward Holmes, an older pupil earning a little money by teaching the younger ones. Also, John Wilson's children and Giles' grandchild appear to be receiving special attention, despite their guardians having to rely on the parish to pay the master.

Quite what arrangements were made for Isaac's early schooling we do not know but his uncle William Ayscough, rector of the nearby parish of Burton Coggles, was a graduate of Trinity College, Cambridge, and may have taken an interest in the boy's lessons. We know he was involved in persuading Hannah that Isaac should eventually study at Cambridge when she was most reluctant to allow it.

With his mother absent, Newton's childhood is shrouded in darkness and these were also dark times for England.

Consequences of the Civil War

After some initial Royalist triumphs, General Fairfax and Oliver Cromwell and their army of Parliamentarians had the ultimate victory. With the attempts to reform religion at the heart of this conflict, it is terrifying to realise that a higher percentage of the male population of these islands was killed or injured in the fighting during the 1640s than in both World Wars. And the king was not spared either. Although he survived the skirmishes and set-piece battles unscathed, eventually, Charles was given as a prisoner to the Parliamentarians by the Scots, in whom he had mistakenly dared to trust.

Eventually, like Archbishop Laud, he was impeached on a charge of treason. Since treason had always been regarded as a crime committed *against* the Crown, how could a king be accused? To make it possible, Parliament redefined 'treason' as a crime against the State and the Commonwealth, i.e. against Parliament as the elected representatives of the people and, therefore, against the people themselves. This time, there would be no concealment of the king's misdeeds by putting his 'evil advisers' on trial. This was personal, with the king in the dock expected to answer the charges against him.

On 1 January 1649, the Rump Parliament – consisting of the few survivors of the Long Parliament who had not died of old age, illness, or as casualties of war, nor been expelled by the Puritans for dissent during Pride's Purge – passed an ordinance for the king's trial. He was charged with subverting the fundamental laws and liberties of the nation and with maliciously making war on the Parliament and people of England.[15] When the House of Lords refused to give its assent to the ordinance reversing the traditional definition of treason, the House of Commons declared itself to be the supreme authority in the land with powers to pass laws without the consent of the king or the House of Lords.

A High Court of Justice was specially convened for the trial to be held in the Painted Chamber of the Palace of Westminster.

One-hundred-and-thirty-five commissioners were nominated to sit in judgement on the king but about fifty refused and several more withdrew after proceedings had begun. Although the trial would be open and public, stringent security measures were enforced. Soldiers were stationed to control the crowds, guards posted on rooftops and cellars searched. President Bradshaw wore a steel-lined musket-ball-proof hat in case any Royalist supporter should make an assassination attempt. The trial opened on 20 January 1649. With quiet dignity, the king exasperated the commissioners, refusing to answer the charges. He declared that he did not recognise the jurisdiction of the court and asked how the House of Commons, recently purged of any Royalist sympathisers, could still claim to represent the people of England.

On 24 January, thirty-three witnesses against the king were heard. The depositions proved the king's personal participation in the war, gave evidence of his approval of various atrocities and demonstrated his intention of stirring up and continuing the conflict. On 26 January, the commissioners drafted the sentence, condemning Charles Stuart, a king no longer, as a 'tyrant, traitor, murderer and public enemy to the Commonwealth of England'. The final session was held on 27 January. Bradshaw's address to the prisoner asserted that even a king was subject to the law and that the law proceeded from Parliament. Furthermore, Charles Stuart had broken the sacred bond between a king and his subjects. By making war on his own people, he had forfeited his right to their allegiance. Declaring Charles guilty, Bradshaw ordered the sentence of death to be read out. Charles, having kept silent throughout after denying recognition of the court, now wished to speak but was not permitted to do so, to his great distress. Instead, he was abruptly led away from the court to await his execution.

A Lonely Childhood

Meanwhile, back in Lincolnshire, although his mother visited him at Woolsthorpe on occasion, unannounced and often for just an hour or two, as a child Isaac Newton must have felt neglected. Hannah eventually had three children by Barnabas Smith who may have accompanied their mother on her brief visits but, otherwise,

Newton can be considered as an only child, left to his own devices for much of the time. Woolsthorpe was set quite apart from the nearest village, Colsterworth, and his grandmother would have considered the children of humble labourers and servants to be unsuitable playmates for her grandson. So as often happens with solitary children with little opportunity to interact with others of their own age, he probably spoke and thought in a manner more befitting an adult and that would make it even more difficult for him to relate to his peers.

Woolsthorpe Manor was not grand but it was stone-built and, by the standards of the day, comfortable, though his grandmother was not affluent. The house may have been thatched at one time, to judge from the steeply pitched roof but by the time of Newton's death, when it was sketched by his friend, William Stukeley, it had a tiled roof and three dormer windows, though no sign of these remains today. Whether thatched or tiled during Newton's childhood, the roof space was designed with access holes for barn owls. We may applaud this as a concession to the wild birds but there was no altruistic purpose: it was intended to attract the owls so they might help keep down the vermin in the attached hayloft and grain store.

Provincial furniture of the mid-seventeenth century was of heavy oak construction and there was little of it. A bedchamber would be furnished with a bed, a storage coffer, maybe a stool and washstand and a chamber pot. Every bedroom needed a chamber pot and we know that Newton purchased one first thing upon his arrival in Cambridge. We do not know what toilet facilities there were at Woolsthorpe, whether indoors or out, since no evidence remains. Most likely, there was an earth closet well away from the house. This usually consisted of a hole in the ground over which was set a board seat with a suitable hole, all within a little hut. A bucket of dry earth stood by to be tipped in afterwards to cover the faeces. Eventually, when the hole was full, a new one would be dug, the hut moved and the procedure repeated. Everything would biodegrade back into the soil or else be used as fertiliser on the crops, along with animal manure. There was no toilet paper: cloths or sponges left soaking in vinegar as a disinfectant, or disposable hay, leaves or moss were probably the best options. People of the time believed bad smells, or 'miasmas' as they called them, were the actual causes of disease so they were suspicious of indoor privies. That said, it was also thought that the ammonia smell given off by stale urine kept moths away, so the indoor garderobe, i.e. wardrobe, if there was one, was the place to hang your best clothes. At the end of the previous century, John Harington, a cousin of Elizabeth I, had invented a flushing loo for her majesty but she never took to the idea, so the rest of society never learned of it. Besides, a loo was only going to be as efficient as the accompanying sewage system – which had yet to be invented. So for country folk, the earth closet was the best and most practical idea, and remained so in some places into the twentieth century.

The hall and the parlour at Woolsthorpe would have been the main reception rooms but the inventory drawn up after Isaac Newton senior died includes beds and chests in the parlour – normally the best room in the house – so clearly the Newtons made full use of every space. In the hall and on the landing there are drawings scratched into the walls, some by young Isaac. This was not the appalling act that it might be today, if a child drew on the walls. With paper still a rare and costly commodity, walls were handy and since they were regularly lime-washed to keep them clean and reduce vermin, a new pristine drawing surface would be created at least once a year. Newton's sketches appear to date from his time at the grammar school in Grantham since they include St Wulfram's Church, which stands opposite the school, and a post windmill that was built nearby during the time of his attendance there. Other graffiti include possible witch marks, intended to ward off evil and witches in particular, these being very much 'in the news' in the mid-seventeenth century.

Witchcraft[16]
Back in 1604, James I – a man paranoid about witches whom he believed had been involved in a number of attempts to assassinate him – introduced *The Witchcraft Act* in England, making hanging the mandatory punishment even for a first offence, however minor the outcome of the supposed criminal act. If the alleged witch was

found to have a mole or birthmark or liver spot upon their body which might be 'the devil's mark', that was sufficient to condemn them to death. The act stated that:

> If any person or persons shall use, practise or exercise any invocation or conjuration of any evil or wicked spirit, or shall consult, covenant with, entertain, employ, feed, or reward any evil and wicked spirit to or for any intent or purpose then they shall suffer pains of death.

During James's reign in Scotland, as many as 4,000 people were believed to have been burnt as witches – an incredible number considering the small population. England, with a far greater population, sent less than half that number to the flames. This was all down to James and his obsessive fears which may be traced back to his childhood. He was persuaded by his Presbyterian tutors that the execution of his mother, Mary, Queen of Scots, had been brought about by witchcraft, as much as by the political necessities of her cousin, Queen Elizabeth. As a result, the boy developed a dark and unhealthy fascination with Black Magic. An English courtier to both Elizabeth and James, Sir John Harington (inventor of the flush toilet, *see* above) later remembered that:

> His Highness [James] told me her [his mother's] death was visible in Scotland before it did really happen, but was spoken of in secret by those whose power of [fore]sight, presented to them a bloody head dancing in the air.

For ordinary people, witchcraft was a way to explain their misfortunes as part of the on-going struggle between God and Satan. If a loved one died unexpectedly, or the hens stopped laying eggs or a child fell ill, it was easier to blame it on a witch's satanic curse than to think that God was not taking loving care of you and yours. Unsurprisingly, witches became scapegoats for all manner of events, from crop failures to lost valuables.

In 1612, there had been the notorious Pendle witch trials in Lancashire. Alizon Device of Pendle cursed a pedlar who refused to sell her any pins. The pedlar collapsed and his son reported it to a local magistrate, Roger Nowell. Alizon lived with her mother Elizabeth, her grandmother Demdike, younger sister Jennet and brother James. Neighbours referred to Grandmother Demdike as a 'cunning' or wise woman. Nowell interviewed Alizon and she confessed to bewitching the pedlar but also accused their neighbours, with whom the family were having a feud, of using spells to kill four people. The neighbours then accused Demdike of witchcraft, so Nowell arrested Alizon, Grandmother Demdike and also their neighbours, Anne Whittle, and her daughter, Anne Redferne.

Elizabeth Device held a celebration on Good Friday, a day when all good Christians should have been in church, mourning their Saviour's death upon the cross. A local constable heard rumours that it was actually a meeting of witches, so arrested everyone present. The family quickly implicated others and all were accused of plotting to kill a man using witchcraft. Elizabeth's nine-year-old daughter, Jennet Device, was called to give evidence in the trial that followed. There had been earlier cases of children appearing as witnesses in trials but the law stated those under fourteen were not credible and could not be sworn under oath. However, in his book *Daemonologie*, King James wrote that 'Children, women and liars can be witnesses over high treason against God.' This influenced the justice system and led to Nowell using Jennet as his key witness.

'At twelve noon,' she said, 'about twenty people came to our house. My mother told me they were all witches. My mother is a witch and that I know to be true. I have seen her spirit in the likeness of a brown dog, which she called Ball. The dog did ask what she would have him do and she answered that she would have him help her to kill.' Jennet then named six people and her mother and brother James. James denounced his mother Elizabeth too but Jennet then turned on him, saying he had been a witch for three years and she had seen his spirit kill three people. Her convincing evidence was believed by the jury and, after a two-day trial, all her family and most of her neighbours were found guilty of causing death or harm by witchcraft. The following day, ten people, including all Jennet's family, were hanged at Gallows Hill.

The clerk of the court, Thomas Potts, wrote a book about the trial. His *Wonderful Discoverie of Witches in the Countie of Lancaster* became popular and his writings and Jennet's evidence appeared in a handbook for magistrates, *The Country Justice,* which was later used in the colonies in America. It became acceptable to use the testimony of children in trials of witchcraft. During the notorious Salem witch trials in 1692, most of the evidence was given by children and nineteen people were hanged.

Twenty years after the Pendle case, Jennet found herself on trial, accused of witchcraft. In 1633, at the village of Wheatley Lane in Lancashire, Edmund Robinson, aged ten, was responsible for looking after his mother's cows. On one occasion, he was late bringing the animals home from pasture and told his mother that witches had abducted him, blaming some of the women of the village, one of whom was Jennet Device. The case was taken before the local justices and the women were found guilty by the jury. But the judges were not convinced and referred the case to the Privy Council at Westminster. Young Edmund and the women he accused made the long journey south to appear in court but, perhaps more scared of the higher authorities than he was of his mother, the lad finally admitted his story was untrue. Late home, he had concocted the whole tale because he knew his mother would punish him. The women were acquitted. However, despite this, Jennet was not allowed to leave Lancaster Castle until she had paid for her board during the time spent there. For Jennet, that was impossible and the last known record of her was at the castle in 1636. King James's obsession was still destroying lives more than a decade after his death but, fortunately, his subjects were becoming more sceptical about the existence of witches.

Widows were always easy targets for such accusations. They might be blamed for bad weather, crop diseases, sick animals, miscarriages or the death of a loved one with no means of proving they were innocent. And every witch had a 'familiar', whether a cat, dog, goat, mouse, bird or frog; bore the 'devil's mark' of a mole, wart or age-spot, and flew on her broomstick. Since animals were everywhere, either as pets, livestock, vermin or wild creatures and everyone has a blemish or two on their body, almost every lonely woman might pass the test for a witch. Flying was another matter. Fortunately for every housewife who owned a broom, by 1712, sanity prevailed. In that year, when Jane Wenham of Hertfordshire was accused by her neighbours of being a witch because they claimed they had seen her flying on her broomstick, a wise magistrate, Sir John Powell, stated in court that, since there was no law against flying, she did not have to answer that charge. However, the jury found her guilty of 'conversing with the Devil in the form of a cat'. Sir John had no time for such nonsense and Jane was released but, unsurprisingly, avoided going home to face her neighbours. In Newton's day witches were still considered very real and witch marks carved on walls and lintels thought to be a simple and free method of protection. Thus they were scratched or painted on window ledges, chimneys and doorways; any point where a witch might gain entry to a building.

The Woolsthorpe Manor House

There is some intriguing speculation that the house at Woolsthorpe is *not* the building in which Isaac Newton was born, despite the story generally accepted and the fact that the *National Trust Guidebook* states that: 'Newton's mother's room, the Red Chamber. Isaac Newton was born here...'

A descendant of the Newton family, Russell Newton, has researched the information concerning the manor house and discovered a different story entirely.[17] The confusion begins in William Stukeley's account of his visits to Woolsthorpe Manor. Stukeley knew Isaac Newton in London and first visited the manor in 1721. Newton was not there at the time but his servants gave Stukeley a tour of the house 'where Sir Isaac was born', as he noted. However, after a second visit a few months after Newton's death in 1727, Stukeley now stated that the house had been rebuilt by Barnabas Smith, Newton's stepfather 'of not so large a form as the old one which was become very ruinous; that wherein Sir Isaac was born'. In other words, despite the National Trust's guidebook claim that Newton was born in the Red Room upstairs in Woolsthorpe Manor, it now seems possible the house in its present form did not exist in 1642.

Furthermore, according to the inventories that accompany Isaac senior's will of 1642 and Hannah Newton's will of 1679 detailing, room by room, the contents of the house, Hannah's list accounts for a house of three storeys, not two, as in the earlier document and the rooms have different names and uses. This may be because Hannah changed things around for her own convenience, but it is hard to equate the two inventories.

Russell Newton has also unearthed a story told by the Atter family of Woolsthorpe. Samuel Atter, who died in 1859 aged 100 years, spent his life at Woolsthorpe and described his father, Lawrence Otter (*sic*) as a tenant of three generations of Newtons, ending with Sir Isaac. Atter tells of two houses on the manor site a few yards apart. The older house, referred to as either Widow Newton's or the Dower house, was later divided into two cottages and Richard Otter – a relative of Lawrence and Samuel – lived in one of them. Therefore, it is possible that the current manor house was not simply a remodelling of the original but a completely new building from the one in which Isaac Newton was born. Whether he first saw daylight in the present building or not, Isaac certainly spent his childhood there, raised in the main by his grandmother, a woman of some education – a fact that considerably influenced his future.

Chapter 3

THE 1650s: THE DISTRACTED SCHOLAR

The 1650s in England saw Oliver Cromwell's Puritan regime in power, firstly as a Commonwealth and then as a Protectorate once Cromwell was created Lord Protector in 1653. The puritanical attitude to religion and life in general made the country stark and austere in so many respects. Young Isaac Newton would certainly have experienced the unadorned, rigorous impositions of Puritanism at first hand in his childhood. There is some doubt as to whether his grandparents, James and Margery Ayscough, who raised him from the age of three, were of this persuasion or not but from 1646 the church that the family attended in Colsterworth was in the charge of Francis Browne, described as a 'Minister of the Word, a Godly and Orthodox Divine'. Having been appointed to the post by a parliamentary committee, 'orthodox' meant Puritan so services in Colsterworth church would have followed the requisite pattern of long sermons, everyone partaking of communion at a plain table and with psalms recited, not sung. Hymn-singing and decorated altars set apart from the congregation smacked of popish idolatry. The service was conducted by a minister; no longer was the title 'reverend' to be used. The parish records were to be kept by appointed representatives and births, rather than baptisms, were recorded.

Barnabas Smith, Isaac's stepfather and Rector of North Witham, began signing himself 'minister' instead of reverend but Isaac's maternal uncle, William Ayscough, having been appointed Rector of Burton Coggles by Charles I in 1642, did not change his signature.[1] This may suggest the Ayscoughs had some Royalist sympathies while Smith was either less committed or more cautious. However, despite any reservations regarding the new Puritan regime, William Ayscough kept his position in Burton Coggles throughout the Commonwealth and Protectorate periods, so he must have refrained from expressing any overt Royalist sentiments. At the end of January 1649, with the execution of King Charles in Whitehall in London, there must have seemed little possibility of any return to monarchy as the state regime.

Uncertainty and Austerity

Whatever anyone's sympathies were at the time, the condemnation of a king as a traitor to his people and his subsequent death on the scaffold must have come as an incredible shock. The uncertainties of a country without a king became apparent in the Commonwealth period that lasted from 1649–53. England was ruled by the military which, although answerable to Parliament in theory, often took action without parliamentary sanction. No one was sure what was going on and the reluctance of foreign rulers to have dealings with the Commonwealth that might collapse into chaos at any time meant a co-ordinated foreign policy was impossible to implement. Without a head of state, with whom could matters be discussed and negotiated? The only solution Parliament could devise at the time was to appoint Oliver Cromwell as head of state as Lord Protector, a title he accepted. Surprisingly, Parliament went a step further in 1657, offering him the hereditary title of king. Cromwell refused, saying he already held the dignity of that office and the name 'Protector' was enough. After all, he had not disposed of one king only to put another in his place but he did agree that the title of Lord Protector should be heritable by the eldest son – a decision that would prove to be the downfall of the regime. However, despite refusing to become King Oliver, he did reside in the former king's palaces, living in royal splendour by all accounts.

Even before the king's defeat, the Parliamentarians had abolished Christmas, causing great popular resentment among ordinary people – Christmas was one of the few remaining holidays since saints' days were no longer celebrated. In December 1643, the apprentice boys of London protested against the shopkeepers who had been told to open on Christmas Day and, in the words of a delighted Royalist, 'forced them to shut up their shops again'. On 24 December 1644, the editor of a pro-Parliamentarian news pamphlet expressed support for the MPs' decision to favour the Puritan monthly fast over the traditional Christmas feast but admitted the common people rejected the idea with incredulous shouts of 'What, not keep Christmas?' Many ordinary people quietly kept Christmas as special each year and in 1647 – despite the fact that Parliament had recently passed a law declaring the celebration of Christmas a punishable offence – a crowd gathered at Cornhill in London and 'set up Holly and Ivy on the pinnacles of the public water conduit'. When the Lord Mayor sent officers to remove the decorations, the crowd resisted, forcing the mayor to rush to the scene with a party of soldiers to break up the demonstration by force. The worst disturbances took place at Canterbury where a crowd of protesters first smashed up the shops which had opened on Christmas Day and then seized control of the city. This riot set off a major insurrection in Kent in 1648 with a series of risings against Parliament and in favour of the king, which Fairfax and Cromwell only managed to suppress with great difficulty.

Following Parliament's victory in 1649, demonstrations against outlawing Christmas became less common but there is no doubt that many people continued to celebrate the day in private. In his pamphlet *The Vindication of Christmas* (1652), John Taylor provided a lively portrait of how, he claimed, the old Christmas festivities were still being kept up. Nevertheless, as time went by, Christmas ceased to be celebrated in the majority of churches. It was ironic though that while the Puritans succeeded in ending the religious observance of Christmas, they failed to suppress the secular, pagan Yuletide festivities that they had railed about for so long. While Cromwell was not personally responsible for cancelling Christmas, both he and the senior members of his regime supported the ban, transacting government business on 25 December as if it were a day just like any other.

The famous diarist John Evelyn noted what happened when he went to church on Christmas Day in 1657:

> I went to London with my wife to celebrate Christmas Day... Sermon ended, as [the minister] was giving us the holy sacrament, the chapel was surrounded with soldiers, and all the communicants and assembly surprised and kept prisoners by them, some in the house, others carried away... These wretched miscreants held their muskets against us as we came up to receive the sacred elements, as if they would have shot us at the altar.

Christmas was not the only casualty of Puritan rule. The theatres were closed and organs removed from churches. Unaccompanied singing in unison was permitted in praise of God but no harmonising.

Puritan demands for the removal of the Church of England prayer book as being too papist and all bishoprics to be abolished resulted in local disquiet in many places and, eventually, the production of locally organised counter-petitions. But Parliament had its way and the English *Book of Common Prayer* of 1604 was outlawed in 1645, to be replaced by the *Directory of Public Worship*, which was more a set of instructions than a prayer book. The *Directory* was never popular. Few churchwardens' accounts record its purchase and the old prayer book was certainly used clandestinely in some places, not least because the Directory made no provision at all for burial services, but the *Book of Common Prayer* would not be reinstated until after the Restoration of the monarchy to England in 1660.

Lodging with William Clarke

In 1655, at the age of twelve, Isaac Newton was sent off to school in Grantham, 7 miles away. His mother, widowed in 1653, had returned to Woolsthorpe, bringing with her Isaac's three half-siblings. But at Grantham Free Grammar School – now King's School (as it had also been known before, until the Parliamentarians abolished the monarchy in 1649) – the term 'free' only applied to Grantham townspeople, so his mother was required to pay for his schooling. This she was not keen to do, despite being more than able to afford the fees. Isaac's uncle, William Ayscough, may have persuaded Hannah to send him and she could have been relieved to get him away from the manor for a while because the boy later admitted to being disruptive at home. In a waste-book which he kept, known as the Fitzwilliam Notebook, Newton wrote a long list of confessions from his past. Despite being nineteen when he compiled the list in 1662, some of his sins must have dated back to before 1653 when his stepfather died because he writes:

> Refusing to go to the close at my mothers command
> Threatning my father and mother Smith to burne them and the house over them
> Wishing death and hoping it to some
> Punching my sister
> Robbing my mothers box of plums and sugar
> Peevishness with my mother
> With my sister
> Falling out with the servants.[2]

Once in Grantham, the lad's 'peevishness' would be someone else's problem. Hannah was friends with Katherine Storer. She had much in common with Katherine, both being left a widow with children. However, Katherine was now married to a wealthy Grantham apothecary, William Clarke, also a widower with children. The couple then went on to have three more children together. Despite this family of nine children, the Clarkes agreed to take on one more and young Isaac Newton became their lodger in rooms above and behind the apothecary shop, next to the George Inn on Grantham High Street.[3] He slept up in the garret – the perfect place, as matters turned out, since it was where Clarke kept his large library of books. Newton was no stranger to books: Barnabas Smith's considerable collection of theological volumes went to Woolsthorpe after his death but Clarke's library had a far wider range of topics, including medicine, alchemy and apothecaries' remedies. Perhaps it was his bedtime reading up in the garret that first inspired Newton's interest in science since copies of books by

René Descartes and Galileo's *Starry Messenger* were there on the shelf to pique his imagination.[4]

We know at some point at around the age of thirteen he discovered *The Mysteries of Nature and Art* by John Bate, first published in 1634, and possibly that, too, was in Clarke's library.[5] It certainly was not a school book and Newton spent 2½d on a notebook to record the interesting passages he read. In its pages were detailed instructions for the construction of mechanical models, including a windmill of a design known as a post mill. Newton was disappointed that the sails would not turn indoors so he invented the mouse-powered mill, with the little animal running in a version of a hamster-wheel to turn the sails. However, 'Mr Miller', as Newton called him, was not always obliging in providing the power upon demand, only working at his pleasure and sometimes eating the grain he was supposed to be grinding.[6]

Bate's book also explained how to make kites, sundials that worked and paper lanterns. These last, Newton made and used to light his way to and from school in the winter, scaring the locals with what seemed to be lights floating in the air in the process. He also constructed a sundial at Colsterworth Church where, for decades, it remained the most accurate time-piece for the village. But whereas other youngsters of his age would have enjoyed seeing the results of mouse-powered mechanisms, flying kites and eerily floating illuminations, Newton took most pleasure in the actual construction.

Ever the perfectionist, it became clear that he had a tremendous talent for making mechanical devices to the highest standard of workmanship. You can almost picture other boys trying to have a go and Newton, never known for his patience with ineptitude, scoffing and sneering at their efforts. He did try to involve his fellows in what he called 'philosophical play' but they preferred rough-and-tumble games to the painstaking, thought-provoking activities that Newton pursued out of school.

The Clarkes were certainly tolerant of their young lodger's activities, allowing Newton to speed along the corridors of the sizeable shop, through the house behind and above the shop in a cart he made.[7] He was permitted to draw diagrams on the walls, fly his kites from the roof, construct models and tinker with potions in the stillroom. To begin with, he seems to have learned far more from William Clarke than he did at school.

Apothecaries were the pharmacists of the day, making up pills and medications and tending the sick and Clarke must quickly have realised Newton had a keen interest in all aspects of the craft and certainly let him help out in the stillroom, if not in front of shop. The boy kept details of the various remedies he made up, including one that involved 300 mashed millipedes in four gallons of ale with a little mint and wormwood added. But apothecaries were not restricted to making medical treatments and Newton's notebook records recipes for things as diverse as fish bait and paint pigments. He also learned some chemical techniques which would prove useful in the future, such as how to use acid to cut glass, and was allowed to experiment with sulphur, mercury and other freely available chemicals, which today would be relegated to the fume cupboard.

The inventory attached to the will of Ralph Clarke, William's father, from whom he inherited the apothecary business in 1630, shows what the shop contained. Apart from such equipment as a number of pestles and mortars of both brass and stone for grinding, weighing scales, weights and measures, the list of stock makes intriguing reading:

Alum, green copperas, brimstone [sulphur], red and white lead. Bay oil and various sugars [sugars were often flavoured with spices or flowers as remedies, or came in grades of fineness, such as loaf sugar in a solid block or powdered sugar], starch, rice and almonds. Liquorice, rhubarb, prunes, raisins, currants, honey and hops. Spices including pepper, cinnamon, cloves and nutmeg as dry ingredients and as oils. Flowers of rosemary, roses [for coughs and blood disorders], celandine [for treating jaundice], gilly flowers [carnations] and hyacinths. Lemon pips and pine nuts. Lemon soup, raspberry soup and the juice of dragon's blood [actually a red tree resin with antibiotic, antiviral, antiseptic and healing properties]. Body parts of crocodiles and other creatures. Minerals. Perfumes.[8]

This mixture of herbs, chemicals, spices and other foodstuffs all for sale together was common practice and, with the ever-increasing trade with the New World, new exotic ingredients were being added to the range. In 1658, the physician Sir Theodore de Mayerne recorded this recipe in his book *Archimagirus Anglo-Gallicus* for what he calls 'London Pye', although it sounds more like a stew or casserole, since he makes no mention of any pastry. It uses a number of the ingredients inventoried in Clarke's apothecary shop, along with some we would find strange and some from the Americas that would have been very novel at the time, notably both ordinary potatoes (described as roots) and sweet potatoes. Incidentally, this is one of the earliest examples of a recipe giving exact quantities; earlier ones are often very vague as to measurements.

Take of marrow-bones, eight; cock-sparrows, eighteen; potato roots, one pound; chestnuts, forty; sweet potatoes, a quarter of a pound; lettuce stalks, two ounces; dates, half a pound; oysters, a peck; citron-rinds, preserved, a quarter of a pound; artichokes, two or three; yolks of hard-[boiled] eggs, twelve; lemons sliced, two; barberries, picked, one handful; gross pepper [pepper corns rather than ground pepper], a quarter of an ounce; nutmeg, sliced [?], one half ounce; cinnamon, whole [the bark], half an ounce; cloves, whole, a quarter of an ounce; a large mace, half an ounce; currants, a quarter of a pound. Liquor it when it is baked with white wine, butter and sugar.[9]

Whether the Clarke family and their lodger ever ate anything like this very spicy and expensive concoction we do not know, but the apothecary would probably have either stocked or been able to acquire most of the ingredients, if a customer ordered them. Marrow bones would be available from any butcher, the cock sparrows netted for free or bought from a poulterer and the eggs might well be from local hens, butter from the dairy and wine from a vintner. Knowing Newton's interest in experimentation, including on himself, he was probably just as keen to sample foodstuffs he had not seen before as to distil millipedes and the like.

While able to learn so much from William Clarke, Newton was a less than star pupil at the Grammar School. Learning Latin and Greek and great swathes of scriptural texts by rote was not inspiring but one aspect of the teaching Newton took to heart and would continue to use throughout his time at Cambridge was the 'commonplace book'. There, the students wrote out selected passages from texts they read for future reference, along with their own notes, annotations and questions raised. As we have seen, he applied this method in studying Bate's book and in the apothecary's shop, but what would have been included in the school curriculum of the time?

Secondary Education

An instruction book drawn up for Newport School in Shropshire in 1656 gives a good idea of what was expected of a grammar school in terms of not only academic education but a grounding in religious principles, manners and the moral virtues of an upright Puritan citizen:

> The first duty entered upon every morning after a short and solemn calling upon God by the Master for a blessing thereupon, shall be the distinct reading of a chapter of the Holy Scriptures by one of the scholars as the Master shall appoint, and afterwards Prayer shall be put unto the Lord for his further blessing upon their endeavours in teaching and learning. And before their dismission in the evening, they shall sing one of David's Psalms as the Master shall appoint and then close the day with prayer and thanksgiving.[10]

Studying the Bible was central to education and it was believed to be so important to understand the text's precise meaning in considerable depth that some schools would have scholars read the Old Testament in the original Hebrew and the New Testament in the original Greek. The point was to avoid any corruption of meaning by other translators who might bias the language in favour of their own opinions. This was one of the Puritans' main arguments against Catholicism; that Rome insisted on using antiquated translations of previous translations that incorporated the scribal errors and misinterpretations of centuries before. To the Puritan mind, every man's own interpretation of the Bible, arrived at through prayer and contemplation, was as valid as that of any ancient churchman and likely more correct.

The Puritan poet and secretary to Oliver Cromwell, John Milton, proposed that 'the Hebrew tongue be gained [learned] that the Scriptures be read in the original by pupils'. That might be possible for boys attending grammar school but what of those who did not have that option? The Puritan Ralph Verney, son of Sir Edmund who died at Edgehill as the king's standard-bearer, wrote a letter in 1652 in answer to a girl who wished to learn Latin, Greek and Hebrew in order to read the Bible in its original languages. Sir Ralph told her:

> Good sweet heart, be not so covetous; believe me a Bible with the Common Prayer [book] and a good plain Catechism in your mother tongue being well read and practised is well worth all the rest, and much more suitable to your sex.

It seems unlikely that Hebrew was on the curriculum at Grantham because we know that Newton taught himself Hebrew later on. Grantham probably kept to Latin and some Greek. Logic, however, was on the curriculum and had always been studied since medieval times. It required the close reading of texts written by classical writers, like Aristotle and Plato, and then reasoning, through argument, to produce a persuasive piece of rhetorical prose to explain the subsequent conclusions.

However in the 1600s, views were changing as to whether this method of teaching was suitable in grammar schools. It would remain a foundation of university education but should not pupils understand the basic facts of a subject before constructing logical arguments regarding it? Was it not tending towards superficial knowledge rather than underpinning the foundations? John Milton certainly thought that the teaching of logic and high-flown rhetoric should be reserved for university education. Other contemporary writers agreed that it was preposterous to teach logic and metaphysical ideas before considering 'the concrete thing itself'. In plain language, how could students rationalise ideas without understanding the substance of the subject?

Nevertheless, the 'disputations' arising from the use of logic continued in grammar schools and Newton might well have been required to take part. The Newport instructions specify how these disputations should be conducted:

> Once in six weeks throughout the year Saturday in the forenoon shall be spent by the upper forms in such exercises as the Master shall appoint, proposing grammatical or historical questions unto one another and making declamations and such like as may tend to the begetting of learning amongst the scholars.

Incidentally, 'upper forms' then referred quite literally to higher forms or benches. In the school hall, new boys sat on the lowest forms at the front and progressed over the years to the tiered upper forms at the back, where the eldest boys sat. It was from the vantage point of the upper form that Newton was able to carve his name on the high window sill where it can still be seen today.

In order to prepare for a disputation, the scholars had to trawl through the classical texts to find support and illustrations for their arguments. For Newton, the spirit of research required for these exercises was something that remained with him throughout his life. But religion, grammar and logic were not the only subjects. Manners and moral instruction were just as important for young gentlemen. In 1633, John Clarke of Lincoln – as far as I know, he was no relation to William Clarke of Grantham – wrote a book of manners for use in schools, covering behaviour in the home and out and about, as well as in the classroom, using the format to teach both Latin and English:

> Daily in the morning, before all things upon his knees he [the pupil] is to praise God and call for grace whereby he may increase in learning and virtue. Which done, he is to come to the school, mannerly to salute his master and his fellows and

diligently applying his learning, lose no time idly in jangling to his own hurt and hindrance of others. He is to have continual practice of Latin speech. [He should be] gentle in word and deed to all his fellows, no busy complainer, nor yet no hider of truth, benevolent, liberal ... a diligent marker of the virtue and good manners of others ... and to fly far from the company of all unthrifty rake-hells.

Grantham Grammar School and the Trigge Library

Newton appears to have avoided the company of 'unthrifty rake-hells' but was not always 'gentle to all his fellows'. Early on in his schooling, having little interest in the uninspiring subject matter, he was bottom of the class. It may have been this ignominious position of an outsider not from Grantham which led to him being bullied. We do not know for certain the identity of the bully but he sat a place above Newton in class. It is possible that it was one of Clarke's stepsons, Arthur Storer. Arthur was two years younger than Newton, so his higher position in class may have rankled and in his list of sins, mentioned above, Newton notes as sin Number 44: 'Beating Arthur Storer'. On the other hand, it could have been Edward Storer who was ten months older than Newton, or some other unnamed fellow. Whether Arthur Storer was involved or not, the two became friends for life and the event changed Newton's attitude to academic learning. According to John Conduitt, Newton's nephew by marriage who recorded many tales told to him by Sir Isaac in later years, the bully was 'much larger' than Newton – a fact which may cast doubt on it being the younger Arthur – and kicked Newton in the belly on the way to school one morning. Newton must have smouldered with anger for the entire day until...

As soon as school was over he [Newton] challenged the boy to fight & they went out together into the church yard [of St Wulfram's across the way]... Though Sir Isaac was not so lusty as his antagonist he had so much more spirit & resolution that he beat him 'til he declared he would fight no more.[11]

Egged on to do worse by the schoolmaster's son, Newton then pulled the bully by the ears to the church building and rubbed his face against the stone wall. There would be no more bullying of the boy from out of town. Neither could he be belittled any longer for being bottom of the class. Having been roused to physical action, Newton now determined to assert his academic prowess to beat the bully in the classroom. Once having set his mind to the required learning, his agile brain and capacity for single-minded concentration meant he swiftly overtook the bully and everyone else in academic achievement, to become top of the class. Though unsurprising to us, perhaps this transformation came as a shock to his contemporaries. And there was no going back once he realised how easy such learning was for him. By this time, he would also have had access to the extensive library of Francis Trigge, housed within St Wulfram's Church and available to the pupils in the grammar school across the lane, although the majority of books there were theological, such as those of Barnabas Smith back at Woolsthorpe.

Francis Trigge was a licensed Puritan preacher, clergyman and rector of Welbourne, 12 miles north of Grantham, during the Elizabethan period, dying in 1606. He was concerned for the better education of ordinary people and set up a library in 1598 with £100 'or thereabouts' to be spent on books for the purpose of

> ... the better encreasinge of learnings and knowledge in divinitie & other liberall sciences & learning by such of the cleargie & others as well as beinge inhabitantes in or near Grantham & the soake thereof as in other places in the said Countie.

A bequest of twenty further volumes were added to the library from Trigge's own collection under the terms of his will when he died in 1606. The library was to be kept in the room above the south porch of St Wulfram's Church with the books to be chained to desks and read there. In theory at least, it was the first public reference library in England and is still in its original setting today, much as Newton would have known it. Although theological texts were the most numerous, they included an unexpectedly eclectic mix, from Calvinist and Lutheran sermons to outspoken anti-Catholic propaganda but there are also anti-Protestant diatribes. As the Trigge Library website says:

> What survives is the whole history of the Reformation, set out in the writings of the men who brought it about or set themselves to oppose it. It is a remarkable collection for students of religious beliefs.[12]

Such books may have set young Newton to rethinking his own theological views.

Apart from the many theological books, there were also printed volumes on medicine, copied from earlier manuscripts by the classical physician and surgeon Galen and others. There were books concerning fourteenth-century legal cases in Italy and other oddities. A catalogue compiled in 1608 and still extant contains 228 titles, although some of these had been bound together. There was also a 'Bestiarium' listed: a medieval book about animals that still included unicorns as existing creatures, not that this is so surprising when in Newton's day the physician and philosopher Sir Thomas Browne still included unicorns in his writings on the natural world, while discrediting the possibility of griffins and sphinxes.[13] Perhaps unicorns were more readily believed in by those who regarded the Bible as correct in every detail, being literally the Word of God to the Puritan mind. Unicorns are mentioned eight times in the Old Testament, so who would dare to doubt their existence? It would be fascinating to know Newton's view on these elusive creatures.[14]

The Alderman of Grantham – the leader of the town council, Grantham's version of a mayor – had charge of the library that was to benefit the townspeople. In 1651 and again in 1657, William Clarke was the alderman and would, no doubt, have adhered strictly to the oath regarding library use and custodianship of the books – he was that kind of man when it concerned civic responsibility. According to Trigge's stipulation, the alderman was to be assisted by the two vicars of North and South Grantham and by the schoolmaster of the grammar school opposite St Wulfram's Church who was to keep the key. The schoolmaster at the time was Henry Stokes. Unlike Clarke and most of the town councillors, who were Puritan supporters of Oliver Cromwell and the Parliamentarian regime, Stokes was a Royalist at heart and quite open about his preference. He attended a town council meeting in 1651, ready to offer his resignation as schoolmaster if Alderman Clarke and the others would prefer a master of their own persuasion.[15] Fortunately for young Newton's future, Stokes was confirmed in his post at the grammar school.

Officially, the school was supposed to accommodate twenty pupils, although John Conduitt later recorded that Newton told him there were between sixty and eighty boys when he was there. That must have made the single schoolroom a cramped space for learning. The master's house next door, where Henry Stokes lived, was larger than the schoolroom. Little wonder that so much emphasis was placed on the good behaviour of pupils. Apparently, there was general concern among educationalists of the time regarding 'cockneys and tidlings wantonly brought up'.[16] Today, the term 'cockney' – once used to refer to those born within hearing distance of the bells of St Mary-le-Bow Church in the City of London and, more recently and less accurately, to those with a London accent – had quite a different meaning in Newton's day. It then meant a spoilt child, usually one raised in an urban environment and, therefore, in adulthood, less hardy and more likely to complain in any situation of adversity, sorrow and war in particular. So it was a derisory term, most probably coined originally by country folk with little respect for town-dwellers. Isaac Newton certainly could not have been categorised under that term. Neither was he a 'tidling'. The OED references the quotation given above as originally dating back to 1520, found in R. Whittington's *Vulgaria*, folio 37v, so it must have been copied into the Newport School instruction book in 1656. 'Tidling' also meant a pampered or spoilt child without the urban qualification; a darling; a young, delicate or puny child, needing special care; a weakling.

Interestingly, there were worries that with pupils required to read, write and speak in Latin during school hours, they might forget how to read and write in English. The queries were raised by Mulcaster, asking, 'How many small infants have we set to grammar which can scarcely read? How many to learn Latin which never wrote a letter?'

If the school bully in the incident described earlier was young Arthur Storer, William Clarke's step-son, that did not prevent Arthur and Isaac Newton from building a friendship that would ultimately span the Atlantic Ocean and last until Arthur died in 1687, in Maryland in North America, aged forty-one. By that date, Arthur Storer had become America's first named astronomer and had supplied data which Newton used in his *Principia,* acknowledging his old friend's contribution when the book was published just a few months after Arthur's death. Newton also referred to Arthur's report of the earliest sightings of 'Storer's' comet at the River Patuxent, near Hunting Creek in Maryland, in the confines of Virginia from 14 August to 18 September 1682. Newton later wrote:

And Mr Storer (by letters which have come into my hands) writes that in the month of December, when the tail [of the comet] appeared of the greatest bulk and splendour, the head was but small and far less than that which was seen in the month of November before sun-rising; and conjecturing at the cause of the appearance, he judged it to proceed from there being a greater quantity of matter in the head at first, which was afterwards gradually spent.[17]

This was the same comet that Edmund Halley predicted would return; thus it became famous as 'Halley's' comet, not Storer's.

Foreign Affairs

While Isaac Newton and Arthur Storer were concerned with learning the declensions of Latin nouns and how to conjugate irregular Latin verbs, the Commonwealth of Great Britain was attempting to make an impression on the world stage. Because of their similar Puritan religious views and republican stance, the Dutch United Provinces were approached early on in the Commonwealth period as likely allies in taking a stand against the monarchies of Catholic Europe. However, republican as they were, the Dutch took a dim view of a fledgling regime that had committed regicide and the English ambassadors arrived in The Hague to a hail of insults and departed swiftly without any negotiations having taken place. Calling the Dutch 'juggling sharks', interested only in themselves, the would-be chief ambassador, Oliver St John, was keen to persuade Parliament to punish the Dutch and since the United Provinces were England's commercial rival, some form of trade embargo was favoured.

In the autumn of 1651, The Navigation Act passed into law. A deliberate snub as well as a blow to Dutch trading practices, the Act specified that all goods imported into Britain from across the world had to be carried in British ships. Since the Dutch made huge profits as carriers of goods for other countries, this put a considerable dent in their commercial dealings. But hitting out at Dutch business enterprises was not enough. British broadsheets vilified the Dutch as renegade, ungodly Protestants interested only in making money. Even more insulting and with no logical grounds but overweening pride, the Act also stipulated that, upon sighting an English vessel at sea flying the new republican flag, ships of all other nations must dip their flags in respect. Unsurprisingly, in May 1652, off the Kent coast, the Dutch responded, not with lowered ensigns but a broadside of cannon shot. The Commonwealth was now at war with the United Provinces.

Naval engagements were fought in the English Channel and the North Sea with the Dutch having early successes under the leadership of Admiral Maarten van Tromp. The English navy had expanded under Charles I and the Commonwealth now reaped the benefits. Robert Blake was a capable commander who had earned his reputation on land, fighting with distinction in Parliament's New Model Army. Now given command of the navy as General-at-Sea – the Commonwealth distained the Spanish title of 'Admiral' – Blake rewrote the book on naval tactics and conduct at sea. He instigated the close formation of 'sailing line ahead', in order to rake the enemy with a continuous broadside of cannon shot. This was a new and devastatingly effective strategy. Over a century later, Admiral Horatio Nelson wrote of his respect and admiration for Blake and his revolutionary ideas on war at sea. In size, the Dutch and English fleets were comparable at about 100 vessels but the English deployed ships to blockade the Dutch ports and the Dutch diverted part of their fleet to escort convoys of their merchantmen, suffering considerable losses. The Battle of Texel was a lengthy engagement, lasting from 31 July to 1 August 1653. Admiral Van Tromp was killed and the Dutch lost thirty men-o'-war; the English lost less than half that number.

Trade had suffered on both sides and the English must have been relieved when the Dutch sued for peace. Oliver Cromwell regretted the waste of effort for both parties, even as his country's coffers swelled with Dutch booty, feeling that if two Puritan nations could not co-operate, it was a pity. Never a supporter of the war, when Cromwell became head of state as Lord Protector in December 1653, peace talks began, culminating in the Treaty of Westminster, signed in April 1654. The treaty was of surprisingly little advantage to English trade. The Dutch were required to cease harbouring Royalist exiles and agreed to honour the English flag at sea. The reason for making so few demands was that Cromwell wanted the Dutch to join in an alliance against Catholic Spain, but they were not persuaded. England's only gain appears to have been an enhanced reputation as a military and naval power worth consideration when other European nations were forming alliances.

Having negotiated trade agreements with Sweden, Denmark and Portugal, the ink had hardly dried on the Treaty of Westminster when Lord Protector Cromwell declared to his Council of State that 'the King of Spain is the greatest enemy to the Protestant cause in the world,' so making war on Spain and the Spanish Empire could be regarded as a crusade to save the Protestant religion. Of course, there was also the commercial aspect to consider: that England felt entitled to a share of the vast wealth of the Americas. It has been suggested that Cromwell was persuaded to a policy of war by representatives of the mercantile community, rather than by religious or military arguments.[18]

The war was fought off the coast of Spain, the Canaries and in the Caribbean, with the island of Hispaniola (Haiti) as the main objective. The success of the war was counted in terms of a Spanish treasure galleon worth £2 million, the almost total destruction of the Spanish West Indies fleet off Tenerife by Robert Blake and gaining the island of Jamaica, which Cromwell described as 'a dagger pointed at the heart of the Spanish Empire'. The failures were more numerous. Hispaniola was never taken and the leaders of the expeditionary force, Robert Venables and William Penn (father of the founder of Pennsylvania), found themselves in the Tower of London for their troubles. Robert Blake died of wounds received in battle in 1657, though his exploits earned him a state funeral in Westminster Abbey, and the cost of maintaining the fleet at sea outweighed the value of the Spanish treasure gained. Worse yet was the number of men's lives lost in the Caribbean to heat and disease, rather than battle, along with deaths from scurvy and infections aboard ship. The war with Spain did not end officially until 1667, when the restored king, Charles II, signed the Treaty of Madrid – by which time England was again at war with the Dutch.

Science in the United Provinces of the Netherlands

Whichever way England's pendulum relationship with the Dutch was swinging during the 1650s and 1660s, both countries agreed on the pursuit of science as beneficial to mankind and, ultimately, leading to a better understanding of God's creation. If navigation, trade, ship construction and cannon manufacture happened to be improved in the process, then so be it. As two Protestant republics, neither had to consider the Catholic Church's embedded doctrines nor the possibility of royal censorship. Ideas could be discussed and published without fear of accusations of heresy, such as Galileo had suffered, nor the banning of controversial texts and being put on the pope's list of forbidden books. When Frenchman René Descartes was ready to publish his work, he took the precaution of moving to Amsterdam before committing his writings to the printing press.

Descartes was more of a theorist than an experimenter. In the field of mathematics, he invented the use of eponymous Cartesian co-ordinates, still employed today as a means of identifying a point on a graph or a map, but his philosophical theories were the cause of great controversy. As a proponent of dualism, he argued that body and soul were two quite distinct entities; that matter and spirit could co-exist, as they did in mankind, yet remained separate forms. The soul or spirit gave rise to personality, belief and even genius – all ethereal, immeasurable qualities – whereas matter was more concrete, definable and could be weighed and described scientifically, being unaffected by spirit. At the most basic level, according to Descartes, the human body, like the rest of the universe, was a machine that functioned and moved as God first determined, awash in the invisible medium of the ether that filled every space in the universe. Such controversial ideas would have caused Descartes no end of problems in his native France but the Netherlands was more accommodating.

The most troublesome part of Cartesian philosophy was its logical conclusion: having designed and caused the mechanical universe and everything in it to begin working, God was no longer required to keep the device going. For many people, to regard God as redundant and unnecessary was anathema. In England, Robert Boyle liked the idea of a mechanical universe but could not support the demotion of God to a mere bystander. His preference was to have God as an overseer, endlessly making minute adjustments and generally tinkering with the works. However, this version also had its drawbacks. God was perfect and his creation must, likewise, be perfect and run forever. How then could it possibly require any tweaking of parts? Isaac Newton was only eight years old when Descartes died but he too would find difficulties with the Frenchman's interpretation of the universe and the role God took in its functioning. For certain, Newton took God far too seriously to think of him as a glorified manual labourer. An older, Dutch contemporary of Newton, Christiaan Huygens, went so far as to reject the belief in God as a result of studying such ideas, although as a far-sighted astronomer, he dared suggest that life on other planets was a possibility, so long as liquid water was present.

The Huygens family of The Hague were at the forefront of progress in natural philosophy. Constantijn Huygens the elder was acquainted with Galileo and became a friend of Descartes. He was wealthy enough to give his three sons a wide-ranging, liberal education, employing excellent tutors from across Europe. The Englishman John Pell taught them mathematics, giving them the advantage of an early foundation in the subject that Newton had to teach himself. Constantijn had a particular interest in the grinding and use of lenses; how they could be used to reveal detail otherwise invisible to the naked eye. His second son, Christiaan, would take this interest much further and become an international scientist in his own right. In the 1650s, together with his brother Constantijn the younger, Christiaan began designing a refracting telescope. They ground their own lenses and achieved a magnification of x50.

With a new kind of eyepiece that he invented, Christiaan made detailed observations of the planet Saturn. In 1655, he was the first to observe the rings of Saturn, although he believed it was solid, 'a thin, flat ring, nowhere touching [the planet] and inclined to the ecliptic', he noted. He also discovered the first of Saturn's numerous moons, Titan. He sketched the Orion nebula and his telescope was of such quality he was able to distinguish that the nebula consisted of individual stars – the brightest area of this cloud of stars is known as the 'Huygenian region' today. Christiaan also observed a feature on the surface of Mars and, by timing its appearance over a number of days, calculated the length of the Martian day. He was accurate to within 7 minutes and published this and his other astronomical observations in 1659, in his book *Systema Saturnium*.

In 1656, ever ingenious, at the age of twenty-seven, Huygens invented the pendulum clock as a more reliable timepiece than any seen before and, the following year, came up with the probability theory involved in games of chance. Fascinated by his pupil's ideas, one of Christiaan's tutors translated the work from Dutch and published it as *On Reasoning in Games of Chance*. With card games a fashionable pastime throughout the seventeenth century, every player should have read it. If they could understand the mathematics, a good many purses would not have been emptied, pulling their owners down into debt. Gambling was a common hazard of the time. Newton's notebooks, kept as a student at Cambridge, reveal that he was not immune to the craze, recording bluntly, 'lost at cards'. We do not know if Newton read Huygens's book on probability theory but the two men would certainly be studying each other's writings in the future, particularly on the subject of optics.

The End of the Protectorate

Young Newton probably had little recollection of the Civil War, having been just six years old when Charles I was executed at the end of January 1649, so the period of the Commonwealth and Protectorate and the austerity of the Puritan regime were simply the way things were to him. Living as William Clarke's lodger in Grantham, in a 'godly' household, Puritan ethics would have surrounded him, but life in England was about to change yet again.

On 3 September 1658, Lord Protector Oliver Cromwell died, most likely from the ague – malaria – a disease prevalent in his home areas of the Fens in eastern England. Apparently, the recent death of his favourite daughter, Elizabeth, had lowered his spirits considerably and two decades of war, stress and heavy responsibility must have exhausted him. Personally, he had never been popular, but even his most fervent critics must have admired Cromwell's ability to balance the military and religious factions of government and, while he was head of state, dissent and disorder were contained by his powerful personality alone. Only after his death was the very personal aspect of the Protectorate revealed.

In accordance with *The Humble Petition and Advice,* the instrument of government that had set Cromwell in place as Lord Protector, his eldest son, Richard, succeeded to the office. Much has been written about how different the country's history might have been if the petition had not stipulated that the eldest son must inherit his father's title. Cromwell's younger son, Henry, was a tried and tested army commander and had been made Lord Lieutenant of Ireland by his father, a post which gave him experience in governing a turbulent land. Charles Fleetwood, husband of Cromwell's eldest daughter Bridget, had vast military experience, was greatly respected by the army and worked alongside Cromwell during the Protectorate years. Either of these two men could have proved successful in the highest office. Not so Richard.

In the early 1650s, Oliver had described his son Richard as 'idle'. Having little interest or acumen for either the army or politics, the younger man preferred field sports and a life of leisure, running up huge debts – altogether an ungodly existence. Despite this, during his last year, perhaps knowing his strength was waning, Oliver deliberately promoted him, appointing Richard colonel of a mounted regiment and a member of the Council of State – the republican version of a monarch's Privy Council – among other offices and at the very end, named him as his successor. Richard was thirty-two.

Richard's appointment as the new Lord Protector went smoothly. Surprisingly, he proved diligent, charming and accomplished at making effective speeches, but trouble was already brewing on two fronts. Firstly, the financial situation of the Protectorate was dire, yet Richard immediately borrowed vast sums of money to pay for his father's state funeral, determined to surpass that of any previous king. Secondly, his office included the rank of Commander-in-Chief of the military, despite having no worthwhile experience of such matters and lacking any respect from his senior generals and captains in the field. The army had no trust or faith in him or his abilities and the religious factions regarded him as ungodly and, therefore, doubly untrustworthy. Their doubts seemed to be confirmed when Richard began promoting civilian politicians and making economies that seemed to be aimed at reducing the power of the generals and undermining the army's position. It was an uneven contest from the beginning. With none of his father's natural authority, the new Lord Protector could not remain long in office.

By April 1659, Richard Cromwell's Protectorate was ended, replaced by the Restored Commonwealth, as it was called.

But this form of government had already proved flawed in 1653, when it was realised that, whatever name was applied to it, a ruling 'committee' required a nominated head. A country needed a Head of State to lead it, someone to negotiate with other Heads of State, to sign treaties and put the seal on new legislation. The title Lord Protector was abolished but something had to replace that office. No doubt, some new title could have been invented, but someone respected and with a recognised authority had to fill the post. Eyes turned to Breda in the Netherlands where a man of suitable age, military ability and charisma had been biding his time for a decade: to Charles Stuart, son of the deposed Charles I, now nominally Charles II.

Chapter 4

THE 1660s: THE STUDENT
OF LIGHT

While the country held its breath in 1659, wondering with what kind of government its future lay – a military state seeming a definite possibility – Isaac Newton's future was equally uncertain. His mother had removed the promising young scholar from Grantham Grammar School, certain he had acquired more than sufficient knowledge for a yeoman farmer. But knowledge was not enough: farming required an aptitude and an inclination for working the land, growing crops and raising livestock. Newton had no interest in such things, keeping his nose in his books when he ought to have been giving an eye to mending fences and securing the pigs. The Manor Court at Colsterworth had fined him on a number of occasions for unrepaired fences that had resulted in his sheep and pigs wandering onto other people's properties and trampling the crops.

With such blatant shortcomings as a farmer, his mother Hannah must have been in despair over her firstborn. When a number of influential men began to persuade her that her son was capable of higher, better things than totalling up crop yields and organising the wool-clipping, she gave in, grudgingly. The first to appeal to Hannah to let her boy return to his education was Henry Stokes, the headmaster at the grammar school. His offer to remit the 40s fee due for a non-resident of Grantham seems to have worked. By the autumn of 1660, Newton had returned to lodge once more with the Clarke family, resuming lessons in trigonometry and land-surveying techniques. But school was not an end in itself.

Concerned for the young man's continuing education, Stokes then enlisted the aid of William Ayscough, Hannah's brother. William was a graduate of Trinity College, Cambridge, and recognising his nephew's potential, he must have had lengthy discussions with his sister, doing all he could to persuade her that Isaac should be allowed to go to university. Hannah was stubborn but, so the story goes, the farm labourers at Woolsthorpe, on hearing of the possibility, were definitely in favour, declaring the lad was 'fit for nothing but the 'versity, anyway'. No doubt, they wanted rid of such an unenthusiastic and incompetent master.

A third man of influence concerning the young man's future appears to have been Humphrey Babington. Babington was Rector of Boothby Pagnell in Lincolnshire, a Doctor of Divinity and a Senior Fellow – later becoming Vice-Master – at Trinity College, Cambridge. He may have known William Ayscough but, more certainly, he was brother-in-law to William Clarke. Apparently, he was a frequent and popular visitor to the Clarke household and could have taken an interest in the budding young scholar who lodged with the family. Duly persuaded, Hannah finally relented but with stipulations. On 5 June 1660, Newton's name was enrolled at Trinity College but despite the family's relative affluence, his mother insisted that he should commence his academic career as the lowest of the low: as a subsizar. This meant the annual fees would be minimal, perhaps as little as £10 for tutorials with £10 for expenses. Used to keeping the estate accounts, Newton recorded his first purchases as a student as a chamber pot, a lock for his desk, a pound [weight] of candles, a quart bottle of ink and a notebook in which to record the clothes he sent for laundering, to be certain they were returned. One month after his enrolment, Newton matriculated – that is, he made his formal entrance into the college – and was promoted to sizar.

A sizar was still no better than a menial servant, earning his keep by emptying the chamber pots and cleaning the rooms of wealthier students. Since many of these 'fellow-commoners' and 'pensioners' were only attending university with the intent of having a good time, study was never high on their agenda. Drunkenness was certainly a feature with the resultant mess to clear up afterwards. However, it has been suggested that, rather than serving other students, Newton may have been the personal sizar to Humphrey Babington.[1] If this was so, his sizar's duties would not have been too demanding, since Babington's fellowship only required his presence in college for a few weeks every year. Even so, to be classed as a menial must have been a galling experience for the young man.

At first, he threw himself into his studies, making copious notes on Aristotle and Plato – the same classical texts studied by medieval students and probably familiar to him from his schooldays. But in-depth notes on Aristotelian philosophy, ethics and logic began to dwindle. His official tutor Benjamin Pulleyn was uninspiring. Known as a 'pupil-monger', Pulleyn simply took on as many students as possible, since they paid their fees directly to the tutor, having about fifty others alongside Newton. The less interest Newton had in the set texts – his notes suggest that he never read them to the end – the more his personal studies diverged from the official curriculum. Two years older than most and with little in common with his fellow students, he became a loner and, despite the reinstatement of Anglicanism as the state religion after the Restoration of the monarchy, he maintained his Puritan attitudes to both religion and study. His work ethic must have been yet another social barrier between him and his feckless fellow undergraduates.

The Restoration of the Monarchy

In the spring of 1660, before Newton went up to Cambridge, Charles II, the king in exile in Holland, watched events across the Channel with avid interest and increasing hope. Richard Cromwell was long gone, doing his best to retire into obscurity and avoid his persistent creditors. The civilian government of England was balanced on a knife edge, fearing military rule on one side or a state of anarchy on the other. Behind the scenes, letters were criss-crossing the seas between Charles and his Royalist sympathisers back home, keeping him abreast of events. As wily a politician as Oliver Cromwell had ever been, Charles had other assets unavailable to the solemn, godly Lord Protector: charm, youth and a lack of inhibition when it came to dealing with the truth. His ability to be sparing with the full facts, if they would upset or offend his subjects or jeopardise his position, was remarkable. He began his campaign to woo back his realm by issuing the *Declaration of Breda* in April 1660.

General George Monk (also spelled Monck), the most respected and moderate of the army commanders, had marched south with his army, from Scotland to London in January. No one was certain whether he came to renew the civil wars or to keep order. Fortunately, it was the latter and this gave a sense of security to the anxious Parliament that reconvened in February. The sitting drew upon the members of what was called the Long Parliament, originally summoned by Charles I almost two decades previously. Therefore, unlike any Parliament which had met in the interim, it had both Royalist and Parliamentarian representatives. A much-reduced assembly due to time passing, none of them could have been in the first flush of youth but all had experienced and survived the war, so they were likely moderate in their opinions and determined that peace would prevail. With Monk maintaining order in the capital, the Long Parliament voluntarily dissolved itself, new elections swiftly taking place to fill the gaps left by departed MPs. The new Parliament – known as the Convention Parliament, since it broke with convention, being summoned by a civil authority, not by a Head of State because there was not one – met in April and the first item for discussion was the *Declaration of Breda*.

Charles and his advisers had drawn up a 'wish list' of promises to tempt Parliament and people to invite him to return to England and restore the Stuart monarchy. A few moments of reasoned consideration must surely have made it obvious that a number of points made in the declaration were impossible to achieve and of those which could, some were quite unlikely. For example, disbanding much of the army was regarded as vital for peace, but soldiers were never going to go home quietly unless they were paid their wages. Army pay was disastrously in arrears with the Exchequer unable to supply the cash required. Nonetheless, in the declaration, Charles merrily declared that he would pay all army arrears. No mention was made as to how the king, penniless himself, would achieve this but it was what everyone wanted to hear. Likewise, the all-encompassing statements that all his father's enemies would be pardoned and the promise given of universal liberty of conscience regarding religion. Another problem which loomed large was that of land disputes. During the war, Royalist estates had been sequestered and bought in good faith by Parliamentarians who now had legal possession. But if the king returned, his loyal Royalist supporters would expect compensation for their recent hard times and want their property restored to them. Charles promised he would put everything to rights with no indication as to how it might be done. Doubts were not to be entertained and the Convention Parliament declared that 'the government of the country properly resided in the King, Lords and Commons'. Charles was formally invited to return and take up his rightful role with virtually no strings attached. The House of Lords was reinstated as the second house of Parliament, to act once more as a check upon the House of Commons, having been abolished under the Commonwealth.

Preparations were swiftly put in hand for the king's homecoming. The English fleet sailed for Holland, carrying a chest containing £50,000 worth of coins as a gift, such that Charles could pay off his numerous debts and array himself as befitted a monarch. The story goes that upon receipt of the money, in childlike delight, he tipped all the coins onto the bed and called his brother James and sister Mary to come look at such a wonderful sight and run their hands through the gold and silver.

On a perfect May morning, Charles embarked on the flagship of the English navy. Originally named *The Naseby,* after the great Parliamentarian victory in the Civil War, this latest design in warship technology and the envy of Europe was hastily renamed *The Royal Charles* in honour of the occasion. Charles returned home at last to the kingdom that for so long, although tantalisingly close, had been beyond his reach. On board, the diarist Samuel Pepys, there in his capacity as Secretary of the Navy Board, was moved to tears by the king's story of his miraculous and perilous escape after the Battle of Worcester in 1651. But the time was not appropriate for sad memories and recriminations, rather one for joyous celebration.

At Dover, General Monk handed his sheathed sword to Charles as a symbol of peace, putting the army under the king's command, and the mayor presented a handsome Bible in recognition of the king's position as Head of the Church of England and to signify God's part in his Restoration. Pepys described in his diary the events of 29 May 1660 that followed after the presentations in Dover:

> From thence ... in our way found the people of Deale going to make a bonfire for joy of the day, it being the King's birthday, and had some guns which they did fire at my Lord's coming by, for which I did give twenty shillings among them to drink. While we were on the top of the cliffe, we saw and heard our guns in the fleet go off for the same joy.

The royal procession rode in leisurely triumph through Kent, from Dover to Canterbury and on to Rochester, where the king spent his first night on English soil in the house of a loyal friend, since known as Restoration House. Pepys stayed there also and noted in his diary his attempts to steal a kiss from a maid in the cherry orchard.

Every town and village was decorated with flags and tapestries hung from windows and crowds cheered until they were hoarse. The king entered London on 30 May to be greeted by the most incredible celebrations. John Evelyn recorded the event in his diary:

> It was a triumph of above 20,000 horse and foot, brandishing their swords and shouting with inexpressible joy; the way strewn with flowers, the bells ringing, the streets hung with tapestry, fountains running with wine; the Mayor, Aldermen and all companies in their livery, windows and balconies

well set with ladies; trumpets, music and myriads of people flocking even so far as from Rochester, so as they were seven hours in passing the city even from two in the afternoon till nine at night. It was the Lord's doing...

At a tavern in Southwark, on the southern side of London Bridge, the proprietor's wife became so excited that she went into labour. The story tells that the king himself halted the procession in order to greet his newest and youngest subject. Having arrived at last at Whitehall Palace, Charles made a gracious speech of gratitude at such a momentous welcome before admitting he was too exhausted to attend the planned service of thanksgiving for his safe return in Westminster Abbey, which was postponed. Instead, he retired to bed, to rest in the arms of his mistress Barbara Villiers. Affairs of state could wait until tomorrow.

A New Era at Cambridge University

Whatever his personal feelings about the return of the monarchy – he never mentions it – the Restoration was most fortunate for Newton. In fact, he might never have gone to the university and remained a disconsolate, anonymous yeoman farmer for the remainder of his life. What a waste of genius and a huge loss to scientific progress that would have been. The revival of Royalist interests saved the situation. Newton's unsung patron Humphrey Babington, as a Royalist, had lost his post at Trinity under the Commonwealth and Protectorate. Now he was reinstated by the new regime. Another man now restored to favour was Isaac Barrow. He too would have a great impact on Newton's career at Cambridge.

Isaac Barrow's childhood had things in common with Newton's. Born in London in 1630, the child's mother died when he was four years old and his father, Kentish linen draper Thomas Barrow, sent him to live with his grandfather in Cambridgeshire.[2] However, unlike Hannah Newton, Thomas decided his son was worthy of a good education and enrolled him at Charterhouse School in London. He was there for two years, learned little and was reckoned such a bully and a troublemaker his father was supposedly quoted as saying that 'should God decide to take one of his children, he could best spare Isaac.' In Barrow's case, a change of school made all the difference. At Felstead School in Essex, under the strict Puritan headmaster Martin Holbeach, Barrow became a model scholar, studying Greek, Latin, Hebrew and logic, excelling in the ancient languages. When in 1642 his father suffered a financial disaster and could not pay the school fees, Holbeach kept him on and, despite his youth, soon after arranged his appointment as a 'little' tutor to one of his schoolfellows, Thomas, Viscount Fairfax of Emely, County Tipperary in Ireland – not to be confused with Thomas, Lord General Fairfax from Yorkshire, who trained The New Model Army that was so significant for the Parliamentarian side in the Civil War.

The following year, Barrow went up to Peterhouse, Cambridge, where his uncle was a Fellow but, since the whole family was open about its Royalist sympathies, both uncle and nephew had to leave. Eventually, Isaac did make it to Cambridge University, to Trinity College, where he paid his way as a sizar, just as Newton would do. Seeing the young man's talent for languages and his Royalist leanings, the Regius Professor of Greek, James Duport, taught Barrow for free, tutoring him in all the Classical languages, in addition to French, Spanish, Italian, literature, chronology, geography and theology.

By the third year, Barrow was also studying arithmetic, geometry and optics; students were discouraged from specialising in mathematics until after they had gained their Bachelor's Degree, which he attained, graduating in 1649 and getting a college fellowship soon after.

As soon as he began working towards his Masters Degree, Barrow turned to studying mathematics in depth and such was his enthusiasm for the subject, he attracted students to hear his tutorials, laying the groundwork for future mathematical studies at Cambridge. He taught himself from Euclid's *Elements*, writing a simplified edition which was published in 1655 and became the standard textbook. A known Royalist, with the Commonwealth regime in place, he was almost expelled on two occasions on the demand of students of the anti-Royalist party.

Fortunately, the Master of Trinity saved him each time and Humphrey Babington could also have added his support. When Duport had to leave his post because of his political views, Barrow also departed, having been awarded £16 per annum for three years – later extended to four – to travel around Europe, reporting back on his research.

Barrow spent time in Paris and then Florence, where much of his time involved studying in the Medici Library. He even made the acquaintance of Galileo's last pupil. He spent eighteen months in Constantinople where he became intrigued by the theology of the local Greek Church. But the money came to an end and he returned to Cambridge in September 1659, just as everything was about to change. Royalists were now returned to favour and Duport was offered his old post as Professor of Greek by the new regime but declined. Isaac Barrow was appointed instead. In a speech he made to the students at the end of his first year, the college must have wondered at the new professor's approach to education. He advised them:

> Continue to stay at home, if you are wise, and apply yourselves to your private studies. Turn over the choicest books you possess or take shelter in the pleasing shade of the library. Muffle yourselves in your snug blankets or sit by your cosy fireside. Consider your health and study at your own convenience.[3]

We do not know if Isaac Newton was one of the students present to hear these words but he certainly preferred the self-taught method of learning. He shared his college chamber with Francis Wilford, a student who was not so inclined to contemplative study. As a result, Newton would go to the 'Walks' – presumably, St John's College Walks that run alongside the River Cam, opposite Trinity College – where he could be by himself to read quietly. On one occasion, a fellow student with the same difficulty regarding his roommate met Newton there and they discussed their problem. The two decided to 'chum together' and 'shake off their present disorderly Companions'. Newton's new roommate was John Wickens, a likewise retiring soul. The two would remain friends for two decades, with Wickens acting as Newton's assistant and secretary for much of their time together at Trinity.

One undergraduate student of the time noted 'I had none to direct me, what books to read, what to seek, or in what method to proceed.'[4] With such a lackadaisical attitude from the tutors, it was no wonder if the students were 'disorderly', as in the case of Newton's and Wickens' previous roommates. But Newton was not held back by the lack of tutorial guidance; rather, he made the most of the freedom to read whatever books intrigued him. He made notes on books written by Galileo, Robert Boyle and Thomas Hobbes, listing the 'philosophical questions' raised by what he read.[5] He studied works by Henry More, a man he had certainly heard about since he was from Grantham and had tutored William Clarke's brother, though they had not yet met in person. Kenelm Digby was another author whose works Newton read and unexpected reading they must have been. Digby was a savant and published on topics ranging from cookery recipes to a treatise on the use of 'sympathy powder', a substance of his own invention which he believed was a means of determining longitude at sea using live dogs. This was not a method for the squeamish and did not work anyway but was taken seriously enough to be considered by the Royal Society and given a trial by the Royal Navy.

Newton's more relevant studies included John Wallis' *Arithmetica Infinitorum,* published in 1655, a book which laid the foundations for Newton's own later work in inventing 'fluxions' – calculus, for which Wallis deserves some credit. Wallis was from Kent and studied at Emmanuel College, Cambridge, graduating in 1637 and receiving his MA in 1640, at which time he was ordained. A skilled mathematician, during the Civil War he used his talent to decipher Royalist coded messages when they fell into Parliamentarian hands. In 1649, he was appointed Savilian Professor of Geometry at Oxford. During his long life, he remained active in the field of mathematics and natural philosophy. Wallis was a founding member of a philosophical group which met weekly at Wadham College in Oxford to discuss scientific matters. The group included Christopher Wren, Robert Boyle and his assistant Robert Hooke, and it would eventually migrate to Gresham College in London and become the Royal Society. However, despite his significant contribution to the group, Wallis could be argumentative and fell out with Thomas Hobbes and the Dutchman Christiaan Huygens, and was a severe critic of René Descartes' works.

Newton also read Descartes' *Geometry*, studying ten pages at a time and testing himself to see if he had understood them fully, before moving on. Clearly, he found Descartes more challenging than Euclid. He purchased a secondhand copy of Euclid's *Elements* at Stourbridge Fair, along with a book on astrology – the latter 'just to see what was in it' – hoping it would give him a good grounding in trigonometry. He read the propositions Euclid dealt with but found the titles of them so self-explanatory, he wondered why anyone would bother writing out the demonstrations to prove them, except for amusement. Having studied Descartes in depth and found Euclid hardly worth the trouble, it was a pity that at Newton's first encounter with Professor Isaac Barrow, he was questioned about the latter, not the former. Unsurprisingly, his answers were not good enough to earn him the scholarship he was hoping for. But it was awarded anyway, so someone must have 'had a word' in the appropriate ear; perhaps it was his patron, Humphrey Babington.

In the summer of 1663, Barrow resigned as Professor of Greek to take up the new post of Lucasian Professor of Mathematics, endowed by Henry Lucas. At the same time, he held the position of Professor of Geometry at Gresham College, bringing him into contact with other members of the fledgling Royal Society.

The Royal Society of London

With the Restoration of Charles II, life returned to something more like its pre-Puritan 'ungodly' state. Theatres reopened and entertainments were legal again. The Puritan regime had encouraged the study of the natural world, regarding it as the physical adjunct to the Bible, enabling mankind better to understand its place in God's creation. But now science could also be regarded as a form of intellectual entertainment, rather than a series of theological exercises.

On 28 November 1660, in London, a committee of twelve members of the Gresham College group announced the formation of a 'College for the Promoting of Physico-Mathematical Experimental Learning'. The group would meet every week to discuss science and conduct experiments. At the second meeting, Sir Robert Moray announced that they had King Charles's approval and a royal charter was signed to that effect on 15 July 1662, creating the 'Royal Society of London' with William, Viscount Brouncker, as the first president. Among those signing the first page of the Charter Book, agreeing to abide by 'The Obligations of the Fellows of the Royal Society' were Robert Boyle, Christopher Wren as Professor of Astronomy at Gresham, Charles Montagu (later Lord Halifax), John Wallis, Christiaan Huygens, the diarist John Evelyn, Kenelm Digby and Henry Oldenburg as secretary. Thomas Hobbes, acquaintance of Galileo and Descartes, as well as one-time mathematics tutor to Charles II, was also a member but never became a fellow, claiming his promotion was blocked by John Wallis because of their personal animosity. Among others invited to join was Isaac Barrow, but he never played a major role and his membership lapsed when he stopped paying his annual subscription. The society's goals were admirable, even if some were unachievable at the time, such as the reduction of the need for manual toil, an increase in longevity and good health for all.

The core activity was the weekly meeting where scientific experiments were performed, observed, witnessed and discussed by members. Volunteers were relied upon in the early days and an extraordinary range of natural phenomena was covered without any coherent plan. Theoretical science, technological advances and outright curiosities all received a hearing, thus the nature of light, the demonstration of a diving bell and the birth of a deformed cow were all topics worthy of consideration. However, the society had its teething problems. Many members saw it more as a social club than a serious institution and tended to draw new members from their own kind. There were difficulties in collecting the membership fees. Those who could afford them were frequently the aristocratic 'social' members, whereas the scholars among the group were often the least affluent, a situation which also led to the increase of those who joined for amusement, rather than the furtherance of science. It was a difficult situation.

Among the society's successes were some of its publishing ventures. The diarist John Evelyn wrote the first book on practical forestry, *Sylva, or a Discourse of Forest Trees,* published by the society in 1664. The following year, Robert Hooke's seminal 'coffee-table' book, *Micrographia,* came out. Lavishly illustrated with drawings done by both Robert Hooke and Christopher Wren, it gave the layman the first ever glimpse of the detailed natural world viewed through a microscope. From a foldout, triple-page spread showing every detail of a flea to the stinging barbs on nettle leaves and the cells in cork bark, the work was an instant bestseller, despite its cost. Samuel Pepys recorded in his diary that he sat up until two in the morning with *Micrographia,* saying it was 'the most ingenious book that ever I read in my life'.

A second royal charter was signed on 23 April 1663 with the king named as the founder. It was now to be known as the 'Royal Society of London for the Improvement of Natural Knowledge'. In November Robert Hooke was appointed as the society's Curator of Experiments. Henry Oldenburg did sterling work as the society's secretary, at first sharing the post with John Wilkins, Oliver Cromwell's brother-in-law and Warden of Wadham College. Oldenburg was from Bremen in Germany and although never a scientist, Robert Boyle had introduced him to the society. He was a professional gatherer of information – an 'intelligencer' being the term at the time – an occupation that could have tipped over into spying. In fact, in 1667, during the second Dutch War, Oldenburg was briefly imprisoned in the Tower of London on precisely that charge, as John Evelyn recorded in his diary:

August 8th 1667. Home, by the way visiting Mr Oldenburg now close prisoner in the Tower, for having been suspected to write intelligence, etc. I had an order from my Lord Arlington, Secretary of State, which made me to be admitted; this gentleman was secretary to our society & will prove an innocent person I am confident.

What had landed Oldenburg in trouble was his extensive network of correspondents across Europe. Without examining every letter to and from foreign countries, the state had no idea what subjects might have been discussed in them. And some might certainly have been regarded as 'intelligence' by a nation at war with a free exchange of ideas on topics such ship construction, navigation and ballistics. Fortunately for the Royal Society, when peace with the Dutch was restored, Oldenburg was released. His friend Martin Lister described how the secretary managed his tasks:

> He held correspondence with seventy odd persons in all parts of the world, and those to be sure with others. I asked him what method he used to answer so great a variety of subjects, and such a quantity of letters as he must receive weekly, for I knew he never failed, because I had the honour of correspondence for ten or twelve years. He told me he made one letter answer another, and that to be always fresh, he never read a letter before he had pen, ink and paper ready to answer forthwith, so that the multitude of letters cloyed him not, or ever lay upon his hands.

With a tremendous ability with languages, Oldenburg decided which letters should be brought to the society's attention, recorded them and published the interesting ones in the society journal, *Philosophical Transactions*. Oldenburg inaugurated this journal in 1665 and it soon had an international following. It was the ideal medium for reporting experimental findings and new ideas and continues to be published today, making it the longest-running scientific journal in the world.

Most of the important players and institutions were now in place for the drama that would unfold, involving Isaac Newton. Meanwhile, having been elected as a scholar on 28 April 1664 (that is, having been awarded a scholarship, so money was less of a problem) Newton began to make mathematical entries in his 'Waste Book', content to study books on subjects that interested him most.

The Trinity College Library

Today, when we think of vast university libraries, it is hard to imagine how few books were available to students such as young Isaac Newton. In 1600, Trinity College Library had only 271 named volumes. This modest collection was augmented in 1604 when John Whitgift, the Archbishop of Canterbury and a former Master of the College, bequeathed 154 medieval manuscripts to the library, fifty-two of which had been 'acquired' from Canterbury Cathedral. A further twenty-two manuscripts came from the same cathedral in the 1615 bequest of Master of the College, Thomas Nevile, who was also Dean of Canterbury, along with 104 other manuscripts and printed books.[6] By Newton's time, Trinity Library owned 500 manuscripts and a total of 2,705 volumes but as a humble sizar student, he would have been limited in his access to what was termed the 'Fellows' Library', permitted on the premises only if accompanied by a Fellow or with special authorisation of the Master. Such lowly students as Newton certainly could not borrow any precious books.

By the time Newton himself became a Fellow in 1667, permitted free access to the library, two-thirds of the books he might borrow were on religious topics and mostly in Latin. Fortunately, by now, Newton was fluent in the Classical languages, including Ancient Greek and Hebrew. Books on what we would term scientific subjects were few. In the library catalogue of 1667, of the total volumes there were less than 200 books in the combined categories of natural philosophy and medicine, and only seventy-six in the section headed 'Geography and Astronomy', which included those on mathematics – Newton's main subject of interest.

Library regulations stated that Fellows could only borrow books with the Master's written permission and keep them for just two weeks, having signed for them in the register.

Fines imposed for failure to return a book on time were stringent, to say the least – 2s 6d per book per week. Any book that was not returned at all, 'imbezelled', as the 1651 regulations stipulate, meant the person responsible 'shall pay the price of the book fourefold'.[7] Interestingly, one of the oldest books in the library, *Fasciculus temporum,* an incunabulum printed in Cologne in 1483, was included in earlier lists but not in the catalogue of 1667. However, it was found in Newton's personal library, centuries after his death, and finally returned to Trinity in 1943.[8] You have to wonder if, at 2s 6d per week, Newton was avoiding the overdue fines by never returning the book at all. Whether he paid the fourfold price for it is not known but there may have come a point where that cost was less than the fines due for lateness.

The Time of Plague

However much time he had spent in the library, the fact was that since the burst of enthusiasm at the very beginning, Newton had all but ignored the set syllabus required for his degree. He had spent the autumn of 1664 reading and making extensive notes on Johannes Kepler's *Optica* and Robert Boyle's *Experiments & Considerations touching Colours,* preparatory to exploring the nature of light and colour for himself, breaking new ground. He had also bought a prism from Stourbridge Fair. Unlike modern pyramidal prisms, Newton's looked like a three-sided glass rolling pin with glass handle knobs each end and no sharp edges. It would enable him to study 'the celebrated Phaenomena of Colours' that so intrigued him; but that would have to wait.

Over the Christmas period of 1664, as the time approached for the Bachelor's examination in January 1665, he had to cram, trying to fill the gaps in his knowledge of the set texts. In those days, examinations were oral, *viva voce,* with the students required to give detailed verbal answers posed by the examiners on the spot. Newton passed – just, 'put in a second posing... which is looked upon as disgraceful' – and received his Bachelor's degree but on examination results alone appeared no better than a mediocre student. Fortunately, Professor Barrow knew the young man's true worth, saying 'he reckon'd himself but a child in comparison of his pupil Newton ... and whenever a difficult problem was brought to him to solve [by a student], he refer'd them immediately to Newton.'

At this point, there were intellectuals with a dim view of how universities regarded those who thought beyond the rigid curriculum of traditional education. A physician, Henry Power, wrote in 1664 concerning his opinion of some of his fellow natural philosophers. In the conclusion to his published work *Experimental Philosophy* – much of which describes in poetic detail the wonders of insect life which he observed under a microscope – he complained that the 'Purple Gowns of Learning' at the least sign of difficulty in explaining any aspect of the natural world, term it 'an impossibility'.[9] By this means, Power claimed, they were stifling both their own curiosity and any attempt by others to solve such problems by further enquiry. Their excuse was that the world 'has long since pass'd its Meridian'. In other words, as we might say: 'the end is nigh', so such efforts were not worthwhile. On the contrary, Power had made his own calculations and concluded that the world would last another 15,000 years, so it was well worth trying to better understand the workings of Nature. Without such efforts, he wrote, we would not have those 'rare Inventions... that have so enrich'd our latter dayes', including 'Guns, Printing, Navigation, Paper and Sugar'. He asked where would we be concerning knowledge of our own bodies if, in his own profession, the heart's function, the circulation of the blood and the lymphatic system had not been discovered and explained? Despite such incredible advances, he noted, there are still those who insist on the 'incurability of Cancers and Quartans'. (Quartans were a form of malarial fever with a four-day cycle of fevers and chills.)

In the early summer of 1665, physicians like Henry Power had more urgent matters to fill their time as London writhed in the grip of the plague. By June, the dread disease had stretched its dark tentacles as far as Cambridge. Colleges were closed on 8 August and the students sent home. Newton returned to Woolsthorpe, taking all his books, notes and paraphernalia with him, determined to continue his studies there. Ever practical, he put up a set of book shelves in his bedchamber to hold his precious volumes and settled down to work. You have to wonder what Hannah thought of her son who spent hours, days and weeks at a time in his chamber, forgetting to eat, wash or change his shirt and doing foolish things, like staring at the sun until it almost blinded him and poking blunt needles into his eye, but nothing whatsoever constructive, so far as she could see.

Servants would find him on a winter morning, sitting in his shirt, writing by the window. They used to tell him dinner was ready half-an-hour beforehand and still it would stand two hours on the table before Newton would come down to eat it and if he found any paper or book to take his attention, the dinner might stand for hours longer, untouched. It was said that the cat grew fat on his discarded meals.

His gruel or milk and eggs that were carried upstairs to him warm for his supper, would often be eaten cold for his breakfast. Hannah was probably glad when her peculiar offspring went off to Boothby Pagnell, to visit his patron Humphrey Babington and to make use of his library and instruments. (When Babington died in 1691, he would bequeath his collection of ancient coins, astronomical, mathematical and musical instruments and music books to Trinity College library.)

Light Experiments

Hannah could not have realised how her son's work would profoundly affect science. What, to her, probably seemed like an utter waste of time, tinkering and fiddling about, was a series of experiments aimed at discovering the true nature of light, as Newton recorded:

> And in order thereto having darkened my chamber, and made a small hole in my window-shuts, to let in a convenient quantity of the Sun's light, I placed my Prisme at its entrance, that it might be thereby refracted to the opposite wall. It was at first a very pleasing divertissement, to view the vivid and intense colours produced thereby.

But for Newton, of course, admiring the beauty of the spectrum, the colours of the rainbow reproduced on his lath and plaster wall, was never going to be an end in itself. He had to understand how the range of colour came from seemingly colourless sunlight. Incidentally, the idea of seven colours in the spectrum was invented by Newton. The visible spectrum is an infinite range of colours, each one shading into the next. It could be defined as simply red, yellow, green and blue but in alchemy – another of Newton's interests – seven was a more significant number, as in the seven planets, the seven known metals, the seven days of the week and even the seven notes in the tonic solfa musical scale, 'doh' being repeated at either end – the actual naming of the notes occurred in the eighteenth century but the idea of 'seven' notes already existed. So what were the seven colours? Red, orange, yellow, green, blue, indigo and violet: if they had been selected from the infinite hues and named in medieval times, the names would likely have been different. Orange and indigo were new words in the seventeenth century, so our rainbow colours are an invention of the time.

The basic theory of light at the time, as discussed by the likes of René Descartes and Robert Boyle, was that white light was pure and simple. They and Robert Hooke were keen proponents of the theory that the effect of colours was an aberration which arose from the interaction of darkness and light. In which case, Newton deduced, should not black print on a white page appear coloured? Since that failed to happen, he not only felt at liberty to propose his own theory, based upon his experiments, but to dispute the explanations of respected thinkers such as Descartes, Boyle and Christiaan Huygens. Like the fictional Sherlock Holmes was to conclude two centuries later, 'having eliminated the impossible, whatever remained, however improbable, must be the truth.'

Newton's prism, as he realised, was 'refracting' the beam of sunlight i.e. bending the rays, and far from being 'pure', the light was a mixture comprising different colours. Each colour was refracted to a different degree by the prism, splitting them up so they became separate and visible. The fact that a prism, a drop of water, the edge of a glass or even a spillage of oil could create a rainbow was not new to science but the colours had been explained away as originating from the glass itself or the water or oil, not from the beam of light. With his prism in place to produce a rainbow on the wall opposite the window shutters, Newton then put a card with a pinhole in the way, allowing only the red light to pass through. The red light alone then passed through a second prism. If the colours were created by the effect of the glass on the light, the red light ought to change somehow and yet it did not. Although the prism refracted it once more, it remained simply red. Newton repeated the experiment with blue light; the result was the same except that the blue light was refracted to a greater extent than the red had been. This is due to the shorter wavelength of blue light but, at the time, it fitted with the idea of light being composed of 'corpuscles': minute globules of light; red being made up of larger corpuscles than blue, it was more 'resistant' to being refracted by the prism.

For the moment, Newton supported the corpuscular explanation for the nature of light, although he would later realise the wave was a better description in keeping with his further findings. In order to complete his current set of experiments, he refocused the whole spectrum of colours through a lens and achieved the gratifying and conclusive result of recombining the colours and producing a beam of white light. What a satisfying moment that must have been and Newton recognised the significance of what he had achieved, referring to it in his writing as the *Experimentum Crucis* – the crucial experiment.

The study of light was not Newton's only field of interest in the months he spent at home. Optics in general involved the construction of instruments, such as microscopes and telescopes. The telescopes of the time made use of lenses to magnify the image and these 'refracting' telescopes had grown longer and more unwieldy since Galileo had first turned his hand-held instrument to the night sky. When the Wadham College group had been active in Oxford in the previous decade, they had planned to create a then state-of-the-art astronomical observatory there and to construct a telescope 80 feet in length. In the event, one of just 24 feet was built. Refracting telescopes also had a great disadvantage in that the lenses created 'chromatic aberrations' – miniature spectrums of colour – that distorted the outer edges of the image. Determined to have a more efficient instrument to view the heavens, Newton ground his own lenses and made polished mirrors, both to exacting specifications, and constructed a 'reflecting' telescope which achieved x40 magnification. The idea for such a telescope was not Newton's; that accolade should go to the Scotsman James Gregory, but Newton's version was a little over 6 inches long, 1½ inches in diameter, beautifully made and gave an image of exceptional quality. It caused great interest when he showed it to his fellow academics after his return to Cambridge.

Yet the investigation of light and making instruments that were both practical and beautiful were not all that Newton achieved at Woolsthorpe. Every aspect of his studies raised questions and observing the planets nightly through his new telescope brought to his mind the problem of planetary motion: why did they move as they did? How did they move and – most important to him – was there a mathematical means of describing the movement? Was there a force of some kind acting upon them to keep them on their respective paths? This last was a vexed question. The science of the day was attempting to shake free of its medieval past, when inexplicable things in Nature could be ascribed to 'invisible forces' without raising eyebrows, yet Newton was beginning to think about gravity as just such an unseen force. As things stood, mathematics was not quite at the point where Newton's theories on such matters could be expressed simply as equations. So, working from the basics that men such as John Wallis had already published, he advanced mathematics in order to make it possible to describe numerically the curved orbits of planetary motion. He called his method 'fluxions'; today we call it differential calculus. His advances in optics, astronomy and mathematics – any one of which would have been sufficient to make him famous among scientists had he published them then – were all achieved in his bedchamber, working alone during the years 1665 and 1666. He said himself: 'For in those days, I was in the prime of my age for invention, and minded Mathematicks and Philosophy more than at any time since.'

A Digression into Fashion

Surprisingly, plague even disrupted fashion in London. Since the French kings Louis XIII and Louis XIV had both suffered from premature baldness, they had taken to wearing wigs and whatever the King of France wore swiftly became the must-have fashion accessory of the royal courts of Europe. In his famous diary, Samuel Pepys first mentions hair pieces, not for men but for women, when a French immigrant, known as La Belle Pierce, brings for Pepys' wife 'a pair of peruques of hair, as the fashion now is for ladies to wear; which are pretty, and are of my wife's own hair, or else I should not endure them'. This was on 24 March 1661 or 1662.[10] He first mentions periwigs – full-head wigs – for men on 9 May 1663 when he went to Westminster:

> where at Mr Jervas's, my old barber, I did try two or three borders and perriwiggs, meaning to wear one; and yet I have no stomach [for it] but that the pains of keeping my hair clean is so great. He trimmed me, and at last I parted, but my mind was almost altered from my first purpose, from the trouble that I foresee will be in wearing them also.

Pepys was finally persuaded that a wig was an essential for a man of fashion when, on Monday 2 November 1663, he wrote in his diary:

> By and by came the Duke [of York, the king's brother], and he walked, and at last they went into the Duke's lodgings. The King [Charles II] staid so long that we could not discourse with the Duke, and so we parted. I heard the Duke say that he was going to wear a perriwigg; and they say the King also will. I never till this day observed that the King is mighty gray.
> Thence, meeting with Creed, walked with him to Westminster Hall ... and thence by coach ... and we light at the 'Change [the Royal Exchange – the fashionable 'shopping mall' of the day in the City of London] ... and so home and carried a barrel of oysters with us, and so to dinner, and after a good dinner left Mrs. Hunt and my wife making marmalett

[marmalade] of quinces, and Creed and I to the perriwigg makers, but it being dark concluded of nothing.

The best wigs were made of human hair; slightly cheaper ones of horsehair, but all were expensive. A gentleman's entire fashionable outfit, consisting of a hat, coat, breeches, shirt, hose and shoes, would cost about as much as the wig alone. It also required constant care from a hairdresser for cleaning, delousing, curling and powdering but at least the gentleman could send his wig for the attention required without personally spending time with the hairdresser. A wig not only concealed greying or thinning hair but, since the gentleman's head was shaven beneath it, the eternal problem of head lice could be dealt with simply by boiling the wig. However, this was not always enough to satisfy the wearer and this is when the advent of plague in 1665 affected fashion. On 3 September that year, Pepys recorded in his diary that he was still attempting to maintain his standards in fashion:

> Up, and put on my coloured silk suit, very fine, and my new periwig, bought a good while since, but darst not wear it because the plague was in Westminster when I bought it. And it is a wonder what will be the fashion after the plague is done as to periwigs, for nobody will dare to buy any haire for fear of infection? That it had been cut of[f] people dead of the plague.

Once Pepys began wearing periwigs, it was difficult to abandon the practice unless a gentleman was prepared to show his own short hair as it grew out, or else went about with a shaven head. Since neither appearance was fashionable – long hair was the badge of the social class with leisure enough to care for it – wigs remained a required accessory, although we know from his portraits that, even in old age, Isaac Newton still had his own hair and did not always wear a wig. But Pepys' portraits tell how the fashions changed. In the 1660s, wigs resembled a normal but coiffured head of hair but if it was difficult to tell an expensive wig from the wearer's own hair, it was not making much of a fashion statement, nor was it indicating the wealth required to afford one. So by the time Pepys had his portrait painted by Geoffrey Kneller in 1686, his wig is ostentatious, expansive and looks nothing like natural hair. But wigs could be problematic, as Pepys noted on 27 March 1667:

> I did go to the Swan; and there sent for Jervas my old periwig-maker and he did bring me a periwig; but it was full of nits, so as I troubled to see it (it being his fault) and did send him to make it clean.

The theft of expensive periwigs in the street became increasingly common in the late seventeenth century and during the eighteenth. One trick used by thieves was to carry a small child on a covered baker's, butcher's or pie-man's tray on the shoulders of a tall man. The child would grab the wig and disappear with it, back beneath the covering cloth on the tradesman's tray. Such ill-gotten loot could fetch an excellent price.

The Wider Situation

Newton returned to Trinity College on 20 March 1666, when the university reopened, believing the threat of plague was over but it was a false dawn. By June, the disease had returned and Newton travelled again to Woolsthorpe where he stayed until Cambridge was back to normal in April 1667. But as he was resuming his academic career, England – and London in particular – had been facing one disaster after another.

The effects of the plague in Cambridge in 1665–66 were light when compared to the devastating toll it had taken on the population of the capital. Those who had relatives in the countryside or elsewhere in the country fled London but thousands had no choice but to remain living in its foetid streets and overcrowded tenements. One who could have left and departed for the comparative rural safety of Woolwich with his wife was Samuel Pepys, but as Secretary of the Navy, he courageously remained at his post in the city. The despair he felt as the plague seized London in its deadly grip is apparent in his famous diary, kept throughout his miserable vigil. In June 1665 he wrote:

> In the evening home to supper; and there to my great trouble, hear that the plague has come into the city; but where should it begin but in my good friend and neighbour's, Dr Burnett's ... the town grows very sickly, and people to be afraid of it; there dying this last week of plague 112 from 43 the week before.

In a letter which Pepys wrote a couple of months later to the daughters of his patron, the Earl of Sandwich, he describes the horrors they had avoided by leaving the city:

> ... I having stayed in the city till above 6000 died in one week of the plague, and little noise heard day or night but the tolling of bells; till I could walk Lumber [Lombard] Street and not meet twenty persons ... till whole families (10 and 12 together) have been swept away; till my very physician, Dr Burnett, who undertook to secure me against infection (having survived the month of his own being shut up) [when his servant had caught plague, *see* above] died himself of the plague; till the nights are too short to bury those that died the day before. Lastly, till I could find neither meat nor drink safe, the butcheries being everywhere visited [by plague], my brewer's house shut up, and my baker with his whole family dead of the plague.

Pepys goes on to tell how grass grew in the empty streets and the deserted courtyard of the Palace of Whitehall, King Charles and the Court having departed to the greater safety of the West Country. Although the mortality rate decreased a little as winter approached, in January the number of fatalities rose again, despite the population being so much reduced. The plague was only to be defeated when the beleaguered city was overwhelmed by a second catastrophe: the Great Fire of London.

In 1660, a Quaker, Humphrey Smith, had published his prediction that London would be consumed by a fire none could quench. He had died in prison in 1663 so never knew how accurate his prophesy had been. On Saturday night, 1 September 1666, about 10 p.m., a fire began in Farriner's ships' biscuit bakery in Pudding Lane. By Sunday morning, when the Lord Mayor came to see what was happening and was asked to give permission to demolish surrounding buildings to create a firebreak, he declared that the fire was of such small consequence that 'a woman might piss it out'. Unfortunately, no woman volunteered her services and the fire spread. The Lord Mayor's refusal was understandable since any properties demolished on his orders would have to be rebuilt at the city's expense but, in the event, hindsight made his decision a disastrous one.

As a strong easterly wind arose to fan the flames, Londoners not immediately affected remained complacent, eating a leisurely Sunday dinner and watching the spectacle unfold. It was the intrepid Pepys who took matters into his own hands and went by boat to Whitehall, to inform the king, believing nothing could halt the progress of the fire 'unless his Majesty did command houses to be pulled down'. King Charles obliged but still the flames spread as sparks blew across rooftops, setting up new blazes streets away from the main conflagration.

On 4 September, Pepys buried his valuables in the garden at his house in the Navy Office buildings in Seething Lane, just west of Tower Hill, including wine and a Parmesan cheese. The rest of his belongings were loaded into carts and sent out of the city. Upon his return, he expected to find his house a pile of ashes but he was one of the fortunate ones: his home remained untouched. Not so St Paul's Cathedral. On the same evening that Pepys buried his cheese, around 8 p.m., bystander William Taswell noticed a burning ember land upon the cathedral roof among scaffolding that had been recently erected so Christopher Wren could make an inspection of the work required to restore or rebuild the old church. Ironically, Wren had reported his findings only a week earlier, advising that the whole building should be demolished and begun anew. His suggestion was swiftly rejected but now Wren would get his way. In half-an-hour, the fire had taken hold sufficiently to melt the lead on the roof. The molten metal poured down into the streets below, preventing anyone from attempting to save the doomed cathedral. The diarist John Evelyn described the hellish scene: 'The very pavements glowing with fiery redness, so as no horse nor man was able to tread on them.'

The area close by St Paul's, centring on Paternoster Row to the north of the cathedral precinct, was then at the heart of England's publishing trade. Scribes and bookbinders had practised their craft for centuries within its shadow. Thus, the publishers of London were among the businesses worst hit by the fire. St Faith's Chapel, in the crypt beneath the cathedral, had provided storage space for their paper, parchment and stocks of books. As molten lead ran down in rivulets, setting all in its path ablaze, so much paper simply added to the inferno. Their loss of stock and business premises meant the publishing trade would take years to fully recover from the disaster. Even in Cambridge, the effects were felt. Had Newton been willing to publish his treatises on optics and fluxions – his *Enumeratio curvarum* was written in 1667 and, if published, would have made his invention of calculus known to the world at a far earlier date – it is doubtful if any London publisher would have taken the risk. Mathematical writings by an unknown Cambridge scholar would be unlikely to make any money for a business currently hanging by a thread.

With the Great Fire extinguished, mainly due to the wind now blowing from the west and thereby sending the flames back across the charred remains where nothing was left to burn, there were weeks ahead of damping down hot ashes, clearing debris from the streets and making safe the crumbling buildings that still stood. As late as February 1667, as Pepys noted in his diary, cellars were yet being uncovered and found to contain still-smouldering ash.

But the capital could not afford to lose its hold on the nation's finances and commerce. The suggestion that the offices of government should temporarily move to York was instantly rejected and served to redouble the city's efforts to restore the *status quo*. It was a tribute to all involved – government and civic authorities, merchants and citizens – that London was back in business so swiftly, even though the infrastructure would take much longer to rebuild. And London's perils were not at an end. While Christopher Wren was appointed as the King's Surveyor of London with Robert Hooke as his civic counterpart, appointed by the Lord Mayor to rebuild the city, and Londoners returned to do business as far as possible, trouble was brewing across the Channel.

Hearing of London's series of disasters, the Dutch, still disgruntled about the treaty following their defeat in the first Dutch War, determined that the following summer of 1667 would be the perfect time to wreak revenge on England, while her authorities were in disarray and her capital city paralysed by the effects of plague and fire. They were not entirely at fault in their beliefs either. Throughout the spring of 1667, rumours were heard concerning the Dutch preparations for war. One informant of such ill news was a woman, Aphra Behn. Born in Kent, raised in Surinam and briefly wed to a Dutch sea captain, now widowed, childless and with a faultless command of the Dutch language, Aphra made an excellent spy. Returning to England from Holland with vital information for the king, the Secretary of State and royal spy-master, Lord Arlington, gave her so little credence that the intelligence was never passed to the king. Lord Arlington has much to answer for. He never paid Aphra's expenses for her time spent in Holland gathering information, though it had been agreed beforehand. As a result, Aphra ended up in prison for debt, eventually buying her freedom with money earned by writing poetry, drama and novels – England's first successful female author.

As a result of Arlington's inaction, the country had a terrible shock when, in mid-June 1667, the Dutch sailed up the River Thames and into its major tributary, the River Medway, as far upstream as Chatham. Chatham was a Royal Navy dockyard and there the cream of the fleet was moored, manned only by skeleton crews because the navy could not afford to pay its seamen. The Dutch set fire to most of the ships but took the flagship, *The Royal Charles,* back to Amsterdam as a prize. The Dutch still celebrate this victory even today. Fearing an imminent invasion, London was in a state of panic and it was at this point that Henry Oldenburg, Secretary of the Royal Society, was arrested as a possible spy and incarcerated in the Tower of London. Samuel Pepys, as Secretary of the Navy Board, was worried that he might also end up in the Tower, blamed for the utter fiasco. Men, money and munitions had been rushed to Chatham and other defensive measures taken but it was all too late. England was saved more by luck than skill – or it could have been sabotage – when the Dutch flagship exploded and sank.

Return to University

Back in Cambridge, on 2 October 1667, Newton was elected a minor Fellow of Trinity College, the position upgraded to a major Fellow on 16 March 1668. On 7 July, he was granted his Master's Degree and a month later made his first visit to London. He would have found the city swarming with bricklayers, masons, tilers and carpenters as the massive task of rebuilding was well underway; the phoenix rising from its ashes. There had been elaborate plans put forward by Christopher Wren and others for a brand new city with wide boulevards and grand piazzas. But commerce came first and merchants and tradesmen were already doing business from makeshift premises set up on the same sites as before the fire. Instead of a beautiful, elegant cityscape, London developed on virtually the same old medieval footprint of narrow lanes and alleyways, St Paul's being the obvious exception. A few major thoroughfares were widened but this caused trouble because nobody willingly relinquished part of their property to make it possible. Robert Hooke, as City Surveyor, had the job of measuring up the land lost by home-owners and calculating the compensation due to them from the civic coffers. To judge from the money he made, the dealings were not always entirely honest on all parties' behalf.

It is not recorded but perhaps during his visit to London, which lasted for six weeks at least, Newton made the acquaintance of some or other members of the Royal Society. Whatever the case, on 23 February the following year, he wrote to Henry Oldenburg, describing in detail his new reflecting telescope. Oldenburg read the letter out at the next meeting of the society and members were eager to see such an instrument for themselves, particularly intrigued that something so small should work at all. It would be another two years before Newton sent them a telescope they could examine and work with. Grinding the lenses and polishing the mirrors, plus the carpentry construction of the tube and stand, and the skilled blacksmith's work to make the gimble and support, all took time and patience.

The year 1669 was yet another landmark for Newton. He had entered Trinity College as a subsizar in the autumn of 1660 – he could have started no lower in the social hierarchy – and on 29 October nine years later, he was elected as the Lucasian Professor of Mathematics. That was an incredible achievement in under a decade. Isaac Barrow had held the post since 1663, the first incumbent since its foundation but, as we have heard, when students asked him complex mathematical questions, Barrow would refer them to Newton for the answer. Recognising the younger man's outstanding abilities in the field, Barrow resigned as Lucasian Professor in Newton's favour. His election was a mere formality. Barrow became Master of Trinity but also took up a clerical appointment as King Charles's Royal Chaplain.

A little before, in July, Newton's mathematical treatise *De analysi* had been sent to the London publisher John Collins, who specialised in the publication of academic papers. It is uncertain who sent it but since Collins had previously seen Barrow's works through the presses, perhaps the ex-professor suggested Newton should deal with him, or Barrow may have submitted it. In either case, the paper was not printed but Collins kept hold of it. Since it contained much of Newton's early work on fluxions, it became a cause of dispute and rancour for the future. In November, Newton went to London again, visiting John Collins in person. The publisher proved very supportive of Newton's efforts in mathematics without going so far as to actually put anything in print. The world still had a while to wait to learn of the work of the new Lucasian Professor at Cambridge.

Chapter 5

THE 1670s: THE PROFESSOR OF MATHEMATICS

In January 1670, Isaac Newton opened the new decade by giving the first of his Optical Lectures at Cambridge. He was assiduous in carrying out his responsibility as Lucasian Professor; sadly, the students were less than enthusiastic in attending the lectures. Apparently, Newton became accustomed to delivering his speeches to an empty auditorium, once the scholars realised the subject was way beyond their comprehension, with 'only the walls to listen'. They must have been the best educated walls in the western world. It was a pity he was unappreciated by the Cambridge students. Elsewhere, his lectures might have been heard by a few who could have understood them. One such rising scholar was Edmund Halley, then studying at St Paul's School in London.

Edmund Halley and John Flamsteed
Edmund (or Edmond) Halley would become an ingenious and incredibly productive member of the scientific community. According to his own account, he was born on 29 October 1656 but no record of his birth or baptism exists, probably because the relevant parish documents were destroyed in the Great Fire of London in 1666. His father, also Edmund, was quite affluent, running a soap-making business, a salter's business and collecting rents from properties he owned in the city. The family had a town

house in Winchester Street (now beneath a nineteenth-century railway line) and a country house in the then attractive rural village of Hackney, 3 miles from London and it was there that Edmund junior was born.

The family fortunes took a downturn when the Great Fire destroyed some of their city properties, reducing the income from rents, but the soap and salting businesses soon recovered and flourished, so young Edmund was able to have the best education.

Unlike Newton – with whom he would have a long friendship – Halley was a star pupil from the beginning. Popular and exceptionally bright, he was chosen as school captain at St Paul's School in 1671, aged fifteen. He was already proficient in Latin, Greek and Hebrew, more than competent in mathematics, understood the basic techniques of navigation and was rapidly developing a high level of skill as an observational astronomer. He went up to Queens' College, Oxford, on 24 July 1673, taking with him a set of instruments, including a telescope 24 feet long (7.3 metres) and a sextant 2 feet in diameter (60 cm), that would have been envied by any contemporary astronomer, to set up his own observatory.

In 1675, John Flamsteed, who was four years younger than Newton, was appointed as the first Astronomer Royal, instructed to equip and man the new Royal Observatory at Greenwich, a village south-east of London where the skies were less obscured by the smoke of the city. He was granted just £100 per annum to cover the expenses and the cost of the instruments. In September 1670, Flamsteed had gone up to Cambridge and entered his name as an undergraduate at Jesus College. Although he was not resident there very often, he was there for two months in 1674, and had the opportunity to hear Isaac Newton's lectures and, hopefully, understood them to some extent.

Meanwhile, Halley was busy studying the stars in Oxford and his astute observations were not tallying with those given in the published catalogue of star positions. In 1675, still only an eighteen-year-old undergraduate, he wrote a letter to Flamsteed, describing his findings and politely asking if the new Astronomer Royal could confirm that his calculations were correct and the catalogue was wrong. Flamsteed obliged: Halley was right and the astronomer at Greenwich was already working on a new and corrected catalogue of the stars in the northern hemisphere for the purposes of navigation. Later that year, when Halley wrote his first academic paper concerning planetary orbits, Flamsteed encouraged him to publish it, even though the young man had not yet been awarded his Bachelor's degree. An outstanding student, Halley would have sailed through the examination for the degree but he was more interested in a new venture in astronomy. If Flamsteed was making a new accurate star catalogue for the northern hemisphere, should not the same be done for the southern hemisphere and who better to do it than Edmund Halley himself? The degree was forgotten for the present.

With Flamsteed acting as the go-between, application was made to King Charles. The king supported Halley's proposal that he should sail to the island of St Helena, the most remote British outpost in the South Atlantic, to carry out his astronomical observations, and instructed the East India Company – a powerful trading consortium – to give the young man and a friend passage to St Helena, which the company controlled, aboard one of their merchant vessels. Halley and his friend, James Clerke, sailed in 1676, taking the latest in scientific equipment with them and funded by Halley's father to the tune of £300 a year – three times Flamsteed's annual funding for Greenwich Observatory. Halley was just twenty years old.

The weather on St Helena was frequently awful and clouds and rain hampered the work. But Halley spent the inclement hours recording wind speeds and direction, information he would use a decade later to produce a paper on the trade winds and monsoons, including the first-ever meteorological chart, a map showing wind patterns around the world. It took more than a year to gather the material and make the calculations required for the star catalogue and Halley and Clerke sailed home in the spring of 1678. The new catalogue was published the following November, so impressive and to such a high level of accuracy that Halley's achievement received the king's accolade. Charles wrote to Oxford University, 'recommending' (i.e. ordering) that the authorities there should award the one-time student an MA, ignoring the strict rules requiring scholars to be resident and attend the university for a minimum number of terms. The university obliged: Halley received his MA on 3 December 1678. Just three days earlier, he had been elected a Fellow of the Royal Society. To have compiled, calculated and published such a document as *The Catalogue of the Southern Stars* in two years was an incredible feat. In comparison, Flamsteed's catalogue for the northern hemisphere was first published in 1712 very much against his wishes because he insisted it was still incomplete. Edmund Halley was one scholar who could have listened to Isaac Newton's lectures and understood what the professor was explaining.

Contact with the Royal Society

Earlier in the decade, although concerned with his lectures and writing another mathematical paper, *De methodis*, nevertheless, in December 1671, Newton had completed the construction of a second reflecting telescope and dispatched it to the Royal Society in London. Upon receipt of the compact but impressive instrument, Seth Ward, the Bishop of Salisbury, who was also a respected mathematician and astronomer, as well as a founder member of the society and Chancellor of the Order of the Garter, proposed Newton for election as a Fellow of the Royal Society on 21 December. With such an illustrious sponsor and the beautifully crafted telescope before them, the members elected the Lucasian Professor in his absence a few weeks later on 11 January 1672.

Emboldened by his election, Newton seems to have been eager to contribute to the philosophical discussions that were a fundamental part of the society's weekly meetings, along with the experimental demonstrations. These were most frequently undertaken by Robert Hooke as the Curator of Experiments, a post he had already held for ten years. Hooke, though an incredibly inventive man who was not afraid to challenge traditional ideas and should be given due credit, was a prickly individual and sometimes over-hasty in his assumptions. He also tended to claim his own priority when others presented their new ideas. For example, when Christiaan Huygens wrote to the Royal Society concerning his invention of the balance spring watch mechanism, Hooke immediately told the members that he had invented precisely the same thing years ago. He then showed them diagrams of his idea. In fact, it was nothing like Huygens's mechanism and the drawings were labelled and explained in code. Hooke refused to decipher the code, saying he would not have anyone steal his invention.

On 6 February 1672, during his first month as a Fellow of the Royal Society, Newton sent Henry Oldenburg his paper on *Light and Colours* in the form of a letter which Oldenburg read out to members and then gave to Hooke for his perusal and critique, aware that the curator also had an interest in the subject. Newton described in his usual meticulous detail all the experiments he had carried out during his sojourn at Woolsthorpe and repeated since, including the 'crucial experiment', explaining his results and conclusions. It was a long letter, written in Newton's tiny handwriting, and would have taken a good deal of time to read, digest and understand. Hooke admitted later, when pressed upon the matter, that he had spent minutes, rather than hours, studying it. He swiftly claimed to have carried out all those same experiments himself long since and far from proving Newton's theory that white light comprised all the colours of the spectrum, they demonstrated Hooke's personal hypotheses to be true: that colours were the result of mixing darkness and light in differing proportions and the glass of the prism itself created the colours seen. What the young professor needed to do, so Hooke declared, was to devise a 'crucial experiment', if he was determined to prove his theory. Clearly, Hooke had misunderstood that just such an experiment had been carried out and fully explained or, more likely, he had not read the whole letter.

Whatever Hooke's opinion, Oldenburg printed a section of Newton's work in the next edition of the society's journal, *Philosophical Transactions,* published on 19 February, making it available to a far wider audience. Christiaan Huygens read it with interest, optics being a subject he had been studying. Less openly critical than Hooke and more restrained in his choice of words, he too expressed doubts as to what exactly Newton had proved about the nature of light. Imagine how shocked Newton must have been when two men, recognised as experts in the field, disagreed with his explanation of the causation of colours. Shock deteriorated into resentment. Newton would not be so eager to send his work to the society in future. Its members were obviously incapable of the level of understanding required to appreciate his painstaking efforts. As for Robert Hooke, his rudeness made an enemy of Newton for the rest of the curator's life and, henceforth, Newton would regard the man's opinion on any subject as worthless.

However, it was too late to withdraw what he had already sent to Oldenburg and in the March edition of *Transactions,* there was published an account of the reflecting telescope and seven further instalments of the papers detailing his optical experiments appeared in the journal throughout the year. Before Christmas, Newton also sent another of his mathematical papers to London, to the publisher John Collins. It contained more of his work on 'fluxions', in particular his 'method of tangents'. Whether he hoped Collins would eventually put all the papers he had sent into one book and publish it is uncertain. Whatever the reason, such a book was never created, although Collins retained the work.

Travel and Communication

All this while, Newton had been keeping in touch with Oldenburg, Collins and others in London by means of letters sent by carriers. For the king's or government's communications there were royal messengers, using relays of horses to get the letters, summonses or writs to their destination swiftly. For the nobility, they might have their own couriers but for ordinary people there were carriers. These might be professionals with a fast horse who would be paid for the service, either by the sender or the recipient. There were mail coaches that covered pre-determined routes, such as London to York or Exeter. Or the carrier could be simply a merchant or carter who happened to be travelling to the part of the country where the letter's recipient lived. Letters went abroad by similar means and communications to or from London and other large towns and cities could be surprisingly efficient.

Throughout the Middle Ages, when England's roads were little more than tracks or what remained of the Roman roads from a thousand years before, wheeled vehicles were used only by workmen carting goods from place to place. When going on a journey, the able-bodied wealthy rode; the poor walked; the elderly or infirm were carried in a litter. This changed in the seventeenth century, when there was some improvement in the paving of roads. Carriages could be hired on London's streets from 1605 and by the 1620s, there were traffic jams in the city and one-way streets had to be imposed. Samuel Pepys, conscious of his rising social status in the Navy Office, was embarrassed in 1667 to be seen in London in a common hackney carriage that anyone could hire. The following year, he acquired a coach and a liveried coachman of his own.

Travel between towns by public transport was still a slow business. The stagecoach, a heavy, lumbering carriage often without any form of springs, was introduced into Britain in 1640. Up to eight of the more wealthy passengers could ride inside; second-class seats were available in a large open basket attached to the back. The least privileged travellers sat on the roof with the luggage, relying on a hand rail to prevent themselves slithering off. This huge, unwieldy vehicle, drawn by either four or six horses, lurched along the roads at an average speed of about 4 miles an hour. The danger of attack by highwaymen was only one of many inconveniences on such a journey. Roadside inns and staging posts were probably comparable to railway stations and motorway service areas today: over-priced and not of the highest standards. However, by Queen Anne's time, the rich, such as young men on their way through Europe on the Grand Tour, could travel in greater comfort, in well-sprung and elegantly upholstered carriages. Their favoured vehicle was the post chaise, introduced from France in the early eighteenth century.

Coaches gradually became more comfortable but there were only blinds at the windows. One day, while travelling in such a coach, when the crowds pelted the open windows with stones and filth, Charles II's mistress, Nell Gwyn – always the comedienne – shouted out: 'Pray good people be civil, I am the *Protestant* whore,' knowing they thought it was the vehicle of the Duchess of Portsmouth, the hated Catholic mistress, Louise de Kérouaille.

From 1680, glass windows kept out the weather – a great improvement for royal mistresses and everyone else. The first simple suspension to protect the passengers against bumps and potholes in the road consisted of leather straps on which the carriage compartment hung from the framework. A German design, called the berlin, introduced curved metal springs to absorb the shocks more effectively. A much lighter, racier two-wheeled vehicle, the gig, was introduced from Paris during the late seventeenth century. Relatively cheap, pulled by a single sprightly horse and driven by its owner, a gig was all too easy to overturn, but it proved popular with young dandies and became the first type of carriage to make driving an enjoyable activity.

At the other extreme from the gig, the more sedate citizens used human rather than animal power for short journeys. A sedan chair was elegant and comfortable and a sedan with wheels, known in Paris as a *brouette*, was pulled through the streets, just like a rickshaw. Despite the comfort, sedan chairs soon went out of fashion, but the carriages evolved into all kinds of vehicles – many of them grand and extremely beautiful – which remained on the streets until finally replaced in the twentieth century by the car.

There were no signposts to point the way in the seventeenth century, so unless the traveller knew the route, he had to hire a guide. Many roads passed through areas that were still thickly wooded and there was always the possibility of an encounter with footpads or highwaymen. These were neither gallant nor romantic, as novels and films suggest, but dangerous criminals, often armed with pistols. Today, footpads would be described as muggers. Hyde Park in London was so notorious for muggings in the 1680s that William III, in 1690, had the road from his palace at Kensington to Whitehall lined with lamps – the first street lights in England. As for highwaymen, they were not always men: Mary Frith, aka 'Moll Cutpurse', was one of the most notorious.

In 1555, an Act of Parliament – still applicable in the seventeenth century – had made the parishes responsible for the upkeep of the highways that passed through their district. Each parish had to appoint a Surveyor of Highways and it was his duty to inspect the roads and, if they needed repair, he could call on each of the parishioners to do six days of road mending. Materials could be legally taken by the Surveyor from anyone's land for this task and stones, rubble or earth would be removed without the landowner being compensated. Naturally, the Surveyor of Highways was not a popular person, as very few wanted to spend six days labouring and his inspections usually meant trouble as he took materials for repair from local landowners. Unsurprisingly, this system did not work too well and meant roads were often impassable in bad weather. Particularly bad were the highways to and from London because they were used the most.

So, in 1656, fed up with the responsibility of maintaining the Great North Road, the people of Radwell in Hertfordshire petitioned the Quarter Sessions for help. As a result, Parliament passed a Bill that gave the local justices powers to erect toll gates on a section of the Great North Road for a trial period of eleven years; the revenues collected to be used for the maintenance of the road. This proved such a success that in 1663, various groups of wealthy landowners were given permission by Parliament to build or improve a stretch of road and then charge tolls to get their money back, thereby making a profit. At first these toll roads were in short sections and acted as short cuts, often bypassing a village and thus reducing its trade – which, again, did not please everyone. At various points along the main roads, houses and gates were set up and a toll-gate keeper lived alongside the route. Toll gates grew in number until by 1872, when the system was finally abolished, there were about 8,000 of them in operation.

A toll gate revolved on a spindle, like a turnstyle, and after the individual had paid his penny, it would turn, allowing access to the new stretch of road. Typical charges in the seventeenth century were 1d for a horse and 6d for a coach. Exempt from the charges were mail coaches, foot passengers and people in a funeral cortege. Because it was possible for daring horsemen to leap over the gates without paying, they were sometimes replaced by what soon became known as 'turnpikes'. A turnpike was simply a wooden bar with spikes on top in an attempt to prevent reckless riders passing through for free.

London Life

In August 1674, travelling by whatever means he preferred, Newton visited London for the third time, so far as is known. He arrived to attend a royal and academic occasion as the Duke of Monmouth, the eldest illegitimate son of Charles II, was installed as the Chancellor of Cambridge University. This may have been a brief visit to the city but the following year Newton appears to have spent some months in London, or else made a number of separate visits. On 18 February 1675, he attended his first meeting of the Royal Society at Gresham College in Bishopsgate. He went again in March and made the acquaintance of Robert Boyle – whom he greatly respected, having read some of his writings – and Christopher Wren. What he made of his first encounter with Robert Hooke in person has gone unrecorded but it was most likely a chilly one.

Robert Hooke was a keen supporter of what might be termed the 'coffeehouse culture'. The first coffeehouse in the Christian world had opened in London in the 1650s, during the Commonwealth. Coffee had originated in the mountains of Ethiopia and gradually spread through the Muslim world of the Ottoman Empire, a suitable non-alcoholic beverage. European merchants brought it home and its quality as a stimulant was quickly realised. Physicians were soon recommending coffee's medicinal virtues as a cure-all and even an aphrodisiac – for men only. William Harvey of 'circulation' fame used to drink coffee with his brother and the ritual was so much a part of their lives, William bequeathed his coffee pot to his brother Elias in his will. Although the Harveys drank their coffee at home, the new idea of a public house which served coffee rather than alcohol soon became popular with the Puritans, who abhorred drunkenness, especially in London. A coffeehouse was not only a place to buy refreshment, going to one was a social event; a male-only meeting place. Another recent innovation was available there too: newspapers for customers to read and share. For those who could not read, articles would be read aloud and the subject matter discussed at length over the coffee.

Members of the Royal Society could extend their normal meetings with informal discussions of the latest experiments at Garraway's Coffeehouse in Exchange Alley, not far from Gresham College. With coffeehouses proliferating across the city, the government did what it could to license such establishments. The trouble was that scientific innovation was not the only topic of discussion in those places. After fifteen years of the returned monarchy, the lustre had faded on the reinstated Crown. Both king and government were suffering from paranoia, fearing plots and sedition at every turn, certain that coffeehouses were at the heart of any treasonous intent.

So convinced were they that this was true that on 29 December 1675 a royal proclamation was printed and put up in conspicuous places that everyone should know the king's order, that coffeehouses throughout the kingdom were to be closed down on 10 January, in less than two weeks' time. The document declared that such establishments were frequented by idle and disaffected persons, as well as taking tradesmen away from their proper employment. Worse still 'divers False, Malitious and Scandalous Reports are devised and spread abroad, to the Defamation of his Majesties Government, and to the Disturbance of the Peace and Quiet of the Realm'. Therefore, it was deemed 'fit and necessary that the said Coffeehouses be (for the future) Put Down and Suppressed'.

Robert Hooke repaired to Garraway's to discuss the disastrous proclamation with fellow-member of the Royal Society, treasurer Abraham Hill. After eating his midday dinner at home in Gresham College, where lodgings went with his post as Professor of Geometry, he returned to Garraway's to meet a friend. Later, Hooke went to the coffeehouse next door, Jonathan's, to talk about his 'new contrivance for flying' with another friend before he got into an argument with three strangers over the earlier royal proclamation.[1]

There were reckoned to be around a thousand coffeehouses in London alone, according to a report of 1673, and their closure would not only put the proprietors out of business but change the social heart of the city. Within the first week of January, Thomas Garraway, owner of Hooke's favourite coffeehouse, and two of his fellow traders had raised a petition to present at Court against the suppression of their means of livelihood. There were three main points to their argument. Firstly, in London at least, coffeehouses were licensed, each licence to run until a given end date. In which case, they proposed, under the law, could their businesses be closed down before the licences expired? Secondly, they were hard-working citizens and was it not unjust to rob them of their livelihoods at such short notice, leaving them with vast stocks of coffee unsold and unsalable, except at absurdly low prices because there would be a glut on the market? Thirdly – and probably most persuasive to the government authorities – there was an excise tax paid on coffee at the point of sale of six pence per gallon, amounting to a lucrative income for the Royal Exchequer. These revenues would be lost if the proclamation came in to force.

The Privy Council received the petition, then sent Garraway and his associates away, so the matter could be debated behind closed doors. When Garraway and one associate, Mr Taylor, were called back, they were required to make concessions, offering to accept that the licences would be reissued at greater cost and have stringent new clauses. Also, they would be required by law to report anything they overheard being discussed in their establishments that might be 'prejudicial to the Government'. They humbly admitted the 'Miscarriages and Abuses committed in such Coffeehouses' and, reluctantly, Garraway and Taylor consented on behalf of their fellow tradesmen to act as spies for the king and to pay £500 to guarantee the coffee-retailers' compliance. All this earned them a six-month reprieve until 24 June: time to sell off their stock and make other arrangements for their future employment. On Monday 10 January, Hooke was back at Garraway's discussing the matter with a one-eyed, itinerant painter.[2]

In the event, the coffeehouses were never closed down, although the threat to do so was revived in 1679. Coffeehouse proprietors were required to report any seditious discussion or libellous papers discovered within two days, either to one of the king's ministers or to a Justice of the Peace. Failure to do so would result in the revocation of their licences. Many fell victim to these unpaid spies, including the Duke of Buckingham and the Earl of Shaftesbury whose political views were broadcast too freely in Jonathan's Coffeehouse. Other establishments, such as the Amsterdam Coffeehouse, became notorious as gathering places for religious dissidents and political fanatics of all kinds but the right of the public to maintain freedom of speech won through eventually.

Coffee was not the only novel beverage in town: chocolate and tea were becoming popular, if only for the affluent. Samuel Pepys sometimes drank chocolate for breakfast with his wife. Tea was also for consumption at home, although some coffeehouses served bowls of tea also. Here is Sir Kenelm Digby's recipe for tea in a form we would not recognise today. It is taken from his cookery book: *The Closet of Sir Kenelm Digby, Kt., Opened*, published in 1671:

> To near a pint of tea take two yolks of new-laid eggs and beat them very fine with as much sugar as is sufficient for this quantity of liquor. When they are very well mixed pour your tea on the eggs and sugar and stir them together. In these parts we let the hot water remain too long soaking upon the tea. The water is to remain on the tea no longer than whilst you can say the Miserere Psalm very slowly.

While Hooke and his friends were worrying about their favourite coffeehouses closing down, Isaac Newton was in London with other, more spiritual matters on his mind. Since medieval times, when universities were first founded to train men for the priesthood, it had been requisite for scholars to take minor holy orders around the time they received their Master's Degree.[3] This antiquated regulation was still enforced in Newton's day but he had not complied and there were deeply personal and religious reasons why. Now, as both a fellow and a professor, the matter of his taking holy orders had become urgent. Newton must have explained his reasons for not doing so to Isaac Barrow, but he was taking a grave risk. His beliefs were not only unconventional; they were heretical. At some point, Barrow took the problem to the very top: to King Charles as Head of the Church of England. If Barrow had told the king the full story – if Newton had confided everything to him – Charles could have had the young professor arrested as a religious dissenter. Fortunately, the king was more tolerant than his forebears, whatever he was told. Though he remained in London for months, awaiting the king's decision, Isaac Newton was eventually excused, permitted to hold his post as Lucasian Professor *without* taking holy orders.[4] However, the requirement was not rescinded for others.

Unorthodox Beliefs

As Lucasian Professor, he had a comfortable suite of chambers between the chapel and the main gateway of Trinity College, on the first floor. There, he had access to the stairs to an upper gallery where he set up his telescope to observe the heavens, while at ground level he had a small garden in which to stroll and think, and some kind of shed to use as his laboratory. His friend John Wickins also lived there, acting as Newton's assistant.

Apart from his lecturing duties, giving a course on arithmetic, working in his laboratory and keeping night vigils with his reflecting telescope, somehow, Newton stretched his time to include in-depth study of the Bible and other religious writings. He had always been a Puritan at heart, ever concerned to give God due reverence and respect. In the list of sins he had compiled in his teens, there were numerous confessions to improper observation of the Lord's Day, such as working after midnight on Saturday, failing to give the sermons in church his full attention and thinking too much about subjects other than God. None of which 'sins' are the least surprising in a man with Newton's tendency to become obsessed with whatever work absorbed him at that moment. But then he took his religious studies to a new level, scrutinising texts of ancient wisdom. This was partly due to his interest in alchemy.

Though today we may think of alchemy as a black art, magicians and wizards concerned with inventing the elixir of life to gain immortality, or turning base metals into gold, in the seventeenth century this was not the case. For a thousand years, the practice of this arcane art had been setting the foundations of modern chemistry. Alchemy was a means of unlocking the secrets of matter, discovering how God's creation was put together and thereby exploring the nature of God himself. The twin quests for immortality and converting lead into gold were both the ultimate achievements of perfection – the alchemist's *raison d'être* – the first required the body to have perfect health and a perfect mind; the second a perfect understanding of the nature of the Earth. Alchemy was not a sinister pursuit but it had always been regarded with trepidation by those who did not understand it – which was almost everyone – and kings and governments feared practitioners who might be able to create an invincible army or boundless wealth for their enemies, if they succeeded in solving the mysteries of creation.

Even in Newton's day, alchemy in its ancient form had to be practised in secret. The first Stuart king, James I (r. 1603–25), had been obsessed with witchcraft and the destruction of witches not so long ago and, as we have heard, the physician Sir Thomas Browne was still writing in the 1670s about the existence of unicorns, the flying horse Pegasus, satyrs and the basilisk as likely true, even as he dismissed griffins and sphinxes.[5] Magic was still deemed possible and accusations of sorcery could be made, so care was required, papers kept secret and such matters discussed among only a very few close adherents of like mind.

Newton's biblical studies were also done behind closed doors. His was not the dutiful reading of the Collect for the Day but deeply considered thought on every passage he read. *The Book of Daniel* in the Old Testament and *The Revelation of St John* in the New Testament were especially interesting to him. Both concerned prophesies of the last days – literally, the end of the world as we know it and Christ's second coming. That day was believed to be near at hand by many, with men like Sir Thomas Browne berating learned academics for not passing on their knowledge, or not striving to discover new knowledge because it was not worth the effort, if the world was about to end. No one could accuse Newton of the latter. He was still greedy for knowledge and his detailed calculations proved it was worth the

Above left: Thomas Digges's diagram of the heliocentric universe from *A Prognostication Everlasting*, published in 1576.

Above right: Martin Waldseemuller's map of 1507/8. (Public Domain)

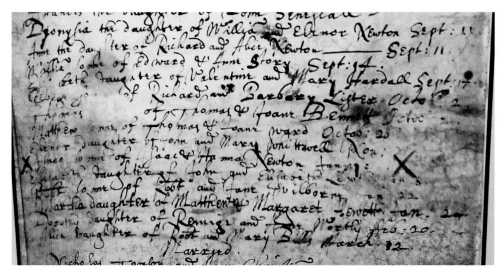

The record of Isaac Newton junior's baptism; held at Grantham Library. (Photograph by Glenn Mount, permission granted for publication in this book, hereafter GM)

Above left: The will of Isaac Newton senior. (Courtesy of Lincolnshire Archives)

Above right: The inventory of Isaac Newton senior. (Courtesy of Lincolnshire Archives)

Woolsthorpe Manor, Colsterworth, Lincolnshire. (GM)

Isaac Newton's bedroom at Woolsthorpe Manor, Colsterworth, Lincolnshire. (GM)

The apple tree at Woolsthorpe Manor, Colsterworth, Lincolnshire. (GM)

Isaac Newton's sundial at St John the Baptist Church Colsterworth, Lincolnshire. (GM)

Right: Site of William Clarke's Apothecary Shop, Grantham. (GM)

Below: Grantham Grammar School, external view. (GM)

Grantham Grammar School, internal view, courtesy of King's School. (GM)

Above: Plaque in the High Street, Oxford, marking the site of the house occupied by Robert Boyle and Robert Hooke. (GM)

Left: St Wulfram's Church, Grantham. (GM)

Trinity Great Court Cambridge. (Courtesy of Trinity College Library Cambridge)

Trinity College Cambridge and apple tree. (GM)

Newton's Note Book. (Courtesy of Trinity College Library Cambridge)

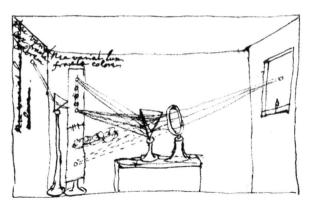

Newton's diagram of his 'crucial experiment', 1672. (Royal Society Publishing under Creative Commons)

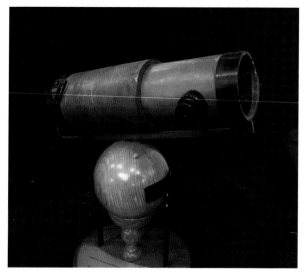

Newton's telescope. Photograph © Andrew Dunn, 5 November 2004. (Creative Commons/ Public Domain)

Above left: Newton's astrolabe at Woolsthorpe Manor. (GM)

Above right: Isaac Barrow, the first Lucasian Professor of Mathematics at Cambridge University. (Wiki Commons)

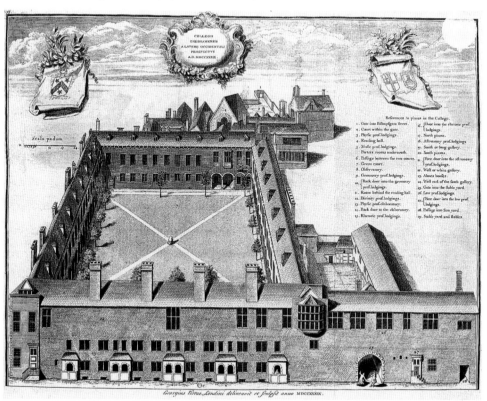

Gresham College. (Welcome Collection, Creative Commons)

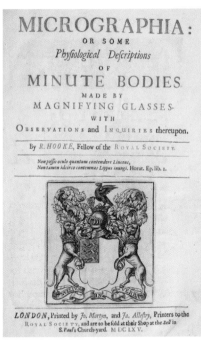

Above left: Sir Christopher Wren by Sir Godfrey Kneller, 1711 © National Portrait Gallery. (Getty Images/The Bridgeman Art Library)

Above right: Front cover of Hooke's Micrographia. (Courtesy of British Library)

Thames Frost Fair by Thomas Wyke 1683–84. (Museum of London/Public Domain)

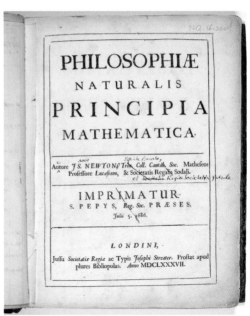

Above left: Edmund Halley by Thomas Murray *c.*1690. (Wiki Commons/Royal Society Collection/Public Domain)

Above right: Front cover of Newton's *Principia Mathematica*. (Courtesy of Trinity College Cambs)

Isaac Newton by
Sir Godfrey Kneller.
Institute for Mathematical
Sciences, University
of Cambridge.
(Wiki Commons)

St Martin's Street, London. (GM)

THE ROYAL SOCIETY'S HOUSE IN CRANE COURT (*see page* 104).

The Royal Society at Crane Court. Wood engraving after (W.H.), 1877. (Creative Commons Wellcome Collection image V0013121)

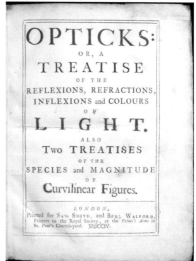

Above left: Charles Montagu 1st Earl of Halifax by Sir Godfrey Kneller.

Above right: Front cover of Newton's *Opticks*. (Wiki Commons/Public Domain)

Below: A copy of Newton's *Opticks* at Woolsthorpe Manor. (GM)

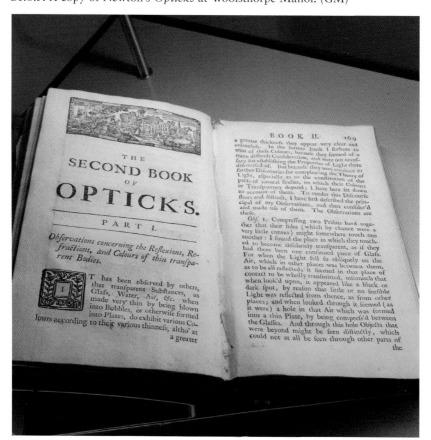

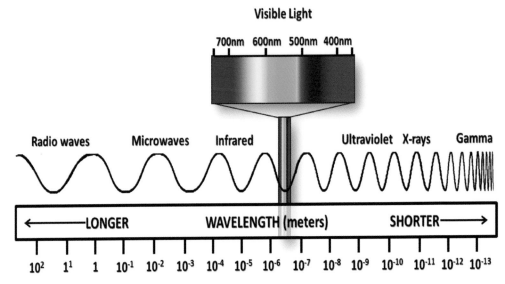

The modern electromagnetic spectrum. (Public Domain)

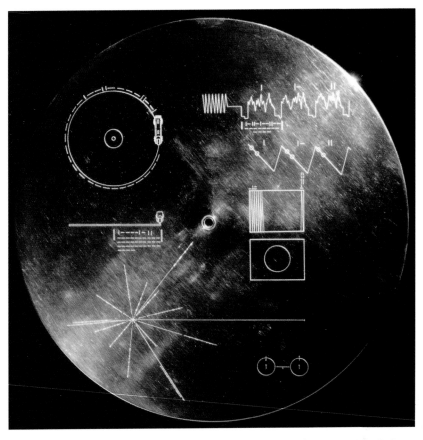

The Golden Record cover sent into outer space on the Voyager missions. (Public Domain)

The Earth taken from the Moon taken during the Apollo 11 mission. (NASA/ Public Domain)

Newton statue in Grantham,
Lincolnshire. (GM)

Newton bust at Trinity
College, Cambridge.
(Courtesy of Trinity College)

trouble to discover it, since he determined that the year 2370 would usher in a millennium of peace for the world.

Beyond his biblical readings, he was also absorbing the writings of the Church Fathers: early Christians who determined the basic doctrines of the Christian belief system. Puritans took the Bible as the one true foundation of their religion but this did not always equate to practice in either the Roman Catholic or Anglican Church. The celebration of Christmas had always been a point on which the Puritans could not agree with tradition: the Bible makes no mention of birthday celebrations for anyone, including Christ, and gives no precise date for his birth. Christmas was the invention of men, not God. The existence of bishops was another issue the Puritans refuted for similar reasons.

Newton was particularly concerned about a theological dispute which had arisen in the fourth century between two churchmen, Arius and Athanasius. Athanasius and his supporters argued that Christ and the Holy Spirit were equal with and part of the 'substance' of God, advocating the divine existence of the Holy Trinity. Arius and his party believed that Christ was not of the same substance as God and nowhere in the Bible was this stated as being so – to the Arians there was no such thing as the Trinity.[6] These opposing arguments were discussed at the Council of Nicaea that met in 325 AD to determine which doctrines orthodox Christianity would uphold, including the idea of the virgin birth, among other issues. The council found in favour of Athanasius, stating the now-accepted doctrine of the Holy Trinity in the words of the Nicene Creed. From his intense personal study and understanding of the Bible and numerous other theological texts, both ancient and contemporary, Newton concluded that Arius was correct; the Church, both Catholic and Protestant, was mistaken, corrupted by Athanasius. Such a belief was a heresy; Arians and Deists (believers in God alone as divine) lived dangerously if they spoke of their ideas unguarded.[7]

The Death of Friends and other Losses

Despite the time dedicated to his arcane studies, Newton was still in contact with the Royal Society in London. In December 1675 he sent Henry Oldenburg his *Hypotheses explaining the Properties of Light* to be read at the society's meeting. This was followed in January and February 1676 by the reading of his *Discourse of Observations*. In June and October that year, further letters arrived for Oldenburg's and the society's consideration: Newton's *Epistola prior* and then his *Epistola posterior*.

Sadly for Newton, he was about to lose two of his most enthusiastic supporters. In April 1677, Isaac Barrow left Cambridge where, as Master of Trinity, he had been urging on the construction of the Wren Library and doing what he could to limit the interference of the king and government in university affairs. Royal appointees to influential academic positions did not always enhance the university's scholarly reputation, nor its puritanical inclination. Barrow visited London and caught what was described as a 'malignant fever'. He had suffered from the complaint before, during his visit to Constantinople, and he dosed himself with opium and fasted, since this same remedy had cured him previously. But on this occasion the remedy was ineffective and the one-time Lucasian Professor of Mathematics died a few days later. He was buried in Westminster Abbey.[8]

In September of the same year, Henry Oldenburg, first Secretary of the Royal Society, also died. This was a regrettable loss, particularly as regards foreign correspondence which Oldenburg had dealt with so efficiently, often replying in the native language of the correspondent. The society appointed a new secretary: Robert Hooke. As far as Newton was concerned, this was an appalling choice. The petulant and argumentative Hooke and the easily offended professor were never going to see eye to eye. As a result, Newton had little contact with the Royal Society for some time, preferring to withdraw to Cambridge, to spend his days studying, lecturing and working in his laboratory.

Little was heard of him for six years but from this period there derive some fascinating anecdotal stories. One tells that he was so obsessed with neatness, a solitary weed in the garden was swiftly removed. He would test the honesty of his servants by leaving open a box of guineas. A calamitous story, told by Newton's relative, John Conduitt, concerned a fire in his study in 1677. Newton returned from chapel to find his notebook of experiments had been burned and so much work was lost. He became upset to the point of near madness and took a month to pull himself together, although as Ackroyd suggests, knowing Newton's penchant for redrafting and preserving past notes, it seems likely that most of what was lost was retrievable from his rough copies which he rarely threw away.[9] Perhaps that task took the month before he was able to calm himself.

His laboratory suffered other fires, for example, the one attributed to Diamond, the dog who again destroyed invaluable notes by knocking over a candle. A chemical experiment to explain the principles of 'that mysterious art', i.e. alchemy, by means of mathematical proofs, also went up in flames and Newton declared he would never do the like again.

Robert Hooke

An interesting character: what manner of man was the Royal Society's new secretary? Hooke was born at Freshwater on the Isle of Wight in July 1635. His father John Hooke was curate at the local church of All Saints. Robert was a frail child, expected to die at any time, at least until he was seven. As he grew stronger, his father hoped he might enter the church but Robert insisted that reading the Scriptures gave him headaches, so he was left to his own devices as far as education was concerned. He preferred dismantling and designing clocks and making model boats – his interest in mechanisms and his manual dexterity was not unlike Newton's. He also searched for fossils in the local cliffs and on the beaches, a fascination that remained throughout his life. Having watched an artist at work one day, he taught himself to draw. With his imagination piqued by art, after his father died in 1648, Robert took his £40 inheritance and £10 given him by his grandmother and went to London. He signed on as an apprentice to the up-and-coming artist of the day, Peter Lely. However, he did not stay beyond a week. He told Lely the smell of paint caused his head to ache. That was the excuse he gave having decided he could teach himself to paint, if he wanted, and would rather save the cost of the apprenticeship.

Instead, Hooke paid to enrol at Westminster School under the famous, forward-thinking Dr Richard Busby. His fellow pupils between 1649 and 1653 included John Dryden and John Locke. There were no more headaches and Robert learned to play the organ, mastered the first six books of Euclid's *Geometry*, became proficient in Latin and Greek, dabbled in Hebrew, Babylonian and other exotic, ancient languages and invented those 'thirty several ways of flying' mentioned earlier. Intelligent and quick to learn any subject so long as it interested him, the unfortunate young man was unprepossessing to look at. In his teens he developed scoliosis and the curvature of his spine grew worse as the years passed. Even friends described him as 'a sorry sight with a thin, crooked body, over-large head, sharp facial features and protruding eyes'. Yet such were his abilities, looks hardly mattered. He went up to Christ Church College, Oxford, but his inheritance had run out, so he paid his way – as Newton would – by acting as a servant to a wealthy student and by becoming a chorister, to earn a few pence.

It was at Oxford that Hooke was adopted by the scientific group at Wadham College and got to know Robert Boyle and Christopher Wren. He also met William Petty, Professor of Anatomy at Merton College. Petty's claim to fame was that he had once received the body of a hanged criminal for dissection, as was the custom, and managed to revive the dead woman. He also protected her, successfully, from those who said she should be hanged a second time and properly. Petty insisted she had already paid for her crime once and it was no fault of hers if the job was bungled.

With the likes of Wren and Boyle, Hooke became a founder member of the Royal Society but, unable to pay the fees, he was appointed to the post of Curator of Experiments, as mentioned earlier. In 1664, he had received a lifetime appointment to a lectureship in mechanics founded – but rarely paid for – by Sir John Cutler. In 1665, Hooke became Gresham Professor of Geometry and lived in Gresham College for the rest of his life. As well as his work as City Surveyor after the Great Fire of 1666, and as the Royal Society's secretary from 1677, giving lectures and presenting weekly experiments to the members, he acted as librarian and keeper of rarities. He experimented and lectured on subjects we would categorise as chemistry, physics, biology, optics, cartography, meteorology and geology. He invented the wheel barometer, the compound microscope, the iris diaphragm for telescopes, a wind gauge, a thermometer using the freezing point of water as its baseline, a weather clock, a hygrometer, apparatus for depth-sounding, a marine barometer, Hooke's Law that 'the power of any spring is in the same proportion with the tension thereof' and the universal joint – no car can be driven without this last. Robert Hooke deserves to be more famous than he is. Newton might have despised him but science owes Hooke so much.

Catholic Plots

Although Charles II had been restored to the throne in 1660 with the promise of religious toleration for all, this never proved possible in the seventeenth century. Certain religions were regarded as too great a threat to a State, which upheld and was founded on the Protestant Anglican faith – Newton's Arianism was a minor problem compared to the ever-present dark spectre of Roman Catholicism. In 1678, when rumours evolved into fact, that the king's brother and heir to the throne, James, Duke of York, had himself converted to the Catholic faith, there was an air of hysteria in England ripe for exploitation. And exploited it was to the full by one Titus Oates, who set the rumour mill grinding in the Amsterdam Coffeehouse, alleging that the Catholic Jesuit priesthood were planning the assassination of King Charles in order to bring the Duke of York to the throne in his place.

Titus Oates was born at Oakham in Rutland and entered Gonville and Caius College, Cambridge, in 1667 but transferred to St John's College in 1669, leaving later the same year without a degree. Never a bright student, his tutor thought him 'a great dunce' but with a good memory. While at Cambridge, he also gained a reputation for homosexuality and being a 'canting fanatic'. On 29 May 1670, he was ordained as a priest of the Church of England, though his claim to being a Doctor of Divinity was false. For a while, he was employed as a parish vicar, during which time he falsely accused a schoolmaster of sodomy with a pupil, hoping to get the man's teaching post. When this did not work out, in August 1676, he joined the household of the Catholic Henry Howard, Duke of Norfolk, as an Anglican chaplain to those members of the household who were Protestants. Although Oates was admired for his preaching, under a cloud, he soon lost this position. Yet the Duke of Norfolk's beliefs may have influenced Oates because, on Ash Wednesday 1677, he was received into the Catholic Church. However, keeping one foot in each camp, at the same time he agreed to co-author a series of anti-Catholic pamphlets with a man named Israel Tonge.

Oates later explained that he had merely pretended to become a Catholic in order to learn the secrets of the Jesuits and that he had heard about a planned Jesuit meeting in London. Oates and Tonge wrote a long diatribe, accusing the Catholic Church authorities in England of approving the assassination of Charles II, claiming the Jesuits were to carry out the task. In August 1678, King Charles was warned of this alleged plot but was unimpressed and handed the matter to the Early of Danby, who took the information far more seriously. As a result, the Privy Council questioned Titus Oates. On 28 September, Oates made forty-three allegations against various Catholics, including 541 Jesuits, many of whom had proved to be his friends in the past, and a number of Catholic nobles. He accused Sir George Wakeman, Queen Catherine of Braganza's doctor, and Edward Colman, the secretary to Mary of Modena, Duchess of York, of planning to assassinate Charles and even Samuel Pepys's name did not escape the list.

Earlier, on 6 September 1678, Oates and Tonge had gone before a magistrate, Sir Edmund Berry Godfrey, and sworn an affidavit, detailing their accusations. After Oates's appearance before the Privy Council on 12 October, Godfrey disappeared and five days later his dead body was found in a ditch at Primrose Hill. He had been strangled and run through with his own sword and Oates exploited this murder to incite the public against the 'Papists', alleging that Godfrey's death was the work of the Jesuits. On 24 November 1678, Oates claimed the queen was in league with the king's physician, attempting to poison Charles but when the king personally interrogated Oates, he caught him out in a number of inaccuracies and lies, and ordered his arrest. However, a few days later, with the threat of a constitutional crisis, Parliament forced the release of Oates, who received excessive praise, a state apartment in Whitehall and an annual allowance of £1,200.

After nearly three years and the execution of at least fifteen innocent men, opinion began to turn against Oates. The execution of the Roman Catholic Archbishop of Armagh was a step too far. On 31 August 1681, Oates was told to leave his apartments in Whitehall, but he refused. Eventually, he was arrested for sedition, received a fine of £100,000 and was thrown into prison. Not until the Duke of York acceded to the throne in 1685, as James II, was Oates retried, convicted and sentenced for perjury, stripped of clerical dress, imprisoned for life and to be 'whipped through the streets of London five days a year for the remainder of his life'. The presiding judge at his trial was Judge Jeffreys, who stated that Oates was a 'shame to mankind', ignoring the fact that he himself had condemned innocent people on Oates's perjured evidence. So severe were the penalties and humiliation inflicted on Oates during his three-year imprisonment, it has been suggested that the aim was to kill him by ill-treatment, as Jeffreys and his colleagues openly regretted that they could not impose the death penalty in a case of perjury. He was eventually pardoned in the reign of William and Mary but his reputation was lost forever. He died in July 1705, obscure and largely forgotten.

A Death in the Family

On 4 June 1679, Newton's mother Hannah was buried at St John the Baptist's Church, Colsterworth, Lincolnshire. She had always seemed more interested in her farm at Woolsthorpe than in her eldest son's academic career. A few weeks earlier, she had rushed to Stamford in Lincolnshire, to nurse her second son, Benjamin Smith, through a 'malignant fever'. Benjamin recovered but Hannah had caught the contagion. Newton was summoned from Cambridge to her bedside but despite making up her medicines himself, using his skills as an apothecary to tend her, she died. He took her home to

Woolsthorpe and arranged for her burial in the church beside his father. They lie there still, Hannah and her first husband, beneath the floor of the Newton Chapel but, unfortunately, their grave is underneath the church organ. Funds are currently being raised to remove the organ elsewhere in the church and refurbish the Newton Chapel as a more befitting memorial to Newton's family.[10]

Newton was now thirty-six years old and he spent much of the remainder of this year in Woolsthorpe, putting the farm in order so it might run smoothly in his absence. As an acknowledgement that the scientific world continued elsewhere, on 24 November he sent the first of a series of letters exchanged with Robert Hooke – perhaps a small gesture of reconciliation – which he described as a philosophical correspondence on the problem of planetary motion. The stars and planets cycled on, despite the death of a loved one. It had been a turbulent decade and the 1680s would prove the same.

Chapter 6

THE 1680s: THE PUBLISHED PHILOSOPHER

In the previous chapter, it was noted that Isaac Newton had begun corresponding with Robert Hooke in London in late November 1679 on the subject of planetary motion, yet the dialogue, which must have fascinated both men, was not particularly amicable between two such temperamental and easily offended personalities. Perhaps it is unsurprising that on 17 January 1680, after just six weeks of exchanging letters, Newton severed contact with Hooke. But the problem of how best to explain why the planets did not orbit the Sun in a circular path, as seemed most logical and had been proposed by Nicolaus Copernicus over a century and a half before, continued to intrigue the world of science. That the planetary orbits were maintained by gravity's force had been demonstrated decades earlier by Galileo, but how did this explain the fact that the orbits appeared to be elliptical, rather than circular? Such motion was even thought to be against God's will since although the world of mankind – everything below the Moon – was obviously imperfect, everything beyond the Moon – the rest of God's universe – was believed to be perfect. Circles were perfect and consistent in form; ellipses were not. Could the problem be rescued, brought back to a perfect state by a mathematically constant explanation? A German astronomer and very capable mathematician believed it could.

Johannes Kepler (1571–1630) wrestled with the data available for the planet Mars. It appeared that Mars not only travelled in an elliptical orbit but its speed was not constant either. When its 'imperfect' orbit brought it closer to the Sun, the planet travelled faster than when it was more distant. After years of deliberations and calculations, in 1618 Kepler produced his three laws of planetary motion. Firstly, that all planets have elliptical orbits around the Sun. Secondly, the closer a planet is to the Sun, the quicker it moves. Thirdly, the square of the time taken by a planet to orbit the Sun once is directly proportional to the cube of the mean distance of the planet from the Sun.[1]

If this third law sounds complex, consider Kepler, Newton, Halley and others as they juggled numbers in their heads and on paper without the aid of a calculator, never mind a computer. It was Kepler's third law and the need to discover the nature of that 'direct proportion' between the time taken by a planet to orbit the Sun and its distance from the Sun that would have some of the most prestigious thinkers of the day scratching their equation-filled heads.

Incidentally, many of us also owe a very practical debt to Kepler. He was the first to realise that, since convex lenses aided those with long sight – a fact known since the thirteenth century – might not concave lenses help those suffering from myopia?

A Time of Comets

The winters of 1680/81 and 1682/83 were good times for those interested in the mysteries of the heavens. From 12 December 1680, Newton began observing a great comet in the sky. It remained visible until March 1681 and Newton corresponded with John Flamsteed, the Astronomer Royal at Greenwich Observatory, on the celestial phenomenon. Newton had his own observatory set up above his rooms at Trinity College and the two men freely compared notes and calculations made concerning the comet, on good terms – for the present. The bright comet was visible even without a telescope and became a talking point across Europe for astronomers and laymen alike. It had first been noticed as early as November 1680, moving towards the Sun and eventually being lost in the star's glare. A little later, a second comet appeared, this one moving away from the Sun. It was the brightest comet in living memory and, in the days before artificial street lighting, could be seen clearly, even in smoky cities like London and Paris.

Comets were still objects of mystery; some regarded them as foretellers of doom, warnings sent by God. No one knew exactly what these fleeting visitors in the heavens were and John Flamsteed's was almost a lone voice in suggesting this second sighting was the same comet, a single object that had changed direction. But even he had no inkling that it could be orbiting the Sun, subject to the same laws of gravity as the planets. Like others, Newton and Halley included, Flamsteed assumed that comets followed parabolic paths. That is, they came from far across the universe and just happened to pass close enough to the Sun to come under the influence of its gravitational pull for a brief time before being flung away, back out into the universe, never to be seen again. Such comets do exist and are termed 'non-periodic'. However, the next comet to become visible in European skies was of a different kind: a periodic comet that would earn enduring fame for the man who realised it would not only return one day but that its return could be predicted with a reasonable degree of accuracy, if never precisely.

During that winter of 1680/81, young Edmund Halley set off on a Grand Tour of Europe, funded by his father, intending to meet with other men of learning. Wherever he went in the early months of his tour, one predominant topic of conversation was the appearance of the 'second' comet. Halley had the opportunity to discuss the subject with Giovanni Cassini, the Italian astronomer and head of the Paris Observatory. Among Cassini's contributions to knowledge were the mapping of France and then of the entire globe, as well as the suggestion – correct, as it turns out – that Saturn's rings comprise myriad tiny particles, orbiting the planet like millions of miniature moons. Halley also visited Holland and Italy before arriving back in London by January 1682.

In the following winter of 1682/83, yet another bright comet appeared in the sky and Halley observed it and studied it in detail,

paying particular attention to the path it took. He wrote to Isaac
Newton about it and they corresponded for years, often touching
upon the matter of comets among numerous other scientific topics.
As an inveterate gatherer of information, Newton accumulated
data on no less than twenty-three comets recorded over the
centuries. Eventually, having so many other projects taking up his
time, he passed all the data to Halley and it was the younger man
who eventually realised that one comet at least seemed to return
periodically. He noted that a comet recorded by Kepler back in
1607 had followed a similar path to the one he observed so closely
in 1682/83 and looking back through the data, there had been yet
another comet in 1531 on the same path. Halley concluded that
all three sightings had been the same comet returning on a cycle of
roughly seventy-five or seventy-six years. In which case, he rather
rashly predicted that it would appear again in 1758/59. If it did,
then the nature of comets would have to be reviewed because far
from being a random occurrence, this one at least orbited the Sun
in the manner of a most eccentric planet. Perhaps other comets
did as well.

Halley's daring prediction proved true: the comet duly
reappeared on Christmas Day 1758, sixteen years after his
death (Halley would have been 102 years old). However, other
astronomers recognised it thereafter, naming it 'Halley's Comet'
and immortalising Edmund Halley in the annals of science – an
accolade thoroughly deserved by the man who could have been
Newton's closest contender for the crown as England's foremost
mathematician and scientist.

Coffeehouse Philosophy

At some point, possibly in January 1684, a few members of the
Royal Society took to meeting in a local coffeehouse to continue
the discussions begun at the society in a more informal setting.
They were Robert Hooke, Edmund Halley and Christopher
Wren. Both Hooke and Wren were deeply involved in the
on-going rebuilding of London after the Great Fire of 1666 with
Wren's most famous project – St Paul's Cathedral – still barely
begun because of lack of funding and continuing disagreements

over the final design. The Church was not proving an easy patron to deal with and Wren had to use every ounce of his diplomacy and tact in an effort to get the building started. One difficulty was that Dean Sancroft and the Chapter of St Paul's wanted a gothic cathedral with a tall spire, as far as possible like the medieval structure it was to replace. Yet their chosen architect had radically new ideas. It was as well that Wren had a regular income as the Savilian Professor of Astronomy at Oxford and occasional payments from the Crown as the King's Surveyor – when the Exchequer remembered and could afford them – otherwise he would have been a poor man, waiting for remuneration from the Church authorities.

The clearing of the rubble of the old cathedral and the levelling of the site were the first causes of delay. Then the stone had to be purchased and shipped from Portland in Dorset. Money was to be raised by imposing a new tax on coal arriving in London from Newcastle, requiring an Act of Parliament which, again, took time. In Dorset, such a huge order for stone meant a new road had to be laid between the quarry at Portland and the coast where the dockyard had to be rebuilt to cope with the larger cargo vessels to ship the stone to London. Despite two foundation stones for the new cathedral having been laid in the summer of 1675 – one by the master mason, Thomas Strong, the other by the master carpenter, John Langland – there was still not a lot to show for almost a decade of work.[2] Wren personally supervised the building work, visiting the site every Saturday and using the fourteenth-century Chapter House that had survived the Fire as his site office until it was demolished in 1714. Despite a shortage of construction labour during the rebuilding of the city after the Fire, he hired only the finest artists and craftsmen.

As the building work progressed behind scaffolding, unseen by the clergy, Wren was able to use the king's warrant as Royal Surveyor to make numerous, surreptitious changes to the design. The final building bears little resemblance to the plan, reverting to the large dome rejected by the Church authorities and adding the grand west main entrance and towers. In fact, Wren had clearly intended to change the design from the beginning, laying eight central pillars with foundations and diameter far greater than required for the design originally accepted by the Dean and Chapter. But with progress so slow, further hampered by French naval activity in the Channel and a disastrous rock fall caused by heavy rains at the Portland quarry, which smashed a crane and other lifting equipment, London employers had a new phrase to describe a lazy employee: 'slower than a St Paul's labourer'. In the 1690s, Parliament even withheld half Wren's wages, blaming him for the lack of available stone.

Despite these problems, Wren had time to take coffee with his friends. Discussions in the January of 1684 had to avoid politics and religion because King Charles was again paranoid about treasonous plans being hatched in such establishments. And no wonder. The previous year, in March 1683, the king and his brother James, Duke of York – after whom New York was named – were staying at the royal estate at Newmarket to enjoy the horse racing there. They must have thought how unfortunate it was that a fire at the king's house meant they had to return home to London earlier than intended.

It was not until June, three months later, that the two men learned how fortuitous that fire had been. Unknown to the royal race-goers, a plot had been afoot to assassinate them both at Rye House, a property near Hoddesdon in Hertfordshire. The scheme was simple: the king and the duke would pass Rye House en route from Newmarket to London. The house was on a stretch of narrow road down which the royal party would have to ride and it was the ideal place to ambush and kill them. Since the fire caused the king to leave earlier than planned, the would-be assassins were not yet in place.

Details of what became known as The Rye House Plot remain sketchy. Perhaps the plotters never got so far as to fully formulate their plan but it appears to have had both political and religious motives. One theory has it the conspirators were anti-Catholics determined to remove King Charles as being too lenient with over papistry. Not only that, but Charles seemed to have no intention of setting aside his brother James – currently his heir to the throne – who openly professed his Catholic faith. Both Parliament and people feared the worst if the country had another Catholic monarch. Queen Mary Tudor, the only other Catholic monarch to rule the Protestant nation, was remembered as causing turmoil, disaster and martyrdom for too many.

Charles had numerous illegitimate children by his many mistresses but no offspring by his wife, Queen Catharine of Braganza. Despite miscarriages in the early years of their marriage, she had been unable to give the king a legitimate heir. There were rumours that Charles might have Parliament pass an act legitimising his eldest son, James, Duke of Monmouth, but this had yet to happen, though the young man was popular, capable and, most important, a Protestant. The Rye House Plot seems to have focussed on Monmouth and he was certainly involved, though not as the instigator.

Party politics also featured with several prominent Whigs implicated. The Whigs identified closely with the Protestant succession. One of the alleged plotters, Richard Rumbold (1622–85), was the owner of Rye House. Although the ambush never happened, the failed plot was revealed in June 1683. Allegations were made that prompted a government investigation and arrests followed. The plotters were accused of scheming to kill the king during meetings at the house of a London wine merchant, at each other's homes and coffeehouses, presumably trying to cover their tracks by varying the meeting place. They were charged with treason.

Monmouth was the most famous of the conspirators but he escaped the law by fleeing the country (some say the king allowed it). Ambitious yet reckless, he may have been brought into the conspiracy by the Earl of Shaftesbury, Anthony Ashley Cooper, who took the precaution of leaving the country before the plot was uncovered. Monmouth's involvement was vital, if the scheme was intended to put him on the throne.

Another of those accused was not as cautious as Shaftsbury. The Earl of Essex was arrested and taken to the Tower of London where he died, possibly by suicide. The politician Lord William Russell; Algernon Sydney, who had fought for Parliament in the Civil War; and Sir Thomas Armstrong were tried, convicted of treason and beheaded. Elizabeth Gaunt, accused of 'harbouring and maintaining rebels', was burnt at the stake but the Duke of Monmouth, Robert Ferguson and Lord William Howard, among other conspirators, escaped punishment. However, an intriguing footnote to the plot is that some historians believe the whole thing was fictitious, made up by the royalist camp to discredit the opposition. That would have been a far more cunning plan. Charles II, buoyed up by the failure of the Rye House plotters and with no legitimate heirs, was able to be even more forthright in upholding his brother's right to succeed him.

Another, far more innocent yet consequential plot was set in motion by Hooke, Halley and Wren over their bowls of coffee in Garraway's one icy January day. London was in the unrelenting grip of the 'Little Ice Age'. The River Thames was frozen over but these three were having heated discussions about planetary motions and the part played by gravity in governing the planets' orbits around the Sun. Everyone accepted that gravity worked but how did it affect large bodies, such as a planet? Halley suggested that gravity would decrease according to the inverse square of the distance of the planet from the source of the gravitational pull: mainly the Sun but with influence from the other planets. Simply put, the inverse square law states that the intensity of gravity, light, heat and other forms of electro-magnetic radiation decrease as the distance from the source increases, according to the formula $1/\text{distance}^2$. Easily written but intensely difficult to work out, taking into account so many variables: the planet's size and proximity to other planets and their masses; the fact that orbits were elliptical, not circular; the presence of moons and whether their influences combined or counteracted each other to affect the planet. It was believed, rightly, though mathematical proof still awaited formulation, that the Moon's gravitational pull on the Earth was sufficiently strong to cause the tides. So many factors had to be considered.

Perhaps unsurprisingly, Hooke claimed he had done the mathematics already and proved that the inverse square law did apply to gravity and this caused the planetary orbits to be elliptical in shape. Wren was doubtful and demanded that the ever-boastful Hooke show him the calculations. He even offered one of his most valuable books as a prize. Hooke could not produce his work and the prize went unclaimed. But Halley was more determined and began an exciting piece of research, showing that Kepler's third law suggested that the inverse square law applied to gravitational attraction and presented his results at the Royal Society's meeting on 24 January 1684.

Back in the coffeehouse, Halley, Hooke and Wren continued their discussions as to whether it could be shown that the inverse square law implies elliptical orbits for the planets but failed to come up with the indisputable mathematical proof. Halley would persevere with the work on these problems but a personal tragedy distracted him during February, March and April, following his father's mysterious disappearance and death during The Great Frost. The young man was then embroiled in litigation against his stepmother over his inheritance. But in August 1684, Halley was again pursuing the problem, still wrestling with the cumbersome calculations. Whether it was his idea or someone else's suggestion, Halley took the pivotal step of visiting Isaac Newton in Cambridge, hoping the talented professor could assist with the mathematics required.

He found the Lucasian Professor in his apartments at Trinity College, no doubt surrounded by piles of notes and books and experimental apparatus. Halley presented his question concerning whether the inverse square laws applied to gravity and, if so, how would that affect planetary orbits, in particular their shape. No doubt, Halley couched his enquiries in suitably humble terms but despite that, Newton must have recognised in him a mathematician of considerable ability – if not quite his equal, naturally – because he willingly discussed the problem with Halley, rather than sending him away. Newton explained how gravity drew the planets toward the Sun, their speed accelerating as they came closer – just as the inverse square law predicted – but then their acceleration would send them hurtling around the Sun like a slingshot and then back out until gravity began to pull them back again: the orbits of the planets would indeed be elliptical.

Newton said he had already achieved the proofs Halley required and also had other highly significant mathematical formulae but did not intend to publish them. Unlike Hooke's claim, Newton's was no idle boast but in among the clutter of his rooms, he said he could not find his calculations. It is possible he knew exactly where they were but, being obsessively thorough about such matters, he would have wanted to check his calculations yet again before showing them to anyone capable of identifying a mistake. No matter; he would either find them or do them all again and send them to Halley in London, confident the younger man would have the mathematical ability to comprehend them. It took time but Newton kept his word and the work he sent would be the basis of perhaps the first truly scientific book with mathematical proofs and maybe the most famous: the *Philosophiae naturalis principia mathematica* or 'Mathematical Principles of Natural Philosophy'.

The Frost Fair

While the coffeehouse meetings were in progress, the country was suffering the coldest winter on record. Thermometers were a recent invention and a universal scale of temperature readings had yet to be established but descriptions of the thickness of ice formed on ponds in a single night suggest the long spell of exceptional freezing weather was unprecedented and has still to be surpassed. December 1683 began with a hard frost, followed by a bitter east wind laden with snow. In London, the snow melted on the 7th but a sharp frost on the 12th was succeeded by a week of heavy snowfall and a north-easterly wind. Places other than London suffered similarly. Bristol suffered badly on the 19th, Durham on Christmas Eve and Oxford had its worst snow on Christmas Day, although London only saw snow showers that day. January saw no improvement and by the end of the month the Thames estuary was frozen a mile out to sea and wagons were hauling goods downriver as far as Gravesend in Kent. The Channel was also frozen on the French side and the packet boats that brought mail to England were frozen in port. At Manchester, the ice was 'half a yard thick and continued till 25 March'.[3]

Undeterred, the people of Leeds in Yorkshire held a frost fair on the frozen River Aire. According to Ralph Thoresby, an ox roast was set up there and various sporting activities organised. In London, John Evelyn's diary provides a wealth of information, noting that brewers and other tradesmen reliant on a water supply were out of work because all the pipes were frozen. He was greatly concerned about

> ...the fowls, fish and birds and all our plants and greens universally perishing. Many parks of deer are destroyed and all sorts of fuel so dear that there were great contributions to keep the poor alive... London, by reason of the excessive coldness of the air hindering the ascent of the smoke, was so filled with the fuliginous steam of sea-coal that one could hardly see across the streetes ... and no one could scarcely breathe.

Evelyn also tells us that 'every moment was full of disastrous accidents' and trees were being cracked asunder by the frost as if by a lightning strike. Despite these gloomy realities, Londoners made the best of the weather conditions. A broadsheet of the time calls it 'Great Britain's Wonder or London's Admiration: a prodigious frost which began about the beginning of December and continued till the fourth day of February following'. The Thames had frozen over before but never had the freeze lasted so long. The river ice was more than a foot thick (30cm) enabling it to be crossed by coach, carriage, sledge or on foot. Enterprising boatmen, robbed of their livelihood otherwise, put wheels under their boats to ferry passengers across the river. By 1 January, a fair and marketplace had been set up on the ice.

King Charles and members of the royal court visited the makeshift town, enjoying eating meat from an ox roast, taking part in a fox hunt on ice and having souvenir cards printed in a booth where a printer had set up his press. The cards proved popular because the printer reckoned to make at least £5 per day at sixpence a time. In other words, he was printing around 200 cards every day and making an excellent income from his ingenuity. Food stalls sold everything from pancakes to roast beef and there were numerous taverns, goldsmiths' shops, a toy shop, coffeehouses, a lottery booth, a music booth and even a brothel: all doing a brisk trade. A circus was put on by a Mister Chipperfield: the first known performance of a family business that still continues today, if in a very different health-and-safety, animal-welfare conscious twenty-first-century format. No such niceties concerned the entrepreneurs who arranged the bull- and bear-baiting spectacles either.

John Evelyn wrote that:

> Coaches plied from Westminster to the Temple ... to and fro, as in the streets; sleds, sliding with skeetes [skates], a bull-baiting, horse and coach races, puppet plays and interludes [short dramatic sketches], cooks, tippling [drinking] and other lewd places, so that it seemed to be a bacchanalian triumph, or a carnival on water.

Others sporting activities, including football and skittles, were being played. The ice thawed a little on 4/5 February and the booths began to be dismantled but it froze again so that Evelyn could still cross in his coach to Lambeth Palace to dine with the Archbishop of Canterbury. On other occasions, he walked upriver on the ice from his home in Deptford.

In Newton's long lifetime the Thames would freeze over again in 1709 but the ice did not last so long as to allow another frost fair that year. However, the winter of 1715/16 was sufficiently severe and long-lasting that the river was frozen for almost three months and a fair was set up. On this occasion, there was far more snow than in 1683/84, 'vast quantities fallen at different times in the season', so that London was described at the time as being 'almost impassable'.

A 'Surfeit of Physicians'

While science in the fields of astronomy and mathematics was making great advances, the field of medicine was lagging far behind. Despite William Harvey having explained the function of the heart and circulation over half a century before and the advent of the microscope revealing such wonders as plant cells and human sperm, in many ways medicine remained in the dark ages, using witches' brews and treatments that fell barely short of torture in an effort to cure the patient.

On 1 February 1685, Charles II had not been well. For some time he had been suffering from recurrent, if mild, kidney infections and a troublesome leg ulcer – probably syphilitic in origin – had kept him from his customary daily walk. However, he spent a lively evening having supper and playing cards with his current mistress and two ex-mistresses. Supper included two goose eggs that may have contributed to the king's subsequent problems. His gentleman-in-waiting and the groom-of-the-bedchamber both slept in the king's room and reported that he passed an unusually restless night. Upon waking, he rushed into the privy closet (his private lavatory) and spent so long in there, his servants became concerned. Only the king's keeper-of-the-closet was permitted to enter this inner sanctum and it took some time to locate him.

Eventually, the keeper arrived and, upon entering the closet, found the king shivering in his nightgown, disorientated and unable to stand without assistance. It is possible the goose eggs had caused diarrhoea and vomiting, leading to dehydration. The king could not seem to speak coherently either. Various sources suggest he had suffered a slight stroke but Brewer believes Charles was in the terminal stages of uraemia – in other words, kidney failure.[4] Uraemia causes the build-up of toxins in the blood because the kidneys no longer function properly and are unable to excrete them as normal. In effect, the body slowly poisons itself. If uraemia was the case, only the modern treatment of dialysis and eventually a kidney transplant could have saved the king. If it was a minor stroke and a stomach upset, he may well have recovered naturally. Either way, the medical practices of the day most definitely made matters worse for the unfortunate monarch, hastening his end in the most humiliating and agonising circumstances. A commentator and wit at the time noted that the king died of a 'surfeit of physicians'. In some ways this was true for the king had more than a dozen physicians to attend him and it seems each one of them had a different favourite treatment to be tried, most of which likely made matters worse, counteracted or even reacted with the other remedies and few at all which could have eased the patient's suffering in any way. If anyone wonders why the receiver of medical treatment is referred to as the 'patient', King Charles's experience is explanation enough.

On that Monday morning, despite the king's obvious indisposition, a group of surgeons came to change the dressings on his ulcerated leg, during which procedure Charles gave 'the dreadfulest shriek' and suffered a series of convulsions. He was pallid and temporarily speechless. His physicians were soon in attendance, including Dr Sir Charles Scarborough who had been his physician during the king's exile and throughout his reign. Scarborough had studied under William Harvey at Oxford, tutored young Christopher Wren who became his assistant for a while, learning the art of dissection, and was a renowned mathematician in his own right. Sadly, none of his skills helped the king whose treatment was as follows:

> The King was bled to the extent of a pint from his right arm. Next the physicians drew eight ounces of blood [another half pint] from the left shoulder, gave an emetic to make the King vomit, two physicks and an enema containing antimony [a poison], rock salt, marshmallow leaves, violets, beetroot, chamomile flowers, fennel seed, linseed, cardamom seed, cinnamon, cochineal and aloes.

All this before noon, as it was noted. Because of the convulsions and inability to speak, it was assumed that the problem lay in the brain. According to medical lore at the time, this was caused by an imbalance of the four bodily humours concentrated in that organ. Bleeding, emetics and enemas were three means of stripping the excess humours from the patient's system in general. When all these treatments seemed ineffective, more targeted remedies were tried to clear the brain of extraneous matter:

> The King's head was then shaved and a blister raised upon his scalp. A sneezing powder of hellebore root [also poisonous]

was given to purge the brain and a powder of cowslip administered to strengthen it, for it was the belief that the nasal secretions came from the brain. A plaster of pitch and pigeon dung was put on the King's feet.

The blister on the scalp was raised by applying cantharides or Spanish fly to the king's shaven head. This was painful indeed. The crushed beetles are toxic, act as both a diuretic and a urinary tract irritant, so further dehydrating the patient. The purpose of the blister was to cause fluid to accumulate on the surface of the head so it could be lanced and drawn off because the fluid was believed to be more of the excess humours afflicting the brain. Likewise, the hot pitch plaster applied to the feet would also cause blisters, this time thinking to draw fluid down and away from the brain. Emetics, laxatives and enemas continued to be administered during the afternoon, further dehydrating and weakening the king. Perhaps all that kept him going was a 'soothing drink composed of barley water, liquorice, sweet almonds, light wine, oil of wormwood (another strong purgative), anise, thistle leaves, mint, rose and angelica'. But this was offset when they gave him a sacred bitter powder (Jesuit's bark or quinine) in a compound of peony water with bryony compound (another purgative) and more poisonous white hellebore.

The next day, Tuesday 3 February, the king suffered another convulsion. His doctors prescribed Jesuit's bark, manna and cream of tartar to be given every 6 hours, *sal ammoniac* (to revive him) in antidotal milk water as required and a julep (a sweetened medication) of black cherry water, lime flowers, lily of the valley (another poisonous ingredient), peony, lavender, powdered pearls dissolved in vinegar, gentian root, nutmeg, cloves and sugar. The surgeons bled him of another 10 ounces and repeated the blistering. They followed this with more barley water with mallow, almonds, melon seeds and the bark of slippery elm (used by back-street abortionists).

On Wednesday, his doctors did not think further medicine necessary until the evening, when they gave him cream of tartar in white wine with senna (another laxative), manna, chamomile, gentian and nutmeg, followed by spirit of human skull – distilled from the skull of a man who had died by violence and not been buried.

On Thursday, the physicians learned that there were cases of fever locally and took precautionary measures, prescribing more Jesuit's bark in antidotal milk water with cloves as a prophylactic. They also administered more spirit of human skull and a remedy called 'Raleigh's stronger antidote' – stronger because it contained more herbs and other ingredients than any other remedy – along with bezoar stone from a goat's stomach (reckoned the 'magic bullet' of the day) and more *sal ammoniac.*

The next day, Friday 6 February, Charles was at his last gasp, though lucid and capable of speech, such that he apologised to his doctors for being 'an unconscionable time dying'. He pleaded with his brother James, Duke of York, not to let poor Nelly (his mistress, Nell Gwynn) starve and confessed that 'I have suffered very much, and more than any of you can imagine. My business will shortly be done.' He asked that the curtains should be opened so that he could see the light of the rising Sun one last time, after which he became acutely breathless and was bled another 12 ounces. He asked to receive the Last Rites according to the Roman Catholic Church, not the Anglican form, and this was arranged by the Duke of York who smuggled his own Catholic priest into the bedchamber by the back stair. Hastily accepted into the Catholic faith, Charles's speech failed, he became unconscious and died just before midday.

Death must have come as a relief to the king. Dr Sir Charles Scarborough performed a post mortem, finding that 'On the Surface of the Brain the Veins and Arteries were unduly full, the Cerebral ventricles were filled with a kind of serous [waxy] matter and the substance of the Brain itself was quite soaked with similar fluid'. This suggested that along with suffering from the uraemia, Charles may also have contracted a cerebral infection, such as a viral encephalitis to add to his problems. Meantime, he left his realm with an equally painful problem: it was a Protestant country that now had a Catholic monarch as his brother succeeded him as James II. There was certain to be trouble in the near future and his subjects faced it with trepidation.

Philosophiae naturalis principia mathematica

Since August 1684, Edmund Halley had been waiting eagerly in London for Isaac Newton to send him his calculations regarding the inverse square law. He no doubt hoped the professor would produce the goods, unlike Robert Hooke who, despite his claims, had yet to show anything by way of the promised proofs. Halley was rewarded in November when a nine-page document was delivered to him by a mutual acquaintance of Newton and himself, the mathematician Edward Paget. The closely written treatise, entitled *De Motu Corporum in gyrum* or 'On the Motion of Revolving Bodies', exceeded Halley's expectations and he rushed off to Cambridge to ask permission, in person, to read the work to the Royal Society at the next meeting.

On 10 December, arriving late from Cambridge, Halley presented the paper as the final item on the meeting's agenda and the few members still present and capable of having the least understanding of it recognised it as a valuable and outstanding achievement. The following February, having been studied by the best mathematicians in the society, the paper was entered into their Register. It was also discussed whether the Royal Society might publish an expanded version, if the ever-reluctant Professor Newton could be persuaded to allow his work to go public. *De Motu* would become the foundation of Book I of the famous *Principia Mathematica*. In the meantime, Newton used the treatise as a basis for his next series of lectures – whether or not any students attended them, or had any comprehension of them if they did come to listen.

It seems Newton had already decided to expand his treatise, perhaps for a further series of lectures, if not for publication. With this in mind, during December 1684 and into January 1685, a flurry of correspondence passed between Cambridge and the Royal Observatory at Greenwich as Newton politely requested the Astronomer Royal, John Flamsteed, to send him a swathe of data concerning star positions and planetary positions relative to one another. Flamsteed happily obliged, despite having no concept of why the professor wanted or could possibly require so much information. When Newton wrote back saying he believed

Saturn's orbit had been miscalculated by Johannes Kepler years ago and must be far larger 'by reason of Jupiter's action upon him', Flamsteed responded 'I cannot conceive of any impression made by the one planet ... can disturb the motion of the other', although he admitted Kepler's figures were somewhat in error. Of course, Newton was correct and pushing the boundaries of science with his idea that gravity could have an effect across the vast distances of space.

The possibility that an invisible force could work in a vacuum over impossibly large distances was a concept which smacked of sorcery and witchcraft. To most scientific thinkers of the day, such ideas belonged in the Dark Ages and there they should remain; it had taken centuries for mankind to fight free of this kind of nonsense. Now one of the country's foremost academics was attempting to revive some archaic 'occult' notions. But Newton's deep interest in alchemical processes enabled him to conceive of the existence of inexplicable, unseen powers and forces. To him, the fact that gravity existed was obvious because its effects were not only observable but mathematically demonstrable. The fact that it could neither be seen nor its nature and origin defined made its existence no less possible than the undisputed existence of God. His best explanation was that 'gravity had its foundation only in the arbitrary will of God.'[5]

In the *Principia*, Newton would explain how gravity not only keeps the planets orbiting the Sun, but holds the Moon in its orbit and, from the vastness of stars to the smallest things, is the reason why an apple falls to earth. He also stated his three laws of motion, the foundation of Newtonian mechanics, as the system became known – a concept which held until challenged by Albert Einstein but, even so, remained perfectly adequate to send men to the Moon in the 1960s and 1970s.

John Flamsteed would not be the only philosopher perplexed by Newton's work. His advances in mathematics, made in order that his calculations could be 'simplified', would confound all but the best academic minds. Some years earlier, he had developed fluxions – we call it calculus – as a shorthand method of calculating curves that were other than circular. Obviously, fluxions were vital in dealing with elliptical planetary orbits but also for more everyday concerns, such as constructing bridges or, these days, to calculate the trajectory of a space craft or probe. Fluxions would be fully explained in Newton's forthcoming papers.

Unfortunately, at this point, a young German, Gottfried Wilhelm von Leibniz, published his *Novus methodus*, detailing his invention of calculus. Although it seems to have resulted from his entirely independent efforts, Leibniz had been acquainted with and visited John Collins, the London publisher of academic books to whom Isaac Barrow has sent some of Newton's mathematical papers in the past. When he learned of Leibniz' book, Newton accused him of the ultimate academic sin: plagiarism. It would cause an infamous priority dispute between the two, which would only end with Leibniz' death. Leibniz always refuted the allegations and John Collins had died in 1683, so could not be consulted.

In the meantime, throughout 1685, Newton shut himself away in his apartments at Trinity to write his masterpiece and conduct experiments, unaware of Leibniz. His new assistant and *amanuensis* was Humphrey Newton, replacing John Wickins who had left Cambridge to take up a clerical post. Humphrey was from Grantham and had probably been recommended to the professor by the new headmaster at the grammar school. If the two were related, it must have been distantly since neither claimed any family connections. Eventually, it would be Humphrey who copied out the final manuscript version of the *Principia* in his neat hand, though he admitted, like much of his master's work, it was something he 'was not able to penetrate into'.

On 28 April 1686, Newton presented Book I of his *Principia* to the Royal Society and by mid-May the society had taken the decision to publish it – John Collins no longer being able to oblige. Halley wrote to Newton with the good news that he had been instructed to arrange the publication and on 30 June, Samuel Pepys, as President of the Royal Society, had granted the licence to publish under the auspices of the society and at their expense. All seemed to be going well. On 1 March 1687, Newton sent Book II of the *Principia* to Halley, followed by Book III on 4 April.

But events beyond his cloistered life in Cambridge did not run so smoothly. Edmund Halley was himself in difficulties. Two years since the death of his wealthy father, his spendthrift stepmother had yet to hand over a penny of Halley's rightful inheritance. By the time the matter had been dragged through the courts, she had spent the money and Halley still had to pay his lawyers' fees. No longer able to afford his fine house in Islington, where he lived with his beloved wife Mary and had an enviable observatory, the couple had been forced to move to a more humble address at Golden Lion Court in Aldersgate Street. This was more convenient for attending meetings of the Royal Society, yet Halley could no longer afford the membership subscriptions. How humiliating it must have been when he was forced to resign his Fellowship and apply for the paid post of Clerk to the Society, in order to maintain the connection. Never one to sulk, he made the best of the situation, proving himself a diligent and conscientious clerk, improving the running of the society's rather muddled affairs and even able to pursue his own research.

Halley was not alone in having financial problems. The Royal Society itself was in a penurious state. Membership had fallen as those who had joined to enjoy the kudos and perhaps out of curiosity, rather than deep scientific interest, began to find other things to fill their time. Of those who were still enthusiastic, some, like Halley, were no longer able to pay and others who could afford the fees were reluctant to, or remiss in doing so. Then, the society had rashly spent most of its budget on the publication of a large format edition of *The History of Fishes* by Francis Willoughby, with hand-coloured plates. Beautiful it may have been, but it sold so few copies the society was left with an embarrassingly large pile of unwanted books. They even attempted to force Hooke as Secretary and Halley as Clerk to accept copies to sell, instead of their salaries. Halley obliged, taking fifty copies instead of the £50 he was owed as his annual payment; Hooke, being more experienced in the wily ways of the cash-strapped society, refused, insisting on having the money due. Determined though to keep his promise to Newton that the *Principia* would be published, Halley scraped together sufficient funds to pay for its publication himself. The book finally appeared in print on 5 July 1687 and, surprisingly for such complex subject matter, copies sold rather well, such that Halley's kindly enterprise earned him a modest profit. The *Principia* was out there in the world, changing mathematics, the study of astronomy and physics forever.

A Catholic King

Beyond everyone's financial circumstances lurked a far greater issue: the country was balanced on the brink of civil war. After the death of Charles II, his brother James became king. Openly a convert to Catholicism, Protestants feared he might attempt to turn the country back to the Roman Church, as Mary Tudor had in the 1550s with disastrous consequences. In the summer of 1685, within months of ascending the throne, James faced a rebellion in Scotland, led by the Earl of Argyll, followed swiftly by a major challenge from his nephew, Charles's illegitimate eldest son, the Duke of Monmouth. The young man was popular and Protestant and could have had a lot of support. He might have made a successful bid for the Crown except that Britain's fear of the consequences of another civil war was even greater than its fear of being ruled by a Catholic monarch. Monmouth's uprising ended in failure at the Battle of Sedgemoor on 6 July as his support ebbed away. Nine days later, Monmouth paid the ultimate price: he was beheaded in London.

James II had won the first two rounds but must have realised his reign was not going to be an easy one. Determined to make any subject contemplating rebellion think again, he appointed Lord Chief Justice George Jeffreys to oversee the trials of all those involved with Monmouth's fiasco. Hundreds of cases were heard in what became known as the 'Bloody Assizes' across the south of England, from Winchester in Hampshire to Wells in Somerset. The law made no distinction between those who had committed treason by taking up arms against the king and those who were merely accessories after the fact. An elderly woman who had helped those fleeing the battlefield was found guilty and condemned by Jeffreys to endure an even more gruesome fate than Monmouth himself. As the final word in brutality, Lady Alice Lisle was supposed to be executed by burning at the stake – a woman's punishment for a political crime. Fortunately, being a 'lady', her sentence was commuted to beheading. Between 24 August and 23 September, Jeffreys and his four fellow judges dealt with more than 1,400 prisoners. Most received the death sentence but fewer than 300 were actually hanged, although in Taunton on the 18–19 September, the hearings earned their name of 'Bloody Assizes' when Jeffreys condemned 144 out of 500 prisoners to be hanged, drawn and quartered and their remains displayed across the country as a warning to others.

Between 800 and 900 prisoners, mostly fit young men or those with a useful skill, such as carpenters and tilers, were transported as slaves to the American colonies where they were worth more alive than dead as a source of cheap labour. Jeffreys shipped them at his own expense but made huge profits on their sales in Virginia and Carolina. Yet others languished in various prisons, awaiting further trial, but this was frequently a shorter sentence as they fell victim to gaol fever – typhus – in the terrible, unsanitary conditions. Jeffreys returned to London in triumph and was rewarded by King James who appointed him as Lord Chancellor 'for the many eminent and faithful services to the Crown'. Others had a less than glowing opinion of him, calling him 'the hanging judge'.

In July 1686, the king set up the Commission for Ecclesiastical Causes and the following 21 April Isaac Newton was summoned to appear before it. Earlier that month, he had been appointed by Cambridge University Senate as one of its representatives in the Father Alban Francis affair. By law, only those of the Anglican faith could attend university – although Newton had done so by keeping his Arian beliefs under wraps – but King James wished to end this monopoly by insisting that Magdalene College, Cambridge, accept a Catholic priest, Father Francis. The Senate was commanded to admit him to the Master of Arts Degree without his taking the required Anglican oath. A letter of refusal was sent to the king. Matters escalated and Vice-Chancellor Peachell, reluctant author of the epistle, accompanied by a delegation, including Newton and his one-time mentor Humphrey Babington, were called to a hearing. Newton was a passionate anti-Catholic and volunteered to help fight the case, arguing strenuously that no one who refused to swear allegiance to the Anglican faith could be admitted. Yet nobody raised an eyebrow at his hypocrisy.

The Commission was headed by none other than Judge Jeffreys and Peachell, as spokesman for the Cambridge delegation, withered before him. Even though Newton had composed his speeches for him, the vice-chancellor was unable to withstand Jeffreys' interrogation. At the commission's third of four meetings, Jeffreys stripped Peachell of his office, his livelihood, even his house. The remaining members made cogent arguments – though Newton never spoke – but the king intended to have the last word. The university lost its case but James was about to lose far more.

In November 1688, the regime changed in a bloodless coup known as the Glorious Revolution. James's Protestant daughter Mary and her Dutch Protestant husband, William of Orange, were 'invited' to come and take the throne. When William arrived, James thought better of contesting the matter and fled into exile. His henchman, Jeffreys, ended up in the Tower of London but died of natural causes before he could suffer a taste of his own medicine.

A Public Profile

Both the publication of the *Principia,* followed by his appearance before the Ecclesiastical Commission, had brought the name Isaac Newton to the notice of people other than academics and members of the Royal Society. As a result, he was offered the post of Member of Parliament to represent Cambridge University in Westminster. Parliament met in December 1688 with the unique task of transferring government from the absent King James to joint monarchs, William and Mary. Newton attended, made copious notes and reported back on the proceedings to the university. However, the only time he spoke in the House of Commons was a quiet aside to an usher, asking him to close a window because there was a draught. But he did make some most important contacts that would affect his future career. He met the philosopher John Locke who would become a firm friend. He dined with the new king, William III, and met Charles Montagu, who would become a friend and patron, as well as Chancellor of the Exchequer.

Chapter 7

THE 1690s: THE ALCHEMIST AND CRIME INVESTIGATOR

So intent, so serious [was he] upon his studies that he ate very sparingly, he often forgot to eat at all ... He very rarely went to bed, till 2 or 3 of the clock, sometimes not till 5 or 6, lying about 4 or 5 hours, especially at spring & fall of the leaf, at which times he used to employ about 6 weeks in his laboratory, the fire scarcely going out either night or day, he sitting up one night, as I did another until he had finished his chemical experiments, in the performance of which he was the most accurate, strict, exact. What his aim might be, I was not able to penetrate into.[1]

This is Humphrey Newton's description of Professor Newton at work: obsessive and utterly absorbed in his chemical processes. To this period may date the possibly apocryphal story of his invention of the cat flap, so that he would not be required to leave his work even for the few moments it would take to let the cat out or in. It certainly sounds like something a man so practical would invent to avoid disturbance in his laboratory. Incidentally, some early texts use the word 'elaboratory', a precursor of 'laboratory', which demonstrates how the word originated because such a place was where current knowledge was elaborated upon and extended.

Newton's fascination with chemistry had developed after he read Robert Boyle's *Sceptical Chymist* but, as with his other scientific studies, Newton read widely around the subject and virtually every available treatise he could lay hands on was perused, annotated and gleaned for any scrap of new information. And then he would push the boundaries as far as he could go. With his mathematics, astronomy and study of light, we know how much he advanced the knowledge of those subjects because his work was published. However, in the field of chemistry, nothing was put in the public domain concerning what he achieved in his laboratory, sweating over his furnace and still, breathing in noxious fumes while his cat – so they say – grew fat on his forgotten meals. Newton never published a chemistry book, yet it appears that he spent decades in pursuit of the subject, perhaps giving more time to it in his later years than he had to his mathematics and optics in his youth. Why was that?

Perhaps the answer lies in the ambiguities of the boundary between chemistry and alchemy. In terms of methods and apparatus, there is virtually no difference between the two but in terms of their history, legitimacy and attitudes to the practitioners, the divide was wide – and dangerous. And beyond doubt, Newton's chemistry had strayed far over that vague dividing line, into the forbidden territory of the alchemist.

Alchemy

The art of alchemy went back to Ancient Egypt although its origins are as mysterious as its practices. It has been suggested that Isaac Barrow and Henry More may have introduced Newton to the subject but this is not certain because, wisely, the information was not recorded.[2] Although the basics of chemistry were evolving from alchemy, the older discipline was regarded as having links to the occult, sorcery and black magic. Its historic aims had been twofold: to discover the secret of eternal life and the means of transmuting base metals into gold. In theory, both were believed possible with the aid of the legendary 'philosopher's stone', though the nature and creation of the stone were equally problematic. The theory was based on the received wisdom that everything on God's Earth was slowly but surely intended to achieve a state of perfection in the end. For mankind, that state would imply perfect health and, therefore, eternal life. In the case of metals, all would eventually become the perfect element: gold. The philosopher's stone, if it could be produced, was simply the means of artificially hastening that process towards ultimate perfection. Perhaps the greatest obstacle to creating the miraculous stone was the requirement that the alchemist himself had to be in a state of spiritual perfection in order to be successful. That impossibility was believed to be the explanation for all past failures. Isaac Newton, never renowned for his modesty, thought he of all people was God's appointee to uncover these secrets.

At one time or another, most European states had made the practice of alchemy illegal. Although emperors, kings and princes might have welcomed the possibility of living for ever and having endless riches beyond imagining, none could contemplate their enemies – or even a lowly subject – acquiring these advantages. One fifteenth-century English practitioner, George Ripley, took the precaution of dedicating his alchemical text to King Edward IV, that the king might have use of them, if he wished and could decipher their meaning. Edward is thought to have 'dabbled' and Ripley's achievements were certainly intriguing. Newton made a close study of Ripley's work, copying out passages from manuscript sources.

George Ripley was a Yorkshireman who studied alchemy in Rome, Louvain and on the Island of Rhodes. While on Rhodes, he created gold for the Knights of St John, producing £100,000 a year to finance their war against the Muslim Turks in the 1450s – so he claimed – but the process was too complex and secret to be divulged. In 1471, Ripley was a canon at Bridlington Priory in Yorkshire where the prior and brethren complained about the fumes and the stenches issuing from his elaboratory. He wrote three alchemical texts: *On the Philosopher's Stone and the Phoenix* was a rehashing of earlier authors' works, so was not too controversial. But his *Compound of Alchemy or the Twelve Gates Leading to the Discovery of the Philosopher's Stone* was original and the first alchemical text to be written in English.

This he dedicated to the king to avoid possible accusations of heresy, sorcery or even treason, since manufacturing gold for personal use was a crime against the state. Ripley's third book was written in Latin, *Medulla alchemiae* (the Marrow of Alchemy), dedicated to the Archbishop of York in 1476 to keep favour with the Church.

The 'twelve gates' referred to in the title of the second book were the twelve chemical techniques then known: condensation, evaporation, sublimation, calcination, distillation, etc. Ripley wrote in English so 'all might read his work' but, of course, he had no intention of revealing his secret formulae. His method of making the elixir of life was explained in a kind of alchemical code, using an artist's palette of colours and a zoo of metaphorical animals:

> Pale & black with false citrine, imperfect white & red,
> The peacock's feathers in colours gay, the rainbow which
>   shall overgo,
> The spotted panther, the lion green, the crow's bill blue as
>   lead,
> These shall appear before the perfect white and many other
>   mo'e.
> And after the perfect white, grey, false citrine also,
> And after these then shall appear the body red invariable,
> Then hast thou a medicine of the third order of his own kind
>   multiplicable.[3]

The point was that only the initiated would understand the code and be able to interpret the method. When Ripley died in 1490 – having failed, it seems, to benefit from his elixir of life – nonetheless, he was far wealthier than a humble canon ought to be. On his deathbed, he confessed to having wasted his life in fruitless pursuits, leaving instructions for all his writings to be burnt. They were based on worthless speculation, he said, not valid experimentation at all. Unsurprisingly, his instructions were not obeyed and his books survived. After all, Ripley grew rich by some means and if not by alchemy, then how? His 'apprentice', Thomas Norton, believed his master had succeeded in transmuting lead into gold and published his own version, which remained in print until 1652, although Norton kept his authorship anonymous by encoding his name in a cipher. Presumably, Newton must also have believed Ripley's work had achieved some worthwhile results, otherwise he would not have wasted his time studying the texts in such detail and copying them into his own notebook.

Newton probably became familiar with elements such as mercury and antimony while working in William Clarke's apothecary shop in Grantham, since both elements were believed to have beneficial medicinal properties. They would have been prepared and sold over the counter to customers. As his interest in the apothecary's craft expanded into the field of alchemy, Newton continued to experiment with antimony and his later notebooks describe in detail how he produced the 'star regulus of antimony'. In this experiment antimony metal is formed with a visible crystalline structure.[4] The process requires the repeated purification of antimony from the ore stibnite by heating it with iron and saltpetre. As the molten metal slowly cools with air excluded by the layer of slag above, the 'star regulus' is produced.

Also, Newton records how he produced 'the net', a purple alloy of metallic antimony and copper. The colour would appeal to any alchemist. He followed the process described by the American alchemist George Starkey – resident in London from 1650 to 1665 – again refining antimony from stibnite using iron but then adding copper. This produces an alloy with the appearance of a regular network of minute crystals on the surface. This is what Starkey termed 'the net'. He explained that this was the 'finely wrought bronze net', which in Roman mythology the blacksmith god Vulcan forged to entrap his wife Venus – represented by copper – and her illicit lover Mars – represented by iron – and thus accorded perfectly with alchemical tradition. Starkey published tracts by Eirenaeus Philalethes, which may be his own pen name or that of a New England Doctor names Childe.[5] The identification remains uncertain but the books, *An Open Entrance to the Closed Palace of the King* and *Ripley Reviv'd* (as in George Ripley), influenced Robert Boyle, Isaac Barrow and Newton among others. Starkey's experimental enquiries caused his downfall when, during the Great Plague in London in 1665, he performed a post mortem on one of the victims and contracted the disease which proved fatal to him.

Having successfully produced the star regulus and the net, Newton realised he could proceed no further with his experiments on antimony and turned his attention to other toxic metals as the bases for his alchemical investigations.

Poisons in the Laboratory

It was suggested at around the time of his fortieth birthday in 1682, perhaps in jest by Newton himself, that his hair had turned completely silver because it took on the colour of mercury, a chemical he was working with a great deal. His hair, though still thick and plentiful, is certainly white in his portrait painted by Sir Godfrey Kneller in 1689 when he was forty-five years old. Through the ages, alchemists believed mercury to be *the* basic component of all other metals. Its fluidity at room temperature imparted to other metals the ability to become liquid when heated. The fact that it can form an amalgam with gold, making the gilding process of other metals possible, also made mercury 'special' since gilding could be a fraudulent means of seeming to transmute base metals into gold – the alchemists' ultimate goal.

However, loss of hair colour is not a recognised symptom of mercury poisoning, but in the 1690s Newton definitely showed signs of reacting to the toxic substances used in his laboratory and his hair was and is an indicator. Mercury, lead, arsenic and antimony all react with the sulphur atoms that are present in keratin: the substance that forms hair and fingernails. Genuine samples of Newton's hair have survived to the present. Most were snipped off as mementoes when he died but a single stray hair was discovered within the pages of one of his notebooks. When analysed using modern techniques in 1979, his hair was found to contain four times as much lead, arsenic and antimony as normal and fifteen times as much mercury.[6] One strand was found to contain toxic levels of both mercury and lead.

Not only did Newton admit in his notes that he evaporated mercury over a fire – the most dangerous way of working with it, inhaling the toxic vapour – but he also had a great fondness for the colour crimson in furnishings and decor. At the time, the most vibrant red paint was made using vermilion, which contained mercury. It is possible the excessively high level of mercury in the hair samples taken on his deathbed was partly due to the bedchamber decor.

Throughout his adult life, Newton appears to have slept little, and had minimal interest in food, as Humphrey Newton related. Neither is there any indication of sexual activity. The first is a symptom of chronic mercury poisoning; the latter two of lead poisoning. He also suffered mood swings and paranoia – again, symptoms of mercury poisoning. In the summer and early autumn of 1693, Newton behaved particularly strangely. In letters written at the time to his friends, Samuel Pepys and John Locke, he complains of poor digestion and insomnia for the past year – a period during which he had become a virtual recluse in Cambridge – daring to admit his 'former consistency of mind' had been lacking recently. That is quite a traumatic admission for a man who believed his thought processes to be all but perfect. He goes so far as to apologise for letters he had written previously, in which he had accused Pepys of saying he had requested favours from King James (this would have been at least five years before, if it happened at all) and that he never wanted to see Pepys again. He berated Locke by letter for trying to 'embroil me with women'.[7] Again, he eventually apologised to Locke as well, blaming a distemper of the head for his appalling rudeness to his friends.

These symptoms – periods of anger, aggression and paranoia, irritability, depression and insomnia – could all be indicative of chronic poisoning with a combination of mercury and lead, with the first predominating. However, certain classic symptoms are absent. He does not mention listlessness and lack of concentration nor loss of memory. He definitely remembered writing those dreadful, accusatory letters and to whom he sent them, even if he was unable to explain why he had done so. Because long-term exposure to mercury affects the brain and nervous system, those afflicted develop hand tremors and their writing becomes spidery. At this time, Newton wrote up some of his alchemical experiments under the heading *Praxis* or 'Doings', pages of symbols and ciphers.[8] They may be almost impossible to interpret but the actual handwriting is Newton's usual tiny, neat script and quite legible. Other symptoms would have been mouth problems and loosening teeth, excess salivation and urination to begin with, although urination decreases as the kidneys eventually cease to function.[9] Newton makes no mention of any such problems but, perhaps, they were too personal and private to be made known, even to friends.

Whatever the true cause and details of his illness in the summer of 1693, thankfully, Newton recovered. At the time, understanding little of the effects of working with toxic metals, those who knew him blamed mental exhaustion and disappointment in a close relationship with a young mathematician.

Nicolas Fatio de Duillier

In March and April 1690, Newton was again in London and met Nicolas Fatio de Duillier, a brilliant young Swiss mathematician, at a meeting of the Royal Society. Newton was swiftly becoming quite a celebrity, not only in Britain but also in Europe since the publication of the *Principia*. Edmund Halley, keen to recoup the money he had spent on its publication, gave it a brilliant, if anonymous, review in the society's *Philosophical Transactions* but others also appreciated it as genuinely ground-breaking work. The French philosopher, the Marquis de l'Hôpital, remarked 'Good God, what a fund of knowledge there is in that book,' enquiring whether the author ate, drank and slept like other men. The Professor of Mathematics at Edinburgh University David Gregory took the trouble to write to Newton:

Having seen and read your book I think myself obliged to give you my most hearty thanks for having been at pains to teach the world that which I never expected any man should have known.[10]

However, there were those who did not admire the *Principia*. In Cambridge, when two students passed Professor Newton in the street, one remarked to the other: 'There goes the man who wrote the book that neither he nor anybody else understands.' Robert Hooke had little good to say about it for his own reasons, at least in private. When a derisory review of the *Principia* appeared in the journal of the Académie Royale des Sciences in Paris, although written anonymously, Hooke was believed to have been the author.

Despite his own growing fame, Newton must have been impressed by the young Swiss. Born in Basel in 1664 and educated in Geneva, Nicolas Fatio de Duillier had the mathematical capacity to be able to understand the *Principia,* and Newton realised this. The young man had already led quite an eventful life. He had become well acquainted with Christiaan Huygens in Holland and would later invent a method of drilling the minute ruby gemstones required for the jewelled movement in clock mechanisms which is still in use today in analogue watches. Fatio worked with Huygens on various topics, including the calculus of infinite series and would share with the Dutchman his list of *errata* which he had discovered in the *Principia,* requiring correction. While in Holland, Fatio discovered a plot to kill the Head of State, William of Orange, and informed the authorities, foiling the assassination attempt.

When William became King of England in 1688, Fatio came to London, perhaps hoping for some reward for previously saving the monarch's life. He was also in search of a patron in Robert Boyle. Fatio had written a paper on the phenomenon of 'zodiacal light' which occurs before dawn when the light from the Sun, as yet unseen below the horizon, is scattered by particles in an interplanetary dust cloud, producing an ethereal glow in the eastern sky. He had discussed this and his ideas on the cause of gravitational pull with Giovanni Cassini, head of the Paris Observatory. With these credentials, once in London he was quickly nominated, seconded and elected as a Fellow of the Royal Society in 1688, attending their meetings quite regularly, even though neither Boyle's patronage nor the king's reward materialised.

After their meeting in June 1690, Newton became very fond of the young Fatio. Much ink has been used in writing about the nature of their relationship, whether Newton was a closet homosexual who had found love at long last or if it was a one-sided infatuation. More likely, nearing his fiftieth year, Newton was beginning to feel his age, becoming aware that, despite his alchemical experiments, he was no closer to achieving immortality than anyone else. When death should catch up with him, that incredible mind and so much knowledge would be lost to mankind and Newton was more than aware of his own God-given abilities. One answer would be to take on a suitable apprentice to study his art, learn from him and, eventually, continue the good work. When Newton asked Fatio to live with him in Cambridge, perhaps that was his intention: to train his successor.

An abrupt break in their relationship occurred in May 1693 and has been blamed for causing Newton's mental collapse as discussed above. The reasons for the break are not certain but Fatio's religious beliefs may have come between them. Newton had calculated to his own satisfaction that the end of the world and Judgement Day were far in the future. This belief was important for the improvement of education, moral behaviour and even the continued rebuilding of fire-stricken London. Yet there were many whose opinion was that the end was imminent, so what was the point in educating young minds, living righteously and building a better world when the Apocalypse could happen any day? It becomes apparent from his actions in the next few years that Fatio was one of those 'millenarians' who believed various doom-laden prognostications of the time. He was arrested as a heretic and supporter of such ideas which, with law and order in mind, the authorities could not allow to go unchecked and unpunished. Although Fatio survived the experience, he discovered that he was mistaken. Judgement Day would not come to pass in his lifetime because he lived to the age of eighty-nine, dying in 1753 at his home near Worcester in England.

Knowing Newton's opinion on such religious ideas, although he must have been disappointed and distressed at the realisation, perhaps it was best that the sorcerer and his apprentice parted company sooner rather than later. They would still meet occasionally at Royal Society meetings as happened in 1717, when Fatio presented a series of papers on the subjects of the precession of the equinoxes and, surprisingly, climate change. He spoke of both matters as being not only of scientific interest but as precursors of the end of time. Quite what the President of the Society, his old friend Newton, thought of these papers is not known.

Sorting out England's Financial Problems

When William of Orange had become King of England in right of his wife, Mary Stuart, in 1688, without a drop of blood being spilt, he was still at heart a Dutchman. He remained more interested in pursuing continental wars in defence of his homeland than his English subjects were willing to finance. In time of war, Parliament would raise taxes to defend England's shores; but whether English taxes should pay to defend the Netherlands, as the king wished, became a thorny issue. Parliament decided they should not; England wanted no part in the foreign conflict. Therefore, some other means of paying for what were called 'King Billy's Wars' had to be found.

A Scotsman, William Patterson, came up with an ingenious solution in 1691. He proposed a scheme whereby funding would come from voluntary public subscription to a 'Bank' and the king could then borrow from this source, running up what would become the national debt, to be paid back at some future date, unspecified. In return for their capital subscriptions, shareholders, i.e. the 'Bank', would be allowed to issue bank notes, trade in bonds and re-lend money elsewhere, using the national debt as security. The idea of bank notes was not entirely new. Since the fourteenth century, the Goldsmiths' Company of London had been issuing notes to clients as receipts for money and valuables given to the company for safe keeping – the goldsmiths having both trust and secure facilities. These receipt notes were used occasionally as 'virtual' money, sparing the client the trouble of retrieving his goods from the company, paying them to his creditor who would then give them back to the goldsmiths to keep safe. Handing over a note was less risky, too, rather than carrying gold and silver around.

Patterson's idea required both government and royal sanction. To get Parliament to agree to the idea it required a political sponsor and it took until 1694 to acquire one: Charles Montagu, the fifth son of the Earl of Manchester. Montagu was a fine scholar and had attended Trinity College, Cambridge, where he made the acquaintance of Professor Newton, twenty years his senior. The unlikely pair became friends and both would benefit from their association.

A Northamptonshire man, Montagu was elected to Parliament in 1689 as MP for Maldon in Essex and his abilities led to a meteoric rise up the government hierarchy. In March 1692, he became a Commissioner for the Treasury and was promoted to Chancellor of the Exchequer at the beginning of May 1694, a post he would hold until November 1699. As Chancellor, Montagu became responsible for the country's finances, which were in dire trouble.

Patterson's 'Bank' would help solve part of the problem: the king's insolvency led to the Bank of England veing set up as a private company, founded by Royal Charter in 1694. Montagu was returned to Parliament, this time as MP for Westminster in October 1695, and embarked upon an incredible effort to sort out the country's other major monetary problem: the state of the coinage itself.

Silver pennies – the basis of the currency system – were notoriously easy to 'clip'. That is, they could be trimmed down. A penny was, literally, a pennyworth of silver. If it was clipped, it lost value. Unscrupulous 'coiners' would trim so many pennies that they had enough silver offcuts to melt down and mint their own counterfeit coins. This resulted in debasing the system twice over: firstly, the legal coins were now underweight and under value and, secondly, there were numerous false coins circulating alongside them. Montagu realised there was only one means of restoring money to its true value and this involved the radical recoinage project. A task of monumental proportions and logistical nightmares, it would require the recall of every coin in the land to be melted down and reminted, while allowing sufficient money to remain in circulation so financial transactions could continue. Not only that, but something needed to be done to prevent the same problem recurring a few years hence.

All this time, Isaac Newton remained at Cambridge, disillusioned and tired of lecturing to empty halls. As his fellow professors were receiving church appointments and rising higher in the realm of academia, having avoided taking holy orders because of his covert heretical beliefs, Newton was ineligible for any such post. If he was going to progress to a more lucrative new position, it would have to be a civil State appointment, unconnected with the Church. We know his influential friends, John Locke and Charles Montagu, had been on the lookout for a suitable post for Newton in London, one worthy of his incredible talents. At the age of fifty-three, thinking his friends had forgotten him in the backwaters of Cambridge, Newton received a letter from Montagu, in his capacity as Chancellor of the Exchequer:

> I am very glad that at last I can give you proof of my friendship, and the esteem the king has of your merits. Mr Overton, the warden of the mint, is made one of the Commissioners of Customs, and the king has promised me to make Mr Newton warden of the mint. The office is the most proper for you. 'Tis the chief office in the mint: 'tis worth five or six hundred pounds per annum, and has not too much business to require more attendance than you can spare.

Montagu had found the perfect appointment: Warden of the Royal Mint at the Tower of London. Mr Overton had been 'promoted' elsewhere, his abilities insufficient to the project the chancellor had in mind. Previously, the position of warden had been a sinecure: a title and a paid office with little actual work required, as the letter above states, and yet Newton's would be the genius behind the recoinage of the entire currency. Fortunately for the whole kingdom's finances, Newton took his work seriously and, as with any task he put his mind to, was obsessive about every detail. Unlike his predecessors at the mint, he earned his salary.

He began his new career, as he so often commenced any new subject, by studying every document he could which might be relevant. The Tower of London was then the repository of royal documents going back to the eleventh century and Newton scoured the dusty archives for all and any information pertaining to the warden's duties in medieval times, long before it was regarded as an idle appointment. Apart from overseeing the day to day business of minting new coins, it seemed it had originally been the warden's task to seek out, apprehend and bring to justice any clippers, counterfeiters and otherwise unlicensed producers of the king's coinage. Until his last days, Newton would proceed to carry out his duties to the letter.

On 19 March 1696, Newton accepted the offered appointment as Warden of the Mint and on 20 April he left Cambridge for London to take up his new position. By August he had settled into his new home on Jermyn Street in London.

Citizen of London

Living in the capital brought Newton to the centre of society, whether for business, scientific matters or pleasure, though he took little interest in the latter. No longer an academic recluse, he threw himself into his work for the mint. It might seem he would now be able to attend Royal Society meetings regularly but two things were against this. For one, his old nemesis, Robert Hooke, would always be there and Newton's dislike of the man had grown into an irrational loathing and contempt that refused to recognise the secretary's many talents and even genius in certain fields of knowledge. Secondly, Newton claimed – whether true or not – that Wednesday afternoons, when the society met, were the very time when his presence at the mint was most necessary and, therefore, it was inconvenient to attend at Gresham College.

Now that he had left Trinity College, he could no longer rely on college servants to see to such mundane matters as cooking his meals, washing his clothes and shopping for household necessities. Newton had probably given such things little thought in the past but in London society he had to look the part of the gentleman he was as he moved among important people and even dined with royalty. He needed someone to take care of his requirements, to entertain visitors and attend to guests. Other men had wives, daughters or spinster sisters; Newton, fortunately, had a capable and attractive niece both to both and ornament his household. Catherine Barton was the daughter of Newton's half-sister, Hannah Smith, and her husband Robert Barton. Catherine was about twenty years old when she arrived in London to live with her uncle. Men such as Jonathan Swift and Voltaire remarked on her beauty when they met her. Others were more deeply touched.

After his wife died in 1698, Charles Montagu began a long-term love affair with her and she went to live with him as his housekeeper. She remained there until his death in 1715, after which she returned to Newton who, by then, was living in St Martin's Street. In his will, Montagu, now Earl of Halifax, bequeathed Catherine a sizable inheritance for 'her excellent conversation', as the Astronomer Royal, John Flamsteed, put it.

At some point while she was living with Halifax, Catherine contracted smallpox. Since London had last seen a case of plague in 1666, smallpox had become the latest scourge of the population. Smallpox was not a new disease but it seems it had recently evolved a new strain, more virulent and deadly than before. Medieval physicians had regarded smallpox as a version of measles, classing it as a childhood disease that might cause scarring and, for a few unlucky victims, prove fatal. Queen Elizabeth I caught it and the kingdom held its breath, awaiting the outcome. She made a full recovery but one of her ladies-in-waiting, Mary Sydney, was so severely scarred, having caught the disease while nursing the queen, Elizabeth banned her from court as too ugly to look upon. Mary became a recluse and took to wearing a mask.

In the later seventeenth century, smallpox had become a killer and the royal House of Stuart was not spared. Charles II's youngest brother Henry had died of it in 1660, soon after returning to England at the Restoration. King William's mother, Mary Stuart – sister of Charles II – had been another victim in the same year. At Christmas 1694, her namesake and niece, the Queen of England and her son's wife, felt unwell. Queen Mary II was as popular with her subjects as her Dutch husband was not. At first, her physicians diagnosed a cold but it seems Mary was unconvinced because she set about burning her most confidential papers and putting her affairs in order. She was right to do so as her condition worsened and the dreaded lesions appeared. England grieved when she died and she lay in state for the rest of the winter so that her subjects might pay their respects. This gave the brilliant composer Henry Purcell time to write a dramatic funeral march and anthems to be sung as she was finally laid to rest. King William was devastated and wise enough to know the people had even less reason to like him now his English wife – his entitlement to the crown – was gone.

When Catherine Barton fell ill with smallpox, her uncle wrote a loving letter to her: 'Pray let me know by your next [letter] how your face is and if your fevour [fever] be going. Perhaps warm milk from ye Cow may help to abate it. I am Your loving Unkle, Is. Newton'.[11] Voltaire insinuated that Newton's appointment at the mint was the result of Catherine's affair with Charles Montagu. However, when Newton first received the post of warden, his niece was still living with her parents in Northamptonshire and was, as yet, unknown to her future lover: Newton was appointed on his own merits and in the nick of time.

Work at the Royal Mint

At the Tower of London, a few tentative efforts had been made to set the recoinage project in motion before Newton became warden. Due to mismanagement at the mint and fraudulent activities among those involved – the temptation of handfuls of old silver coins going into pockets rather than into the furnace to be melted down proved overwhelming for some poorly paid workers – disaster loomed and the urgent project came close to being abandoned. Newton immediately took control, personally supervising the process, keeping detailed accounts of every batch of coins passing in and out of the mint. His knowledge of mathematics proved vital, as did his understanding of alchemical processes. He devised a new 'recipe' for the metals used in the coins. The softness of silver made the clipping of coins easy, so Newton added a dash of copper to the requisite pennyweights of silver, making the coins much harder. To further hamper the clipping, the edge of the coins was milled, given a texture that would be missing if the coins were trimmed. Thus, Newton revolutionised the minting of coins and the Great Recoinage, as it was known, was completed in two years – an incredible feat of logistics.

But overseeing the minting of money was not the warden's only duty. Having read the medieval documents concerning the job, Newton learned that uncovering counterfeiters was an additional duty. In eighteen months, from June 1698 to December 1699, Newton was personally responsible for interviewing more than a hundred informers, witnesses and suspects, leading to the successful prosecution of twenty-eight coiners. Some were just clippers but a few were skilled counterfeiters and one in particular ran a counterfeiting ring so lucrative he became a wealthy man. His name was William Chaloner and he made a worthy and wily opponent for the warden.

Chaloner had begun his career by finding ways to make secondhand clothes look new and selling them as such, until the customer took a closer look. The profits were meagre and, having aspirations to appear as a gentleman, Chaloner turned to a more lucrative method of gaining an income, by claiming the rewards offered for revealing Catholic plots to the authorities. That he set up the plots himself and inveigled hapless Catholics to join him before turning them in, did not bother his conscience, but the rewards were irregular and still insufficient for the lifestyle he desired. The only way to get rich, he realised, was to make the money himself. His audacity was breathtaking. He petitioned Parliament, claiming that someone – unnamed – working at the Royal Mint was supplying counterfeiters with the dies and the tools they needed. The dies were the negative impressions of the heads and tails sides of the coin. If Parliament approved, he would not only inspect the mint and advise on improving the processes, he also had a means of manufacturing coins that were impossible to fake.

The implication that the mint was aiding and abetting the forgers and the suggestion that Chaloner had a foolproof plan for foiling them must have made the prickly Newton so angry, he determined to see the man go to the gallows. In those days, counterfeiting coin was a crime of high treason for which the punishment was hanging, drawing and quartering. But conviction was always difficult, no judge wishing to condemn anyone to such a gruesome end without absolute proof. Newton would find that proof – eventually.

All this time, Chaloner was improving his own method of coin production. Having no interest in silver pennies and shillings (worth 12 pennies), he would produce gold guineas worth 21 shillings. The most difficult part of the process to achieve was making the dies for the coin press. The more perfect they were as copies of the ones used at the mint, the more difficult it would be to identify the guineas as forgeries. Chaloner found an accomplice in Thomas Taylor, a print seller and superb engraver of detailed maps and images. Selling such things was no way to become wealthy and Taylor was persuaded to join Chaloner, creating dies as good as the originals at the mint. Having spent a year passing off French 'gold' pistoles worth 17 English shillings without anyone suspecting fakery, in 1691, the pair moved on to casting guineas.

Chaloner ran a counterfeit ring of perhaps six people. Having produced the guineas in adulterated silver using Taylor's dies, they were then given to Patrick Coffee and Joseph Gravener to skim with a layer of gold as thinly as possible. When finished, Thomas Holloway and his wife Elizabeth would discreetly deliver them to other villains, at a cost of 11s per coin, to be put into circulation. Apparently, Chaloner could hardly keep up with demand and was soon spending his new wealth on wine, women and a house in keeping with his ill-won affluence.[12]

For Newton, the crime most in need of resolution regarded the possible involvement of employees at the mint, whether stealing and passing on tools and equipment to counterfeiters or forging coins on their own behalf or minting legitimately at the Tower but producing underweight or adulterated coins. All these possibilities undermined the trustworthiness of the institution of the Royal Mint. He began by questioning inmates of Newgate Gaol, that London hellhole that was virtually a death sentence in itself, since more prisoners died of disease while incarcerated than lived to meet the hangman. Anyone connected to coining, particularly those who had mentioned connections with the mint, was interrogated at length by Newton who became a frequent visitor at the prison. The accused had nothing to lose and possibly a pardon to gain, if they named names. Some said that tools and dies had been stolen from the mint; others that mint employees had sold them to outsiders. Stories conflicted and each villain was eager to name his fellows as the instigators. In this circle of misinformation, Chaloner was questioned and named, among others, a Mr Chandler, which happened to be his own *nom de guerre*. Such was the web of intrigue Newton would have to unravel but he had no intention of wasting time on the minor players; he was in pursuit of the spider at the centre of this tangled web of criminality.

Pursuing Criminals

To avoid complications regarding the extent of his jurisdiction as warden, Newton got himself appointed as a Justice of the Peace for the seven counties surrounding London but, even so, he sent his agents nationwide. Some of them went rogue and ended up in Newgate alongside those they were meant to be investigating. Agents and informers could not be trusted but Newton, always a man who worked best alone, was unperturbed. Thomas Levenson in *Newton and the Counterfeiter* has a fine turn of phrase to describe him: 'Newton, only months removed from the life of a Cambridge philosopher, managed incredibly swiftly to master every dirty job required of the seventeenth-century version of a big-city cop.'[13]

Being able to produce guineas indistinguishable from the real thing to most people's eyes was difficult to achieve but matters were about to become much easier for Chaloner. The government, desperate for its subjects to lend money to the cash-strapped Treasury, invented the Malt Lottery. Big business was unwilling to trust the government but small investors with a few guineas to spare might do so, if the incentives were tempting enough. In April 1697, the Treasury began selling 140,000 lottery tickets at £10 each, promising not only cash prizes but regular interest payments to the holders, funded by a tax on malt and beer production. Syndicates were formed: people clubbing together to afford the £10 cost of a ticket. The Royal Navy bought over a quarter of the tickets available to use to pay its employees' wages.

At this point, Chaloner was as short of money as the Treasury he would defraud. Newton had succeeded in bringing him to court and the term he spent in Newgate, awaiting his day before the judge, had emptied his purse. At the trial, witnesses suffered sudden bouts of memory loss or failed to appear and, much to Newton's frustration, the case failed for lack of evidence. Chaloner went free but was so destitute he had to produce a few poor quality pewter shillings in his fireplace. They just were not good enough to pass even a cursory glance and he re-melted them and tried again. But then he got hold of a genuine lottery ticket. By now, these were being exchanged like currency, every bit as spendable as guineas and it would be far simpler to print off forged tickets by the ream instead of manufacturing coins. A few reasonable-looking shillings bought Chaloner copper plates and engraving tools and he set to work to reproduce the perfect negative images of both sides of the ticket – he had learned the craft well from Thomas Taylor.

Newton, meanwhile, was building his case, interviewing wives and widows of Chaloner's previous associates, but he had yet to catch the man with any incriminating tools, dies or caches of forged coins in his possession. As Warden of the Mint, Newton was less concerned with the Treasury's lottery scheme than with ending any fraudulent activity at the mint. However, when Thomas Carter was arrested by Treasury officials for passing forged lottery tickets, Newton was there to interrogate him the moment the suspect mentioned Chaloner's name. Chaloner was apprehended and, by now, Newton had so many witnesses against him, a jury could not fail to be impressed by weight of numbers alone. But it was still not concrete evidence of counterfeiting – all such tools and equipment were long gone. Carter though, hoping his sentence might be reduced, told Newton all about the lottery fraud.

John Lawson, a recent arrival in Newgate, was well respected in the underworld of coining and counterfeiting but since his arrest his fellows in crime had taken everything he possessed, leaving his family to starve. Lawson would be the warden's man, heart and soul, in exchange for charity towards his children. Newton arranged for Lawson to share Chaloner's cell. Chaloner, eager to impress Lawson, divulged names, dates and accomplishments. He boasted that he had already bribed at least half 'the good men and true' on the two juries likely to be hearing his forthcoming case – one for the City of London and one for Middlesex County, depending on where the crime was committed. And, if that failed, he still had his trump card to play. The engraved plates for the lottery tickets were still out there, a threat to Treasury finances which could cost hundreds of thousands of pounds, if anyone found and used them. Lawson told Newton every word he heard.

To Lawson, Chaloner proclaimed himself the master forger and king of counterfeiting but, becoming anxious as the trial approached, he wrote letters to Newton, blaming everyone else involved, saying he did not have the skills or knowledge required and was merely a go-between, a minor cog in the forgery mill. Newton read and filed the correspondence but did not reply. Then Chaloner wrote to a judge, listing the services he had done the Crown in the past, unmasking plots, revealing the illegal activities at the mint and offering to improve the coining processes there. It did not help. On 3 March 1699, Chaloner stood in the dock at the Old Bailey, charged with having counterfeited more than a hundred silver and gold coins on various dates. He pleaded 'not guilty'. The printer and engraver, Thomas Taylor, was a key witness, his testimony bulked out by Katherine Coffee who described in detail Chaloner's production of French pistoles. Elizabeth Holloway and Thomas Carter's wife added further incriminating stories. Newton was succeeding in overloading the jury with information of Chaloner's crimes, throwing everything into the mix. Oddly, all the crimes reiterated had occurred in London, whereas the jury sitting was that for Middlesex County, which covered West London cases outside the city. In theory, Chaloner could have asked for a mistrial, or the judge could have declared it so. Neither did.

The jury wasted little time. A few minutes were spent conferring in open court before they returned the verdict: 'guilty of high treason'. The following day, Chaloner was sentenced to death by hanging at Tyburn. Newton had his man at last. Lawson, as Newton had promised, was released, although within the year he was back in Newgate on fresh charges and there was no avoiding the hangman a second time. Chaloner, grasping at straws, having sent a begging letter for mercy to Newton, finally revealed where the engraved plates for the Malt Lottery tickets could be found and named a journeyman smith at the Tower as the supplier of coin dies to counterfeiters. It was too late. Chaloner was hanged until dead on Tyburn gallows on 22 March. The Warden of the Mint did not trouble to attend, although he had watched the execution of other coiners he successfully prosecuted.

Other Pursuits

Newton's work at the mint went on. However, his mathematical pursuits were not entirely abandoned. On 30 January 1697, Newton received a letter from a European mathematician, Johannes Bernoulli, challenging him, publicly, to solve two calculations concerning the paths of heavy bodies. The equations had confounded lesser men but, as Catherine Barton recalled: 'Sir I. N. was in the midst of the hurry of the great recoinage [and] did not come home till four [p.m.] from the Tower very much tired, but did not sleep till he had solved it which was by 4 in the morning.' He returned the answer immediately and Bernoulli admitted Newton's superior mind, recognising the solution 'as the lion is known from its claws', resulting in the equations becoming known as 'the lion's paw problem'.

Having published the *Principia* in 1687, Newton was now working on a new, corrected and expanded edition. To improve the accuracy of his calculations regarding the effects of the Moon's gravitation pull on earthly tides, he required up-to-date information on the positions of other heavenly bodies which might enhance or diminish the Moon's influence. With no time to carry out his own stargazing and record years of observations, he turned to an old friend, the Astronomer Royal, John Flamsteed. In December 1698, he visited Flamsteed at the Royal Observatory at Greenwich to discuss the matter. They parted on amicable terms with Flamsteed promising to send the information in due course.

Meanwhile, Newton's reputation on the Continent was now riding so high that he was elected as a Foreign Associate of the Académie des Sciences in Paris in February 1699. Not to be outdone, the Royal Society in London elected him onto the Council before the end of the year, although Robert Hooke could not approve the promotion. But all was not proceeding smoothly abroad. The German mathematician Gottfried Wilhelm Leibniz was about to cross swords with Newton in an acrimonious dispute concerning the invention of calculus and the conflict would span the following decade.

Chapter 8

THE 1700s: THE MASTER AND PRESIDENT

Newton's success in the recoinage project and bringing counterfeiters to justice brought him promotion and on 3 February 1700 he was appointed Master of the Mint. This office was even more of a sinecure than the post of Warden might have been, had Newton not taken up his responsibilities with such earnestness. He still went to the Tower of London almost every day and his attendance there on Wednesday afternoons made it problematic for him to be at the Royal Society's weekly meetings at 3 p.m. – if that was the real reason. It seems odd if the Master of the Mint was unable to rearrange his diary to suit himself, since Thursday afternoons were free of obligation. Newton was a member of the society's Council, the body that considered which scientific endeavours it was willing to put its name to and looked into the suitability of proposed new members. Once deemed worthy of membership and, no doubt, his ability and willingness to pay his weekly 1s subscription had been taken into consideration, at a subsequent meeting a ballot was held to elect the candidate, or not.[1] In those days, who voted for whom in the parliamentary elections was public knowledge but the Royal Society was ahead of its time in electing members by secret ballot. Identical little paper scrolls were prepared – twice as many as members present at the meeting. Half the scrolls were marked with a cross and placed in one pile; the other half bore some other mark and went in a second pile. Every member took a scroll from each heap, placed one in an urn and discarded the other in a box. The votes in the urn were then counted: a cross indicated approval. The candidate for membership had to receive a cross from at least two-thirds of those present in order to be duly elected.[2] The result was announced there and then.

Isaac Newton, in theory at least, still held the post of Lucasian Professor at Mathematics at Cambridge although, in practice, William Whiston gave the required lectures as Newton's deputy. As a professor, Newton was eligible and duly elected as an MP for the university in November 1701. However, just two weeks later, on 10 December, he resigned as Lucasian Professor, severing his ties with Cambridge academia. Whiston succeeded to the position in 1702 and remained there until 1710.

The Last Stuart Monarch

The year 1702 saw other changes. William III died on 19 March, unlamented by the people. A month before, he had suffered a fall from his horse when his mount caught its foot on a molehill and stumbled. The king broke his collar bone but seemed to recover. When he died of a feverish chill four weeks later, probably pneumonia, the 'little fellow in the velvet waistcoat' – the mole – was cheered and celebrated as having rid the country of its 'foreign' king, who spent the kingdom's cash on foreign wars of little interest and less benefit to his subjects. Unlike his beloved wife Mary's state funeral, William's was brief and simple and passed almost unnoticed. The country was eager to greet its new monarch: Anne, Mary's younger sister.

Anne was also married to a foreign prince, George of Denmark, but unlike Mary she had no intention of ruling jointly with him. Anne would be queen regnant and George would merely be her consort. She was being pragmatic; having witnessed William's unpopularity, she would not force another foreign king upon her people. Besides, much as she undoubtedly loved her husband, he was not the stuff of a good king. Fifteen years her elder, he drank and ate to excess and, although trained as a soldier, neither Charles II, James II nor William III had deemed him fit for military command. A prince without portfolio, there was little for George to do but indulge in gluttony. However, he was extremely active in the bedchamber, getting his wife pregnant at least seventeen times in eighteen years. A healthy crop of heirs to the throne would have ensured the continuation of the Stuart dynasty but from so many pregnancies, Anne and George produced just one likely heir. The succession of miscarriages, still births and infant deaths must have been traumatic for them and seemed to unite them in grief. Their hopes lay in William, Duke of Gloucester, and he was not a particularly strong child either. A day after his eleventh birthday in July 1700, William fell ill. His mother nursed him through five days of delirium until he died. She was too stunned even to weep.[3]

Therefore, as Anne came to the throne in March 1702, despite the celebrations, it was already accepted that she was the last of her line of unfortunate Stuart monarchs. The previous year, Parliament had passed the Act of Settlement, naming the House of Hanover as her heirs. George of Hanover had come to England in Charles II's reign with the possibility of marrying Anne. Anne detested him on sight and her deep dislike of the Hanoverians never wavered. George returned home and found another bride: Sophia. Sophia was the youngest daughter of Elizabeth Stuart, once known briefly as Queen of Bohemia. One of Sophia's brothers had been Prince Rupert of the Rhine, cousin and courtier to Charles II. Had Rupert or his brothers been living, they would be Anne's heirs but Sophia was the last of these second cousins. Other heirs, closer by blood, were available but had to be avoided on religious grounds. Wanting no more Catholic monarchs, the Act of Settlement stated that only Protestants were eligible and, what was more, they had to marry a Protestant spouse. Only Sophia fitted those criteria.

Return to the Royal Society
By now, Newton was rising high in London society and, of necessity, had to look and play the part. In the autumn of 1702, approaching his fiftieth birthday, he sat for the artist Sir Geoffrey Kneller, to have his portrait painted. In this case,

he appears to have bowed to fashion and wears a flowing auburn wig but does not look comfortable.[4] In most of his other images, his hair is his own.

At about this time, he published a paper entitled *Lunae theoria,* his theories concerning the Moon. What his old adversary Robert Hooke thought about it was immaterial. Newton was the coming man. On 3 March 1703, Hooke died and, at a stroke, Newton's relationship with the Royal Society transformed: there was no reason now for him to shy away from presenting papers and attending meetings because his most vociferous and blatant critic was no longer present. Newton promptly determined that now was the time to publish his work on optics, completed years before. When he had sent his paper concerning the nature of light and colours to the society in 1672, Hooke had made derisory remarks about it, insisting the theories were wrong – as he himself had long since proved. Christiaan Huygens had at least been polite about his disagreement with Newton's hypotheses. Newton had never forgiven Hooke's rudeness and since science was coming to agree with Newton's work, that simply confirmed Hooke's incompetence, to Newton's mind at least. Now the matter was ended with Hooke's death. The ultimate accolade came on 30 November 1703, when Newton was elected President of the Royal Society.

The Eccentric Dr Hooke

Robert Hooke had lectured to the Royal Society on an incredible range of topics during his long career. Some subjects were far ahead of their time and controversial. The Bible was then accepted as true, incontrovertible history but Hooke had his own opinions. Even though he was not reticent in making his ideas known, in the early 1690s the Archbishop of Canterbury had awarded Hooke an honorary doctorate. As a child, living on the Isle of Wight, Hooke had been fascinated by the fossils he found in the limestone cliffs. When he became Curator to the Royal Society, other intriguing finds had come his way, including a giant nautilus shell and bones of what appeared to be hippopotami, yet they were found in England. While others explained such things as 'anomalies' put there by God to test mankind's faith, or washed here by Noah's Flood, Dr Hooke wanted a scientific explanation.

His first hypothesis accounted for the remains of strange sea creatures stranded in solid rock. Taking the second verse in the *Book of Genesis*: 'And darkness was on the face of the deep', he theorised that 'the deep' meant, in the beginning, the Earth was covered in water. This was not the forty-day inundation of the Flood but lasted for aeons, before any dry land emerged. To those who believed the world had been created in 4004 BC, such a time scale was not only absurd but heretical. In his lectures, Hooke did not deny the Bible version but said it was the ancients' attempt to tell the story of Creation in simple terms that primitive peoples could understand. But mankind had progressed since then and new, rational explanations were now possible. Such explanations may well have been possible but they were still not acceptable to the majority of laymen and clerics.

Neither was his second hypothesis any better received, to account for the bones of creatures from tropical lands being found in chilly England. Hooke explained that, from time to time, the Earth shifted slightly on its axis, changing the climate zones. He not only proposed that the climate could change, he even thought this would cause species to adapt to the new environment, pre-empting Charles Darwin by almost two centuries! Neither the world nor the society was ready for such ideas and Hooke's theories were dismissed as fantastical and simply wrong. By the turn of the century, Hooke was still lecturing on the age of the Earth and how land was formed by the action of volcanoes and earthquakes but his eyesight and his health were failing.[5]

In other theories, Hooke was less perceptive. He had a crazy idea that the day should be divided into 29 hours. He believed advanced cancers could be cured by smoking tobacco. One abiding concern was his own health. Having been a sickly child, perhaps that was not surprising but he blamed earthquakes for some of his ailments. With official medical treatments frequently doing more harm than good, like many of his fellows, Hooke often self-medicated, experimenting with a cocktail of quack remedies and lethal drugs and noting the effects in his diary. Symptoms, doses and results were recorded meticulously. He also recorded how his friend and one of the founding members of the society, John Wilkins, took such experimenting too far and poisoned himself with opiates. Having no faith in physicians, Hooke took drugs daily to alleviate a host of minor complaints and ward off kidney stones and gout, both of which ailments had carried off many of his acquaintances.

Whatever remedies he took, eventually he lost his battle. Dr Hooke died at the age of sixty-seven in his rooms at Gresham College. His possessions were those of a pauper, his clothes in rags, his body hunched and infested with lice. His household inventory listed bedding, storage chests, chairs and tables, kitchenware and odds and ends: nothing impressive. An assortment of old clothes included three pairs of breeches, nine waistcoats, shirts and male undergarments. One surprise was the discovery of three pairs of women's stays and a petticoat. Other oddities were several hundredweight of scrap metal down in the cellar, a couple of broken harpsichords, more than 3,000 books, and bits of scientific equipment, such as telescope lenses. It was all just a mess of belongings of a poor, sad old man – until a great iron chest was opened. Within was discovered £8,000 in money and another £300 worth of gold and silver objects. By today's reckoning, Hooke was a millionaire but since the most he had ever earned, officially, was £80 *per annum*, his riches were something of a mystery.

Scientific Innovation

Hooke had been an innovator of new ideas but throughout the seventeenth century he was by no means the only one. Some inventions which we may think of as being quite recent in fact date back to the second half of that century. The French Huguenot Denis Papin had been working on producing a vacuum by means of an air pump, alongside Hooke and Robert Boyle. In doing so, he invented the pressure cooker. His demonstration of the apparatus to the Royal Society took a more congenial form than the usual Wednesday afternoon meetings: Papin invited the then President of the Society, Christopher Wren, and a few other members to dinner. They dined on pigeons and rabbit cooked in his new pressurised device. The meal was reported to have been a great success and even the bones were tender enough to eat.

Another Frenchman across the Channel, Blaise Pascal, was only in his teens when he invented a kind of calculating machine to assist his father who had the task of working out tax returns owed to Louis XIV. Involving numerous cog wheels, in the days long before mass production, Pascal had to cut every one individually. Having realised such a machine was a possibility, an Englishman, Samuel Morland, simplified and improved the mechanism and his device can still be seen in the Science Museum in London. For those more concerned with letters, rather than numbers, sometime in the 1660s an anonymous Englishman patented a design, with detailed drawings, for the production of a typewriter. For some reason, there is no record that the invention was ever actually manufactured but modern designers have constructed it from the diagrams and it worked. What a boon it might have been to the letter writers and thesis compilers of the time.

It was the custom to have some form of after-dinner entertainment for guests. Making music and playing card games were popular pastimes but there were more scientific amusements. After Hooke published his *Micrographia,* peering down a microscope at anything from flies to flower petals, pearls to pins, became the fashionable way of amusing guests. One novel diversion seems to pre-date future technology: a flying mechanical bird. It contained a tiny water boiler and when steam was released from its tail end, it was propelled along a wire stretched across the room. As to whether this precursor to the Age of Steam actually functioned, there is only the word of the Marquis of Worcester who claimed to have seen it working.

Diners were known to enjoy viewing painted glass slides, joined together in sequence and passed in turn before a candle, its light enhanced by a globe of water and concentrated by a lens, as Hooke had done to improve the lighting of specimens under the microscope. The images were then magnified and focussed onto a white sheet pinned to the wall. Newton's 'crucial experiment' had combined with Hooke's innovation to produce the first slide shows.

The Little Ice Age also led to innovations that had begun back in 1626, when one of the originators of the experimental method, Francis Bacon, had wanted to prove that snow would help preserve a dead chicken. The cold kept the meat fresh but did the man no favours. As a result of his endeavours Bacon caught a chill, which developed into pneumonia and he died. However, noting the preservation possibilities of snow and ice, by the eighteenth century every great house that had sufficient space in its grounds had an icehouse constructed. If properly built, the packed ice and snow within would last from one winter to the next and was used as a refrigerator to store food throughout the warmer weather. The keeping of ice also made possible the invention of ice cream and sorbet. The earliest recorded ice cream recipe dates to 1665 in the handwritten recipe book of Lady Anne Fanshawe. Her choice of flavourings was unusual – not vanilla, strawberry or chocolate, but mace, orange-flower water or ambergris. However, it is known that ice cream was often served to Charles I two decades before Lady Anne noted down her recipe for 'icy cream', as she called it.

There were other innovations which the English were slower to take up: table forks, for example. These utensils were widely used on the Continent to avoid soiling fingers and fashionable frilled cuffs when dining but in the 1660s Samuel Pepys still failed to see any reason for using a fork when fingers and napkins were available. By the 1700s, though, the use of forks had become the norm in all but the poorest households, which could not afford such luxuries when fingers cost nothing. However, when setting the table, unlike today, forks were placed with the prong tips touching the tablecloth. So what might Isaac Newton and his associates have had served for their meals?

Food on the Table

For Samuel Pepys at least, breakfast was a makeshift affair. His diaries are most informative as he records that breakfast consisted of 'last night's turkey pie and a goose', or herrings. On another occasion he went to a tavern with friends and they consumed 'a great deal of wine, a barrel of good oysters and anchovies'. On other mornings, he simply had a cup of chocolate at home with his wife. For the less affluent, weak beer and a slice of bread and butter would have to suffice. Sometimes, Pepys had a second breakfast, his 'mid-morning draft' as he called it. This was often a social event with friends, much like a modern coffee morning.

The high point of the day's culinary efforts was the midday dinner, although by the mid-1700s, fashionable diners were taking this meal later and later. Dinner was not, as we expect today, an orderly procession of courses: soup, fish, meat, dessert and cheese. This style of dining was known as *service á la Russe* and only became fashionable in the nineteenth century. In the seventeenth and eighteenth – as for centuries before – courses were all mixed up, each consisting of savoury and sweet dishes from which the diner chose what he fancied. Every year in March, Pepys gave a special anniversary dinner to celebrate his having survived an operation to remove 'the stone'. In 1663, the menu for twelve people consisted of:

A fricassee of rabbit and chicken, a boiled leg of mutton, three carp, a side of lamb, roasted pigeons, four lobsters, three tarts, a lamprey pie, a dish of anchovies, good wines of various sorts, vegetables and a banquet of sweetmeats.

Unlike in earlier periods, vegetables were no longer regarded as fodder for the poor only. Better off people, like Pepys, were eating them too. Pepys's friend and fellow diarist John Evelyn published a book in 1699 entitled *Acetaria – A Discourse of Sallets,* that is, 'salads'. To Evelyn, salad did not consist mainly of lettuce and tomatoes but rather of a wide range of fresh and pickled ingredients. He describes how to pickle gherkins (gurkems) and cauliflower but also more unusual foods, such as cowslips, elderflowers, mushrooms, melon and spinach. But this is not just a cookery book; Evelyn looks into the science behind healthy eating, at least according to the ideas of the time, referring to what the ancient physicians advised. Evelyn says he compiled the information because:

> It being one of the inquiries of the noble Mr [Robert] Boyle, what herbs were proper and fit to make sallets with and how best to order them? We have here (by the assistance of Mr London, His Majesty's Principal Gard'ner) reduc'd them to a competent number, not exceeding thirty five; but which may be vary'd and inlarg'd, by taking in, or leaving out, any other sallet-plant...[6]

Evelyn suggests dressing the salad with three parts good 'oyl-olive' to one part 'sharpest vinegar', lemon or orange juice with salt, pepper and grated dry mustard. To garnish, he lists hard-boiled egg yolks, thin slices of horseradish, red beet (beetroot), barberries, etc.[7] A popular dish of the late-seventeenth and early-eighteenth century was an *hors d'oevre* which made use of any leftovers. It combined 'bland' and 'sharp' foods so it was not only a good mixture of flavours but accorded well with the medical theories of the day, regarding a 'balanced' diet. The ingredients for 'Salomongundy' could be any or all of the following:

Bland foods –
Hard-boiled eggs with the yolks and whites separated.
Cooked chicken meat or slithers [*sic*] of cooked veal, pork, duck or pigeon
Cooked white fishes or cooked herring
Lettuce, chopped or sliced fine
Chopped celery and cucumbers
Artichoke hearts and raw mushrooms
Soft cheeses
Boiled onions, either small and whole or large and sliced

Sharp foods –
Anchovies – essential!
Any kind of pickle

Diced fresh or pickled lemon
A sharp oil and vinegar dressing

The ingredients should be arranged on a platter and decorated
with fresh herbs and flowers.[8]

To accompany the new beverages of tea, coffee and chocolate,
cakes and biscuits began to appear in their lighter, modern forms
and less like the boiled puddings of earlier times. Some locally
invented recipes became so popular they can still be purchased
today: Banbury, Eccles and Chorley cakes, Bath and Chelsea
buns still bear the names of their places of origin. But puddings,
boiled in cloths, still thrived in their own right. A Frenchman,
Monsieur Masson, visiting in the 1690s wrote: 'Blessed be he that
invented pudding, for it is a Manna that hits the Palates of all
sorts of People; ah! what an excellent thing is an English pudding!'
Puddings could vary from light, creamy custards to substantial,
generously fruited oatmeal. The boiled 'pud', savoury, sweet or
a mixture of both, was the mainstay of English cookery, yet the
visiting Frenchman would have found much that was familiar to
him because hefty puddings were often served alongside the dainty
portions of French *á la mode* cuisine that was all the fashion at
society tables.

Whereas the austere and underweight William III had a partiality
for a Dutch dish of clear fish soup, known as 'water sootje', his
successor, Queen Anne, loved her food. Her master cook Patrick
Lambe records a number of recipes for 'pulpatoon', which must
have been a royal favourite. Pigeons, quails, partridges, turtle
doves, buntings, larks or hen chicks could all serve as the main
ingredient. The birds were first browned in butter and then encased
in a raised pie. However, instead of ordinary pastry, the crust was
of forcemeat, made with minced veal, breadcrumbs, suet, onions,
beaten eggs, butter, parsley, thyme, lemon and seasoning. Before
the pie crust was sealed with its lid of forcemeat, a *ragoût* of
thick stock, chopped veal kidneys, mushrooms, onion, olives and
chopped chestnuts was poured around the birds, with some of the
liquor reserved to be served as gravy. Anne's obesity problem was

not entirely caused by her health problems, if such rich dishes were presented as often as Lambe implies.[9]

A less exalted diner, Richard Bradley, Professor of Botany at Cambridge, supplemented his meagre income by publishing recipe books. He had lived in London as a child and became fascinated by gardening, enthusiastically studying plants. Though he never attended university as a student, his first publication, *Treatise of Succulent Plants*, got him noticed by influential patrons and with their support he was proposed and elected a Fellow of the Royal Society in 1712, aged twenty-four. He went on to investigate and write papers on subjects related to his interests, including the use of fertilisers and plant hybridisation. As a result, Cambridge University took the unprecedented step of creating a professorship especially for him in 1724 – the first chair of botany – and promised to found and fund a botanical garden at the university. This did not happen and Bradley's income was minimal. Having realised he could earn a better income from popular publications, he continued to compile gardening and cookery books, leaving his students to their own devices and neglecting to give lectures.

In his book *Country Housewife and Lady's Director* Bradley often gives the sources of his recipes: 'Stew'd Beef Steaks' comes from the Spring Gardens at Vauxhall, one of London's most popular places of entertainment. Rich and poor alike gathered there to dance, listen to music, to see and be seen, to drink and to dine. The thin slices of steak are first boiled until tender in dry white wine and water, a little wine vinegar, chopped bacon, onions, lemon peel, a few anchovy fillets, parsley, thyme, sage and a bay leaf. The steak slices are then dried, tossed in flour and lightly fried in butter. They are then removed and the cooking juices added to the butter and flour in the pan to thicken and make a sauce.[10]

'Potatoe-Pudding Baked' is a simpler recipe which Bradley had from 'Mr Shepherd of Windmill Street'. It consists of mashed potato into which is added finely grated carrot, orange juice, butter, eggs, orange flower water, sugar, salt and pepper. The mixture is then oven-baked until golden. Another he discovered at 'The Devil's Tavern' in Fleet Street, London. He must have liked this recipe as he calls it 'Richard Bradley's Stewed Cucumbers'. The cucumbers are treated much like the stewed beef above, being first cooked with onions in wine – red this time – for 10 minutes, then dried off and fried in butter. As with the beef, the cooking liquid is then thickened to make a sauce.

Newton, never known as a gourmet, or even having much interest in food, must have dined well enough when entertaining important friends such as Charles Montagu. When alone, his tastes were frugal. Breakfast of bread and butter and a cup of orange tea would suffice. Unlike other gentlemen of the coffee-drinking, claret-swilling fraternity, Newton mostly drank water. He refused to eat black pudding because it was made with blood, nor rabbits which were killed by breaking their necks and not bled out, adhering to biblical principles, rather like a modern-day Jehovah's Witness.

Dutch Courage and Gin Lane

While various members of the Royal Society were enjoying their cups of coffee, the poorer Londoners could not afford such a luxury. Isaac Newton may have preferred water but for many this was a drink to be avoided. There were a number of reasons for this, not least the suspicion that it made you ill, which, with insanitary water supplies, could often be the case. No one had yet realised that boiling water could make it safe to drink – unless Newton had already made the discovery. Also, tradition had it that the poor of France lived on frogs' legs and water, while Englishmen ate roast beef and drank beer – so that was reckoned another reason not to drink water since the English had looked down on the French as a matter of course since medieval times. However, in Newton's day, an alternative cheap drink was becoming popular: gin.

Distilled spirits had been around for centuries, as every alchemist knew, but a Dutch physician, Franciscus Sylvius, was credited with having been the first to flavour alcohol with juniper berries for medicinal purposes in 1550, thereby inventing gin. The English first got a taste for gin while fighting in the Netherlands against the Spanish in the early stages of the Thirty Years' War (1618–48). (During the latter years of the conflict, Englishmen were more concerned with the Civil War at home and few were fighting abroad.) Medicinally, gin was supposed to calm the nerves and warm the blood, so it was ideal to drink it before a battle. This may be the origin of the term 'Dutch courage'. When they returned home, the English soldiers had no intention of giving up their newly found tipple so brought it back with them.

Charles I had granted a royal warrant to the Worshipful Company of Distillers in 1638, giving them a monopoly on the distilling trade within 21 miles of London and Westminster. But the gin industry did not take off until the arrival of another Dutch 'import', William of Orange. William and Mary passed legislation encouraging the distillation of gin and other spirits during their reign. A licence was not required, so anyone could set up a still at home. Gin was so cheap in comparison with beer and with the water often unsafe, it became the most affordable drink for the poor of London. By the early eighteenth century, London was home to thousands of 'dram shops' and figures suggest that an incredible ten million gallons of gin were being distilled in the capital each year. The city became obsessed with gin.[11]

Between 1700 and 1760, London was involved in an intensely destructive love affair with gin, popularly known as 'mother's ruin'. By the time of Newton's death in 1727, there were estimated to be 7,000 legal gin shops, and countless other illegal drinking dens. Drunkenness became the curse of the capital, causing violence, widespread addiction and social deprivation. For many working-class Londoners, gin became a necessity rather than a drink. It eased their hunger pangs and blotted out, at least temporarily, the horrors of life in the slums; a cheap balm that cost a few pennies and was available on any street corner. Thomas Fielding later wrote about the devastating effects on what he termed 'inferior people' in his political pamphlet of 1751, *Enquiry into the causes of the late increase of Robbers*:

A new kind of drunkenness, unknown to our ancestors, is lately sprung up among us, and which if not put a stop to, will infallibly destroy a great part of the inferior people. The drunkenness I here intend is ... by this poison called Gin ... the principal sustenance (if it may be so called) of more than a hundred thousand people in this Metropolis.

William Hogarth had been born in London in 1697, the son of a school teacher. Although by birth he would have been regarded as lower middle class, his family fell on hard times and his father was imprisoned on account of his outstanding debts. Young William served an apprenticeship to an engraver and went on to become famous for his prints. It is believed the straitened circumstances of his youth led to his works of social criticism, as in the series of images for *A Harlot's Progress*, *A Rake's Progress* and *Marriage A-La-Mode*. Most relevant in this case are his paired prints: *Beer Street* and *Gin Lane*. They were produced in 1751 in support of the Gin Act, an effort to reduce the sale of the distilled drink by showing the merits of drinking beer contrasted with the evils of gin consumption.[12] However, as the year 1704 began, with Newton now President of the Royal Society, his mind was on matters other than what was served for dinner or in his glass.

A Revival in Philosophy

In February 1704, Newton finally published the first edition of his *Opticks*, originally sent to the Royal Society as a series of papers three decades earlier. It was printed in English, not the usual language of science: Latin. This may have been because, although Hooke was no longer there to criticise it, other natural philosophers across the Channel would eagerly take his place. By printing *Opticks* in English, Newton was partially limiting his readership to his fellow countrymen, most of who regarded him as infallible and would not dream of finding fault in the master's work. Only after the English edition had been perused, applauded and approved did the author risk foreign criticism by publishing a Latin edition, including additional 'Queries', in 1706.

Query 31 posed the hypothesis that there may exist a 'unified theory', relating gravity, magnetism, light and electricity to each other – a theory scientists are still working on today, which demonstrates the farsightedness and daring of Newton's thinking. He delegated the publication of the Latin edition to a young French Huguenot mathematician Abraham de Moivre (also Demoivre). De Moivre was ideal for the task: a devoted disciple yet brilliant in his own right. Perhaps he was, to a degree, Fatio de Duillier's replacement as Newton's apprentice.

With *Opticks* safely printed, in April, Newton again travelled down river from London to Greenwich, to discuss further the astronomical data he required for a new edition of *Principia* from the Astronomer Royal John Flamsteed. The information had not been forthcoming, as promised on his earlier visit and Newton, though endlessly patient when working through baffling equations, had little patience with people who failed in his expectations. Newton had also sent Flamsteed a copy of the new publication, whether as a gift or incentive, he must now have regretted doing so. When he enquired what the astronomer thought of it, Flamsteed found fault, not only with Newton's descriptions of the stars in *Opticks,* saying he had given them larger dimensions than was their true size, but claimed he had found mistakes in the *Principia* also. 'Why did I not hold my tongue?' Newton is said to have wondered, when Flamsteed continued to recite a list of supposed errors in both books. Newton left, telling Flamsteed to 'get on with his catalogue' – a reasonable statement today but then an insult: only servants and underlings, never gentlemen, could be given so direct an order.

To add further insult, Newton arranged for a grant of £180 to be paid to Flamsteed for his assistance in helping him to calculate the positions of the Moon, planets and comets – Newton was not particularly interested in the catalogue of the stars themselves. Among gentlemen, information was exchanged without payment. In arranging the grant, Newton not only made Flamsteed seem less of a gentleman but was treating the Astronomer Royal as an assistant to be paid a wage. It was true that Flamsteed had little money – out of his official annual salary of £100, he had to hire his assistants and buy his own equipment, which could be very expensive – but to be relegated to a mere servant of Newton's was an unbearable indignity. In January 1705, Newton recommended the publication of Flamsteed's *Observations*. This was not the full catalogue but contained the information he was so eager to get hold of.

Queen Anne's husband Prince George of Denmark, having little to occupy him otherwise, had something of an interest in scientific matters. Newton, now moving in the most elevated circle of society, persuaded the prince that having his name attached to a star catalogue in perpetuity would preserve his illustrious reputation as a farsighted man of knowledge forever. The prince agreed to become the patron for the production of the catalogue. Flamsteed was not consulted and a triumphant Newton could now add royal patronage to the list of reasons for the urgent completion of the work. But Flamsteed, ever the methodical perfectionist, refused to be hurried: the catalogue was still incomplete and to rush it would lead to errors being made. Newton and Prince George would have to wait. How galling it must have been when Flamsteed heard that on 16 April 1705, the insufferable, ill-mannered President of the Royal Society had received a knighthood from the queen to add to his list of accolades: Sir Isaac. But the honour was conferred for his services at the Royal Mint, not for his contributions to science.

In March 1706, Flamsteed came to Sir Isaac's house in Jermyn Street, with other interested parties. Details were agreed upon for the publication of the catalogue, yet Flamsteed recorded that he, whom the business most concerned, was consulted least of all. Disputed observations and delayed delivery of the manuscript copy continued. However, Newton was also preparing the lectures he had given as Lucasian Professor at Cambridge for publication. They needed a great deal of revision and correction before they could be made public. Newton knew there were numerous errors in the original texts to be put right and he willingly settled to the task. He was as much a perfectionist as Flamsteed and readily admitted to his mistakes, so long as he was the one who identified them; he would not have them pointed out by others. The lectures were published early in 1707 under the title *Arithmetica Universalis*.

In April, Sir Isaac took the Scottish mathematician David Gregory to visit the Royal Observatory at Greenwich and, no doubt, to give Flamsteed another reminder of his tardiness. But the astronomer was about to be given a reprieve – in 1708 Prince George died, his patronage ended and the star catalogue project was suspended. Newton was furious; Flamsteed continued working at his own slow pace. As president, Newton went so far as to remove the astronomer from the fellowship of the Royal Society for failing to pay his subscriptions. If every member who failed to pay had been struck off, few would have remained to attend the meetings but Flamsteed was singled out for punishment and made to serve as an example. Still angry but undeterred, Sir Isaac turned to the queen in her grief, suggesting she might insist on the project's completion by royal command, to honour her consort's memory. Anne agreed. Flamsteed realised that failing to obey a royal command could have far worse consequences than annoying Sir Isaac. His appointment as Astronomer Royal might be terminated. At the time, Edmund Halley, who had previously looked up to John Flamsteed as his mentor and supporter, seemed to have tired of the elder man's stubborn procrastination. The two were no longer friends and since Halley seems to have been an affable fellow, something serious must have turned their relationship sour.

An Adventurous Fellow

Edmund Halley had become simply the Clerk of the Royal Society as a result of his changed financial circumstances since his father's death, yet he had managed to continue with his own scientific research in a number of fields. During the late 1680s and early 1690s, he published a series of papers, particularly on mathematical topics – at which he was brilliant – and astronomical subjects, discussing his findings at society meetings, despite his diminished status. Also, like Robert Hooke, Halley was having difficulty reconciling his findings in the real world with the Church's insistence that the Earth had been created in 4004 BC. He thought it might be possible to calculate the age of the Earth, if he could work out how long it would take for the sea to become as salty as it is, made so by the minerals washed into it from the land by the rivers, assuming the sea had once been fresh water. So many things would have to be taken into account: the variations in rivers' flow, the solubility of minerals in the bedrock beneath the water, the varying salinity of seas across the planet, etc., but even so, Halley realised that less than 6,000 years was by no means time enough. As with Hooke's, Halley's hypothesis that the biblical timeline was wrong, tentative as it was, would make him most unpopular with the Church authorities and his fellow members of the Royal Society.

The younger man's heretical ideas may well have offended the staunch puritanical beliefs of Flamsteed. It is, perhaps, surprising that Newton, with his similar austere outlook, did not also take offence at Halley, yet they remained friends. There was also a rumour dating back to Halley's youthful travels to the South Atlantic. Flamsteed no doubt utterly disapproved, if it was true, that Halley had fathered a child with the wife of a childless couple during the long voyage. There were stories of sexual encounters during his Grand Tour of Europe to add to Flamsteed's disgust at his one-time protégé. Were these reasons enough to estrange two men who had once admired each other?

Meanwhile, maritime matters had intrigued Halley ever since his voyage to St Helena to map the southern stars. In 1691, he demonstrated how a diving bell that he had designed could be of use to the navy, working from an Admiralty ship off the coast of Sussex in southern England. Robert Hooke had actually invented a similar contrivance twenty years before and, for once, had the paperwork to prove it, but it was Halley who put it to practical use. While working with the Admiralty, Halley heard that the post of Savilian Professor of Astronomy at Oxford University had fallen vacant. Eager for some academic preferment, not to mention income, Halley applied for the position. He failed to achieve it and must have been dismayed to learn that Flamsteed had been the most vociferous opponent to his appointment.

The recent publication of a paper that explained how Halley's observations of the transit of Venus across the Sun's disc could be used to measure the distance of the Earth from the Sun, employing the phenomenon of parallax, may have aroused professional jealousy in the Astronomer Royal against the younger man. Halley's mathematical calculations were extremely accurate, his explanations clear and to the point; such an admirable piece of work went unmatched by anything Flamsteed produced. Perhaps the accumulation of 'misdeeds' – heretical ideas, immoral behaviour and professional slight, added together were sufficient to turn Flamsteed's friendship to enmity. Whatever the truth, Halley's renown was enough that he no longer needed the other's patronage.

In 1694, Halley had published a completely original paper concerning the monsoons and trade winds, including the first known meteorological chart. He also considered whether magnetic variation across the globe might be a means of determining the correct positions of ships at sea, if accurate charts could be drawn up. Since the professorship was denied him, Halley would follow a career that went along a more adventurous path than peaceful academia. Some few years earlier, Halley had sent a formal proposal to the Admiralty requesting a ship be made available to him for a voyage of scientific investigation. No details survive as to what precise researches were proposed but they must have been deemed of use to the navy because, in the summer of 1696, Halley received a royal commission from King William, appointing *him* – a landlubber without any naval experience – as master and commander of the ship *Paramour*. Such an appointment had never been known before nor since but was made because the Royal Society was supposed to be financing the expedition, so one of their own should be in overall charge, nominally at least.

Further delays meant the ship was not ready to sail until October 1698, when Halley received instructions to embark on a year-long voyage to study and measure magnetic variations around the world, thereby providing another aid to navigation and a method of fixing positions at sea. The instructions were not a surprise to him since Halley had drafted them himself. What was a surprise and an unpleasant one was the nature of the first officer the Admiralty supplied. Lieutenant Edward Harrison no doubt expected to captain the ship, since the commander was untrained in seafaring and a stranger to ordering sailors to their duties. Harrison already had a chip on his shoulder regarding the Royal Society because he had submitted a paper on the problems of reckoning longitude and had it rejected by that august body as worthless. Therefore, having been snubbed, he had no intention of taking orders from the society's clerk.

On the voyage to the West Indies and Brazil, Harrison caused a catalogue of difficulties for Halley, yet always stopped just short of open disobedience and mutiny. Despite these problems, Halley fulfilled all his experiments but, as the *Paramour* turned for home, it seems Harrison gave Halley an ultimatum of some kind. It must have been along the lines of 'if you call yourself a captain, then you sail the ship.' Harrison went off to sulk as his ultimatum rebounded: Halley navigated the Atlantic without difficulty and brought the ship home safely, without the lieutenant's assistance. Harrison was court-martialled for his pains. Halley took the opportunity of improving his status: 'Captain' Halley resigned as the humble Clerk of the Royal Society and resumed his former position as a Fellow.

His seagoing career was unfinished. Soon after returning home, Halley set off on a second voyage – without Harrison – sailing so far south in the Atlantic that the ship encountered icebergs. In 1701, he commanded an Admiralty ship to study the tides in the English Channel. This was genuine scientific work but with a hidden agenda: to survey French ports and harbour approaches for use in time of war. Halley's thoroughness and discretion earned him royal notice and in 1702 the new queen appointed him as an envoy to Vienna, to advise the Austrian Emperor on harbour fortifications in the Adriatic. When he returned to Austria, to check the work was being properly conducted, the emperor expressed his pleasure by presenting Halley with a diamond ring. Both visits involved travel across Europe and meetings with eminent people, including dinner with the future Kings of England, George I and George II in Hanover. But it must be that rather more was going on behind the scenes because, upon his return to London, in January 1704, the Chancellor of the Exchequer was ordered to pay Edmund Halley the sum of £36 for his expenses 'out of the secret service'. Spying and espionage had been added to his *curriculum vitae*.

The year 1703 brought Halley the chance to attain his ultimate academic wish when he was chosen to replace John Wallis as Savilian Professor of Geometry at Oxford, despite Flamsteed's efforts to prevent it by complaining that 'he now talks, swears and drinks brandy like a sea-captain,' which was unsurprising in the circumstances. In November, Halley was elected to the Council of the Royal Society, the same day his good friend Isaac Newton became its President. Installed in the professorship in 1705 and becoming a Doctor of Civil Law in 1710, Dr Halley abandoned adventure for the quiet life. In 1705, he published his calculations concerning the comet of 1682 that would ultimately bear his name, making public his certainty that it would return at a predicted date.

A Synopsis of the Astronomy of Comets also set out evidence that the so-called 'fixed' stars, previously believed to be firmly attached to a single crystal sphere, actually moved independently, gradually changing their positions. Polaris, the Pole Star, had not always pinpointed north: this was more revolutionary stuff. But unlike the case with some of Halley's (and Hooke's) ideas, the world was on the cusp of outgrowing the old model of the universe that described the heavens as a series of concentric crystal spheres, like the layers of an onion. Having left behind the geocentric view of the Solar System, it no longer made sense to maintain the Earth at the centre of anything but the Moon's orbit, never mind the rest of the star-studded universe. The crystal spheres were about to be relegated to the realm of poetry; science had no further use for them. Halley's version of the astronomical positioning of the stars was generally acceptable to all but the most confirmed romantics.

Earthly Conveniences

While the likes of Newton, Flamsteed and Halley were concerned with unravelling the secrets of the universe, other ordinary people went about such mundane activities as shopping. In 1705, in Duke Street, not far from Newton's house in Jermyn Street, lived Hugh Mason. He ran a stall in St James's Market but to increase his profit margins also rented his spare rooms to William Fortnum. William had come to London following the Great Fire of 1666 to make his fortune as a builder. He then progressed to working on the high-class buildings going up in the newly fashionable district of Mayfair but, apparently with time on his hands, he also took a post as a footman in the royal household.

There was, among other perks of the job, one which continued into Victorian times: that of the queen's half-used candles – thousands of them weekly – being given to the servants to use. Many underlings gave the top-quality candle remnants to their families to sell on but William suggested he would buy them off his fellows to save them the trouble. William took the candles home to Duke Street where Hugh Mason melted them down and made new high-quality candles to sell on his market stall. The pair made such a fine profit that they went into business together in 1707, opening a proper retail premises and branching out into top-of-the-range grocery produce. The famous partnership of Fortnum & Mason was born, although the likelihood of finding any royal candle remnants on the shelves in such a grand emporium today is doubtful.

One of Fortnum & Mason's claims to fame is that the company invented the Scotch egg. In 1738, realising the shop was in the perfect position to supply travellers leaving London for all points west, William came up with a number of ideas for food that could be eaten conveniently in a moving stagecoach. The best of his developments was to hard-boil an egg, wrap it in sausage meat, then coat it with breadcrumbs and deep fry it. Scotch eggs have remained popular snacks ever since.

In the last year of the decade, Sir Isaac moved from Jermyn Street to a new house in Chelsea, although he did not find the place much to his liking nor so convenient for work at the Royal Mint at the Tower, so his sojourn there was brief. By October 1709, Flamsteed's tardiness with the requisite data notwithstanding, Newton was writing to Roger Cotes regarding a new edition of the *Principia*. Cotes would do for the *Principia* what De Moivre had done for *Opticks*. Newton was the master of his art but would leave the laborious tasks of editing, rewriting, correcting and dealing with publishers and printers to his disciples. All was set for another prosperous decade.

Chapter 9

THE 1710s: THE FAMOUS PHILOSOPHER

Deciding the house in Chelsea was inconvenient, in September 1710 Newton again moved to a new house, number 35 St Martin's Street. One of a row of terraced houses built in about 1695, his new abode had plenty of room on three storeys and was within walking distance of the Tower of London for his daily commute. It was a long walk but Newton, as a country squire, was used to striding along and, even in his eighties, preferred to go on foot, if at all possible, rather than by sedan chair, as his physicians advised. Unfortunately, the house in St Martin's Street was demolished in 1913 and the Westminster Reference Library built on the site, the library entrance porch overlaying the footprint of number 35. However, panelling and fittings from the 'fore parlour' were rescued and reconstructed as the Isaac Newton Room at Babson College, Wellesley, Massachusetts. Sir Isaac remained at St Martin's Street until 1725, when it was thought the rural situation of Kensington would benefit his health, but he kept the house until his death.

Religious Studies

Besides attending to business at the Royal Mint, Sir Isaac had numerous other projects in hand. During 1710, he published the paper *De natura acidorum* (Concerning the Nature of Acids), based upon some of his alchemical experiments, together with other mathematical treatises, as well as keeping an eye on the progress of Roger Cotes with the new edition of the *Principia*. Throughout his life, he had studied the Scriptures assiduously. His belief that the doctrine of the Holy Trinity – that the Godhead comprised three elements, God the Father, God the Son and God the Holy Spirit – was the invention of the early Christian Church and not evidenced in the Bible was arrived at following years of diligent theological research.

Back in 1690, he had sent a letter to his friend John Locke that included his *Historical Account of Two Notable Corruptions of the Scriptures*, a paper refuting the Trinity that he wished Locke to arrange for publication on the Continent. The outcome could be serious for him if it was published in England and in 1692, as a Latin version of it was ready to go to press in France, Newton hastened to suppress it and stopped its publication. Like his other religious works, it would not be published until after his death. He was right to worry about the consequences of making his Arian views known. In 1710, his friend, fellow Arian and successor as Lucasian Professor at Cambridge, William Whiston, dared to speak openly of his beliefs and was dismissed from his post. The blind mathematician Nicholas Saunderson replaced Whiston as Lucasian Professor, keeping the Newtonian perspective flourishing without any further religious controversy. Meanwhile, Sir Isaac himself wanted to keep his place in society secure and knew silence was the only solution.

The earliest writings of the Christian faith were not the only religious subjects Newton studied. Pre-Christian belief systems also intrigued him. He had conducted three separate projects during the 1680s and 1690s. He examined the ancient Egyptian ideas about Nature that had been brought to Greece by Pythagoras and others, neatly combining both his interests in religion and alchemy. He analysed primitive Sun-worshipping cultures, which he saw as logical precursors of Copernicus' heliocentric universe. Temples to the Sun, including Stonehenge in England and others in ancient lands, such as Canaan and Assyria, long before Moses' time, were sites where man's earliest religious beliefs had been practised. Newton collected reports from as far afield as India and China, concerning evidence of ancient sun worship across the Old World. He concluded that the Sun was the deity of man's instinctive monotheistic religion, the earliest 'representation' of God. His third project worked towards mapping the spread of peoples – and therefore their religious beliefs – across the world, originating from the sons of Noah.[1]

Since Noah had practised Judaism and the dispersal of his descendants might be viewed as the earliest diaspora, Newton studied the Jewish faith, as well as Christianity. His library contained the Bible's Old Testament in Hebrew, along with copies in English, Latin and Greek. By making comparisons between the Hebraic version of the Old Testament, the Greek version of the New Testament and their later Latin and English counterparts, Newton could trace the origin and development of 'erroneous' ideas, like Trinitarianism, through time.

In Sir Isaac's lifetime, there were many who believed the End of the World – Armageddon – was fast approaching. Having witnessed the execution of a king, the Great Plague, the Great Fire of London and freezing winters, perhaps it was unsurprising that some saw these events as having been foretold in the prophesies of *The Book of Daniel* and as evidence that they were living through the 'Last Days' described in *The Revelation of St John the Divine*. Such a belief could have worrying consequences. As mentioned previously, there were a number of academics who viewed educating the next generation as a waste of their valuable time, since the young would not have cause to use the knowledge gained as the world was about to end any day. Others had similar ideas concerning planning for the future. Why set money aside for an old age, or store food stuffs for a winter that would never come? Newton determined to refute such fatalistic attitudes by making the definitive calculations concerning the End of the World.

Even so, he actually gives more than one possible date – 2034 and 2060 AD being those closest to his time. If either was to prove correct, they were far enough in the future that nobody should abandon forward planning or the proper upbringing and education of the next generation. According to Newton, preparation for those times was even more important because they did not indicate the total annihilation of mankind but a new beginning: 'The Second Coming of Christ'. He anticipated The End of the World 'as we know it' and the foundation of God's Kingdom and Paradise on Earth.[2] Rather than a doom-laden belief, he saw hope for godly mankind and only the wicked would suffer.

Moving the Royal Society

Newton was not alone in requiring a new home. By 1710, Gresham College was in need of repair and the Mercers' Company, as Gresham's trustees, wanted the Royal Society to vacate the premises so building work could begin. The society had been given notice seven years earlier in 1703, a few months after Robert Hooke's death. Their meetings took place in Hooke's rooms, where he lodged as one of the Gresham professors, but the trustees demanded Hooke's keys be returned to them and the society was told to find alternative accommodation. Members were unhappy at being forced out of their 'home' and, besides, there was no money to finance the move or buy new premises.

However, with Isaac Newton now presiding over the society's membership with his friend Hans Sloane as secretary – a post he had previously shared with Hooke – the impecunious situation was about to change. In the meantime, armed with a sizeable list of excuses as to why they could not move, the society clung on at Gresham for a further seven years, meeting in the same rooms, which were now the lodgings of Dr John Woodward as a Gresham professor who was also a Fellow of the Royal Society and on the Council. Newton put his considerable administrative and organisational skills to work as soon as he was elected President and supported by Hans Sloane, membership fees, backdated for up to a year, were gathered in. Money was invested in property and by September 1710, the society was a well-financed institution. Its reputation as a scientific body had also been rescued, for it had begun to acquire a name as a club for dabblers and crackpots. Newton changed that by raising the standards of papers read out and by expelling members he found unsuitable, though failure to pay fees was often just an excuse to be rid of those the President disliked, such as John Flamsteed.

Newton also changed the structure of the meetings. They became far more formal and there were rules concerning conduct of members. When a paper was being read aloud, there was to be no talking, whispering or laughter. Another member whom Newton disliked and Sloane detested was John Woodward, whose rooms at Gresham they were using for the meetings. If Woodward was expelled he would hardly allow the society to continue to do so. Woodward, Sloane and Richard Mead were all medical men but whereas Sloane and Mead were Newton's supporters, Woodward was not and Newton put his name on a 'hit list' of members he wanted voted off the Council at the next election. Newton was insistent on regular attendance at meetings; as President, he was present at 161 out of 175 meetings, most of his absences occurring due to ill health in his last years.[3] However, for some reason he was not at the meeting on 8 March 1710 when things became very heated.

Hans Sloane was reading a paper to the membership, sent by the French Académie des Sciences, concerning gall stones as a possible cause of colic. If Newton had been presiding, decorum would have been maintained but, in his absence, Woodward interrupted the reading, saying Sloane was making no sense, perhaps because he was reading it in French. He also questioned Sloane's knowledge of anatomy and declared that gall stones did not cause colic. According to the minutes of the meeting, Sloane laughed and pulled a face and Woodward's temper got the better of him. Quite what happened then is not recorded but we know Woodward was capable of going beyond the bounds of sensible behaviour because he later fought a duel with Richard Mead.

Richard Mead had been born in Stepney, just outside the City of London in 1673. He studied medicine at the Universities of Utrecht and Leiden before gaining his MD in Italy. Returning to England in 1696, he set up in medical practice in Stepney. Mead was elected a Fellow of the Royal Society after publishing a paper, *A Mechanical Account of Poisons*, in 1702, and became a governor of St Thomas' Hospital in 1715. Mead was a close friend of Dr John Radcliffe, the royal physician, succeeding him in the post after Radcliffe's death in 1714 – just in time to attend Queen Anne on her deathbed – but going on to serve George I, his son Prince George and daughter-in-law Princess Caroline. His other patients of note included Isaac Newton, Dr Samuel Johnson, Alexander Pope and Sir Robert Walpole.

As a Fellow of both the Royal Society and of the Royal College of Physicians from 1716, Mead was recognised not only as an expert on poisons but on smallpox, among other subjects. It was his knowledge of and work with venomous snakes and a dispute over methods of treating smallpox that led to a major disagreement with Dr John Woodward in 1719. The argument degenerated into a fistfight outside Woodward's lodgings in Gresham College. Newton must have been appalled at such misbehaviour between two Fellows that was likely to bring the Society's good name into question. However, Mead was his friend as well as his personal physician and was known for his philanthropic deeds. He became a founding governor of the Foundling Hospital and its medical advisor. His house close by, in Great Ormond Street, would become the famous Hospital for Sick Children after his death in February 1754. He was buried in the Temple Church but there is a marble monument to him and a bust by Peter Scheemakers in the north aisle of Westminster Abbey. This last is ironic because Mead's rival, John Woodward, had been buried in the same aisle in 1728 and also has a monument sculpted by Scheemakers.

John Woodward had been born in Derbyshire in 1665 and was taught medicine by Dr Peter Barwick, one of Charles II's royal physicians. Despite not having studied at university, in 1692 he was appointed Professor of Physic at Gresham, elected to the Royal Society the following year and granted his doctorate by both the Archbishop of Canterbury and Cambridge University in 1695. Apart from medicine, he seems to have been as interested in botany, geology and the classification of fossils – of which he had a remarkable collection – writing papers on hydroponics, rock strata and two volumes on the fossils of England. His medical treatise *The State of Physick and of Diseases ... Particularly of the Smallpox*, published in 1718, was the issue that brought him into dispute not only with Mead, but with Mead's friend and fellow royal physician, John Freind (*sic*). Apparently Woodward and Freind publicly accused each other of killing their patients.

Returning to the problems of the Royal Society being no longer welcome at Gresham College and being wary of upsetting Woodward as their host there, all difficulties would be resolved if a new and permanent venue could be found for society meetings. Sir Isaac made a unilateral decision and simply announced that he had found and intended to purchase suitable premises at number 2 Crane Court, off Fleet Street, to the west of the city. The house had once belonged to Nicholas Barbon (aka Barebone), a qualified physician who, in the aftermath of the Great Fire of London in 1666, had become a builder and speculator. His knowledge of economic theory, and the destruction of the fire, led him to set up the Phoenix Fire Office, an insurance company and the first of its kind. However his extensive building projects were often underhanded, if not illegal, but he was by that time wealthy enough to buy his way out of judicial hearings.

When the property at Crane Court came up for sale in October 1710, Sir Isaac bought it for £1,450 out of society funds. Members were dismayed that they had not been consulted and, having viewed the place, complained that it was small, cramped, dilapidated and inconvenient, hidden at the end of a 'court' that was little better than an alleyway. Their objections were overruled by the President. Hasty renovations were carried out on the interior and the first meeting was held there on 8 November. Sir Christopher Wren was commissioned to build a 'galleried repository' in the garden behind to house the collection of specimens and curiosities. However, some pieces in the collection were found to be mouldy, rotten or crumbling to dust and were discarded before the move, as was an item of greater significance: the only known portrait of Robert Hooke. All other portraits of the society's elite were transferred safely and it must be conjectured that the loss may have been orchestrated to please the President.

To enhance the outward appearance of Crane Court, Newton ordered the porter at the door to wear an appropriate gown and to carry a staff topped with the society's arms in silver. To gain prominence on Fleet Street itself, a lamp was lit at the entrance to Crane Court whenever a meeting was held. Inside, the meeting room was not spacious but Newton, again, would impress his authority. The President would sit at the head of a green baize-covered table, his back to the fireplace, flanked by the Secretaries. Before him on the table during every meeting he attended lay the society's grand mace, which he had designed and commissioned. After his death, his successor as President, Hans Sloane, abolished this practice immediately he was elected to office. Cramped it may have been but Crane Court would serve as the Royal Society's home for sixty-five years until 1775, when Somerset House in the Strand was offered as an alternative. Formerly a royal residence, it was no longer needed after George III and Queen Charlotte acquired Buckingham House – now Buckingham Palace.

The Calculus Priority Dispute
An intellectual argument had been simmering for more than a decade concerning who had invented 'fluxions' or 'calculus': Newton or Gottfried Wilhelm Leibniz. Newton claimed he had worked out 'the method of fluxions and fluents', as he called it, years earlier in 1665 – his *annus mirabilis* – but first mentioned it in the *Principia* published in 1687.[4] He then partially explained his 'fluxional notation' in print in 1693 but only published a full account, claiming his invention, in 1704, in *De Quadratura Curvarum* which appeared as an appendix at the back of *Opticks*, although it was first written back in 1691. In the meantime, Leibniz had begun setting out his version of calculus in 1674, although its earliest use is identified in his notebooks of 1675, and published as *Nova Methodus pro Maximis et Minimis* in 1684, a paper explaining and demonstrating his method. In terms of actual publication, Leibniz had won the priority dispute but Newton could not let the matter rest.

Leibniz was born in 1646 in Leipzig, where his father was Professor of Moral Philosophy at the university so, unlike Newton, even as a child he was expected to follow an academic career – no farming for young Gottfried. His father taught him to read before he was old enough for school and he proved an able student. He was allowed access to his father's library and claimed to have taught himself Latin.

At the University of Leipzig, he chose to study law. By the time he had written his doctoral thesis in 1666, he had to take on a tutorship to earn some money because he was in debt. However, when the time came for his graduation, there were so many doctoral candidates that summer Leibniz, being one of the youngest at just twenty, was told he would have to wait until the next graduation day. He was most annoyed and, for reasons never explained, blamed the Dean's wife for the personal slight. Instead of waiting, he took his ready-written *Dissertation on the Art of Combinations* to the less popular University of Altdorf and graduated there. Impressed with Dr Leibniz, Altdorf offered him a professorship but his love of academia had been blighted at Leipzig and he determined on a career in law.

He became somewhat of a jack-of-all-trades at the Court of Hanover. Alchemy, politics, mining, religion, foreign visits, librarianship, legal cases – Leibniz seemed to busy himself with so many projects, he became renowned for rarely completing anything successfully. With a brilliant mind and an exceptional imagination, he had countless ideas for improving everything, from mining techniques to cataloguing books, from binary notation to political machination but, unlike Newton or Robert Hooke, he had neither the manual dexterity nor persistence to apply his inventiveness to practical purposes. But the one 'invention' he pursued to its conclusion was calculus: both differentiation and integration.[5]

In 1673, Leibniz had visited London and the then Secretary of the Royal Society, Henry Oldenburg, introduced him to the society and to John Collins, known for his publication of academic works. At the time, Isaac Barrow, the Lucasian Professor of Mathematics at Cambridge and young Newton's mentor, had sent some of his protégé's papers to Collins with a view towards possible publication in the future. After Leibniz's visit, Collins continued to correspond with him, telling him of mathematical ideas and advances in the Royal Society. When Leibniz sent an abstract of his calculus to Oldenburg, the secretary knew enough of mathematics to realise that although the German used a different form of notation, his technique was basically the same as Newton's fluxions and fluents. Both Oldenburg and Collins did all they could to persuade Newton to publish first but Hooke's earlier criticism of his paper on the *Theory of Light and Colour* had put the Cambridge scholar off publishing anything. Perhaps if Collins had admitted his contact and correspondence with Leibniz, Newton might have realised why it was a matter of urgency to get his work in print and establish his priority of invention. But Collins said nothing, concerned for his reputation if other academics learned that their papers were not confidential in his hands, as his trade would suffer. Seventeenth-century publishing was always a risky business anyway.

Still unaware of Leibniz's particular interest in calculus, Newton was persuaded to write a letter to the German, to assist with the other's 'mathematical queries', which only he could possibly answer. Newton agreed, after much coercion. Unsurprisingly, the letter became two detailed treatises of eleven and nineteen pages of close-written script, summarising his work on infinite series but only mentioning that he would not 'proceed with the explanation of fluxions' for fear his methods would be stolen. Thus, the true reason for the letters was not fulfilled and his painstaking correspondence achieved nothing – all because Oldenburg and Collins dared not tell Newton the full story.

In 1677, Leibniz was again in London. Collins had not learned his lesson and invited him to visit his print works – at which time it was later said the young German was at liberty to look at any work lying around, including Newton's. Leibniz admitted that he looked but claimed there was nothing of interest to him. In 1684, when his calculus ideas went public in *Acta Eruditorum*, Leibniz had no idea of the shock and outrage it caused in London and Cambridge. Newton claimed that Leibniz's work was 'pure and unmitigated plagiarism', stolen from *his* papers.[6] It was not. Even if the idea had been copied, the notation was completely different to Newton's and, in fact, easier to use – which is why Leibniz's version of calculus is the one still used today.

On the Continent, interest in calculus was spreading. Guillaume l'Hôpital (1661–1704), a young Frenchman, requested Johannes Bernoulli to teach him mathematics by correspondence. Bernoulli was one of few men who fully understood calculus and he used Leibniz's methods. In 1698, in Paris, l'Hôpital published the first text book on the subject, *Analyse des Infiniment Petits pour l'Intelligence des Lignes Courbes*, using Bernoulli's letters as source material – a fact he acknowledged. However, his presentation and explanations were far more accessible and 'user-friendly' than anything written by the experts in the field: Newton, Leibniz or Bernoulli, so l'Hôpital's version became the text that was used to teach differential calculus and popularised Leibniz's forms of notation across Europe.

The truth seems to be that the invention of calculus was the next logical step in the advance of mathematics; two men achieved what was required quite independently and by employing differing methods. But neither could concede the priority of discovery to the other, although Leibniz appeared the more reasonable, willing to accept and announce calculus/ fluxions as parallel creations. This was not good enough for Newton and so began forty years of dispute and bad feeling between the Englishman and the German that would expand to include their supporters and countrymen and even extend beyond the grave. While Newton was the wronged hero on this side of the Channel, on the Continent, he was regarded as the villain. The mathematician Johann Bernoulli went so far as to suggest Newton had plagiarised Leibniz. In 1699, Nicolas Fatio de Duillier joined the dispute, taking his old friend Newton's side. In addition, a decade before, de Duillier had sent Leibniz a paper of his own, concerning another method of calculus, only to have it dismissed as unworkable by the German, so this was an opportunity for revenge. De Duillier did not hold back:

I now recognise, based upon the factual evidence, that Newton is the first inventor of calculus, and the earliest by many years; whether Leibniz, the second inventor, may have borrowed anything from him, I should rather leave to the judgement of those who have seen the letters of Newton and his other manuscripts. Neither the silence of the more modest Newton, nor the unremitting exertions of Leibniz to claim on every occasion the invention of calculus for himself, will deceive anyone who examines these records as I have.[7]

In early March 1712, after a further acrimonious exchange of correspondence between John Keill – one of Newton's more active supporters – and Leibniz, the German wrote to the Royal Society, declaring he would 'appear like a suitor before a court of law' in defence of his claims to priority. Newton obliged, setting up a committee of members to hear the evidence, examine the priority dispute between Newton and Leibniz and present a verdict. In this, Newton was far exceeding his authority as President and the committee of eleven men was selected by him. Eleven men, note; not a jury of twelve and just to be sure the adjudication went in his favour, six – a majority – were his most loyal followers, including Edmund Halley and Abraham de Moivre.

To make certain he had the last word on the committee's conclusions, Newton wrote up their report himself and published it under the title *Commercium Epistolicum* within six weeks of the committee's inception and just one week after the appointment of its final three members. The reported ended: 'For which reasons we reckon Mr Newton the first inventor and are of the opinion that Mr Keill in asserting the same has been in no way injurious to Mr Leibniz'. This is what was noted down in the *Journal Book* of the Royal Society. Leibniz had no chance of winning this so-called court case. Later, Newton went so far as to deny he had any part in the committee's judgement. In January and February 1715, he had an *Account of the Commercium Epistolicum* printed in two consecutive editions of the society's *Philosophical Transactions,* adding character assassination to the demolition of Leibniz's intellectual reputation. Newton denied its authorship but the numerous technical references could only have been his.

By this date, Leibniz's own patron, George, Elector of Hanover, was King of Great Britain. He did attempt to reconcile his two warring subjects, ordering Newton to write to Leibniz. Newton obeyed his king but the letter was much the same as what was written in the *Commercium*, if using different words. No one remaining in Hanover had much interest in Leibniz any longer. Friendless, he died in November 1716 with a solitary servant to attend his funeral. But European scholars kept his priority claim alive, despite the third edition of the *Principia*, (published in 1726), having every last reference to Leibniz erased by Newton.

Meanwhile in July 1713, the second edition of the *Principia* was published, making use of data connived from John Flamsteed. The new *Principia* had been edited, corrected and seen through to publishing by Roger Cotes. Within two years, Cotes was dead and Newton remarked cryptically, 'If he had lived we might have known something.' But another problem had been highlighted recently in which Sir Isaac, the Royal Society, Queen Anne, the Admiralty, John Flamsteed and Edmund Halley would all have a role to play. However, the most significant part was played by a dead man: Admiral Sir Cloudsley Shovell.

The Longitude Problem

Cloudsley Shovell was born in 1650 and joined the Royal Navy as a young officer in 1664. He earned a recommendation for bravery by swimming from one ship to another to carry a message while under fire during the Dutch War of 1666–67, was made a second lieutenant in 1673 and given his own command as captain of the *Sapphire* in 1677. His rapid rise through the ranks saw him knighted for various acts of gallantry and courage in 1689, made a Rear Admiral in 1692 and appointed Commander-in-Chief of the British fleet in 1704.

In October 1707, he was leading home a squadron of twenty-one ships, after a series of victorious encounters with the French Mediterranean fleet, when they became engulfed in fog for twelve days somewhere off the west coast of France. Fearing his ships might founder on the rocky coast, Sir Cloudsley summoned the navigators from each vessel to be rowed over to his flagship, HMS *Association,* for a consultation. The general opinion was that they were safely west of the Brittany peninsula and all was well.

But one man disagreed. An unnamed seaman on *Association* had kept his own reckoning of the fleet's position throughout the foggy voyage. Subversive navigation by an inferior was considered a mutinous offence in the Royal Navy since it could lead to dispute between officers and crew. Even knowing the penalty for this was death, the seaman was so certain the navigators were wrong and believing the ships were in imminent danger from the rocky outcrops of the Scilly Isles, he approached the admiral and told him of his calculations. Outraged, Sir Cloudsley had him hanged for mutiny there and then and never even noted the sailor's name in the logbook. A few hours later, at 8 p.m. on 22 October, the seaman was proved correct when *Association* struck the Gilstone Ledges off St Agnes Island, one of the tiny Scilly Isles about 20 miles from the south-west tip of Cornwall. The flagship sank within 4 minutes with the loss of all hands, 650 men, although the admiral, who had long ago proved himself a strong swimmer in a period when few seamen could swim at all, was washed ashore alive.

Meanwhile, before the rest of the fleet could react and avoid the same fate, *Eagle* and *Romney* suffered a similarly rapid end; a fourth ship sank more slowly. Twenty-six men were saved from a watery grave by other ships pulling them from the sea but 1,647 souls were lost. Perhaps as he lay, gasping and exhausted, on the shore, Sir Cloudsley had time to reflect upon his catastrophic misjudgement. But what could he have done when the 'dirty weather' had made it almost impossible to fix their position at sea precisely? His thoughts were never recorded because, so the story goes, a local woman, beachcombing along the sands for loot washed up from the wrecks of the previous evening, found him collapsed and, thinking he was dead, tried to take a valuable emerald ring from his finger. He struggled feebly to prevent her but she 'extinguished the flickering life' and took the gem. Three decades later, on her deathbed, she admitted her crime to a clergyman and showed him the ring. What happened to the ring afterwards only the clergyman may have known.

It was this disaster and the loss of so many lives, caused by errors made in reckoning both latitude and longitude, that would ultimately bring the longitude problem to the attention of Parliament. It had always been possible to measure latitude, i.e. a position north to south, by the height of the Sun above the horizon at midday, although of course that required clear skies which Sir Cloudsley had not had for twelve days. Nothing could be done about the weather; that was just bad luck but there was no way, even in the best weather, of calculating longitude. Knowing longitude would make accurate positioning possible, east to west. The Earth's circumference is 360° and for every 15° travelled to the east, an hour is gained; for every 15° west, an hour is lost.

At the time, the Prime Meridian was taken as an invisible line running from the North Pole to the South through the Canary Islands.[8] Eventually, the Greenwich meridian was established at the Royal Observatory with the invisible line running north–south through Greenwich taken to be 0°. This would mean, for example, if it was 12 noon at Greenwich but at a ship's location in the Atlantic, the Sun's position was measured as being at 9 a.m., then the vessel must be 3 hours or 45° west (3 x 15°) of Greenwich and its position could be marked on the chart accordingly. The difficulty lay in knowing the correct time back at Greenwich. In 1714, pendulum clocks and pocket watches were becoming increasingly accurate but both became unreliable on a pitching, rolling ship subject to vagaries of wind, sea and weather. If only someone could invent a means of measuring time precisely in such adverse conditions, Parliament promised the incredible sum of £20,000 for a solution that worked, the enormous reward reflecting the magnitude of the problem to a seafaring nation.

The urgency of the need was brought to Parliament's attention by a petition signed by 'Captains of Her Majesty's Ships, Merchants of London and Commanders of Merchant-Men', reminding the government that not only Royal Navy vessels were at risk; Britain's trade relied on merchant ships for its prosperity. When the petition was presented in May 1714, it took just a few weeks – a rapid response in parliamentary terms – for a committee to be set up to look into the problem. Sir Isaac Newton was first called as an expert to explain the current ideas for methods of determining longitude at sea but he became a permanent member of the Board of Longitude on which he would serve for seven years. He spoke of several projects which seemed theoretically sound but had proved impractical: to use an accurate timepiece; to observe the eclipses of Jupiter's moons; by knowing precisely the timings for positions of Earth's Moon and a new idea proposed by William Whiston and Humphrey Ditton.

Whiston, having been ousted from his post as Lucasian Professor of Mathematics because of his unorthodox religious views, was probably in need of both occupation and remuneration. Ditton was Master of Christ's Hospital Mathematics School in London and the two friends put their analytical skills to solving the problem by what was called the 'thunder and lightning' method. They knew the sound of cannon fire could travel surprising distances – it was reckoned that during the Dutch Wars, cannon fired in the Battle of Lowestoft, off the Norfolk coast, had been heard in the middle of England. Whiston and Ditton proposed that signal ships should be stationed at specific known points across the oceans to fire exploding shells at every midnight. By timing the gap between seeing the shell explode and hearing the explosion – like counting the seconds between lightning and thunder to estimate how far away a storm is – other ships could reckon their distance from the nearest signal ship and gauge their position on the charts. As with the other suggestions, this sounded reasonable at first hearing, but mariners were quick to point out how wind, rain or fog could muffle both sight and sound and Edmund Halley gave first-hand accounts to the committee. But a far greater difficulty probably never occurred to Whiston and Ditton: the signal ships themselves.

For one thing, holding a stationary position in the middle of the ocean would be an insurmountable problem for a vessel powered only by the wind and sea anchors could not be made strong enough or long enough for the great depths in the mid-Atlantic, for example. And who would supply the thousands of ships required? Who would man the signal ships, remaining at sea indefinitely, and how would they be re-provisioned and repaired without returning to port every few months and thus breaking up the signal network? What about acts of piracy or war destroying them, or the possibility of an enemy discharging a similar signal from an unauthorised location? Ultimately, this idea was as unworkable as the others and, worse still, would cost exorbitant sums of money.

Sir Isaac and Edmund Halley both favoured reckoning longitude from the timings for positions of the Moon, if John Flamsteed ever completed his star catalogue. Of the 400 copies of the version Newton had succeeded in rushing into publication in 1712, before Flamsteed was ready, the Astronomer Royal had managed to acquire and burn 300 of the imperfect, unfinished catalogues. The hope that every ship's navigator should have a copy was not about to materialise. Second best, Newton believed, would be an accurate seagoing clock but he was not confident that such an instrument was possible. In 1721, he wrote to the Secretary of the Admiralty:

A good watch may serve to keep a recconing at Sea for some days and to know the time of a celestial Observ[at]ion: and for this end a good Jewel watch may suffice till a better sort of Watch can be found out. But when the Longitude at sea is once lost, it cannot be found again by any watch.[9]

Meanwhile, the committee drew up a Bill and presented their findings to the House of Commons. The Bill passed swiftly on to the House of Lords and went before Queen Anne on 8 July 1714 to receive the royal assent. It was now an Act of Parliament: the Longitude Act, setting up the official Board of Longitude to assess and award prizes to anyone of any nationality who could find a means of solving the problem – £20,000 for a method accurate to within half a degree of longitude; £15,000 for an accuracy within two-thirds of a degree and £10,000 for an accuracy within one degree. The answer lay years in the future and even then Parliament did its best to avoid presenting the prize, but a version of John Harrison's Chronometer saw Captain James Cook safely around the world in 1772–75, without ever failing to keep accurate time.

A New Ruling Dynasty

A few weeks after putting her name to the Longitude Act, on 1 August 1714 Queen Anne died and was succeeded by the House of Hanover, a branch of the family she had loathed. Anne had been ailing for years but the previous December had suffered a serious bout of fever and never fully recovered. Her list of health problems was long and included arthritis, gout, obesity, alcohol dependency, confusion, failing eyesight, anaemia, renal and liver damage, one often adding to the severity of another.[10] Had Anne died of fever that winter, the new monarch would have been Queen Sophia but she – the only remaining sibling of Prince Rupert – passed away in March 1714, so Anne was succeeded by Sophia's son George, the Elector of Hanover, as George I. He made no secret of the fact that he preferred to live on his German estates, rather than in England, and never made any attempt to learn English or the ways of government or to get to know the people of his new kingdom.

When immediately informed of Anne's death, having been warned that it was imminent, it took George almost six weeks to arrive in England with a large entourage and one of his mistresses. She was created Countess of Darlington and the other, his favourite mistress, became Duchess of Kendal. George spent most of his time with these two women who were branded rudely as the 'ugly old trolls': the Maypole and the Elephant. Aged fifty-four and with little but his Protestantism to recommend him to his new subjects, King George had no interest in them or the country's problems, leaving his ministers to run the government and bother him as little as possible. With an inactive Head of State, English politics degenerated into a state riddled with bribery and corruption. The Prince of Wales might have taken the matter in hand during his father's frequent absences in Hanover but the king did all he could to exclude his son and heir from playing any role in government. The hatred between father and eldest son would be a recurring feature in the Hanoverian dynasty.

Despite this, George, Prince of Wales, and his wife, Caroline of Ansbach, were more interested in their adopted country and often entertained the aristocracy and gentry since the king did not wish to acquaint himself with the English nobility. Sir Isaac was a popular visitor at their court and Princess Caroline would have conversations with him, making an effort to improve her English. Caroline had formerly been tutored by Gottfried Wilhelm Leibniz at the Hanoverian court. He had believed in and taught her the Cartesian view of the universe, expounded by René Descartes, which ran contrary to the Newtonian model. The princess preferred Newton's explanations and even attended meetings of the Royal Society to enhance her knowledge, which would have saddened her old tutor before he died in 1716.

Caroline also took a deep interest in Newton's chronology of the world and asked if he would give her a copy. Newton obliged but stressed that it was solely 'for her own use'; it was not meant for other eyes. However, a young cleric, Antonio-Schinella Conti, came to England in 1714 to view a solar eclipse and decided to stay in London. He was a friend of both Caroline and Leibniz and hoped to become better acquainted with Sir Isaac. Conti acquired a copy of Newton's chronology and sent it to Monsieur Fréret in Paris.

Fréret was an antiquarian who disagreed with Newton's chronology, which he translated into French and published. Newton eventually received a copy of the French version of his work and printed his response to it in the Royal Society's *Philosophical Transactions* in 1725. He was livid and accused Conti of breaking his word before refuting all Fréret's objections and commencing a new and expanded work on the subject. Sir Isaac intended to have the last word; *The Chronology of Ancient Kingdoms Amended* would be published in 1728, a year after his death.

On Friday 22 April 1715 (on the Continent, using the Gregorian calendar, the date was 3 May), London witnessed the first total solar eclipse visible in England since 1104. Edmund Halley drew up diagrams predicting the path across the country that the total eclipse would take – either side of this route, the eclipse would be partial. His predictions proved accurate and it was hoped this would dispel the superstitions about such an event, proving it was brought about neither by magic nor miracle but was simply a predictable natural phenomenon.[11] Foreign scientists were invited by the Royal Society to come to Crane Court to view the eclipse. Willem Jacob 's Gravesande came as a member of the Dutch delegation to welcome the Hanoverian king officially but took the opportunity to watch the eclipse with the Royal Society. He became friendly with Newton, remained in London and joined the society. Later, when he became a professor of mathematics, astronomy and philosophy at Leiden University in 1717, the post enabled him to promote and champion Newton's ideas in Europe.

Edmund Halley had arranged for other observers across Britain and Europe to time and measure the eclipse systematically, so this became the first co-ordinated scientific programme of its kind. The weather obliged; the skies were cloudless over the city of London and Halley collected reports as they came in from across the country and abroad. As a scientific event, it was a great success but, surprisingly, it was not until the nineteenth century that similar co-ordinated observations made at different locations and the subsequent sharing of information became standard procedure.

Deaths and a Family Wedding

One person of significance in Sir Isaac's career and social life died in May 1715: Charles Montagu, the Earl of Halifax, his patron. He was only fifty-four years old. This meant that Newton's niece Catherine Barton had lost her lover and she may have returned to live with her uncle for a while. She was now a wealthy woman since the earl had left her well provided for in his will and, despite her previous relationship with Montagu, her marriage prospects were good.

Two years later, in 1717, Catherine married John Conduitt. He had been born in London and was baptised at St Paul's, Covent Garden, on 8 March 1688. After attending Westminster

School, he was chosen as a Queen's Scholar to go up to Trinity College, Cambridge, from 1705 to 1707, although this was after Newton had left his post as Lucasian Professor. However, though a promising student, Conduitt never graduated but joined the British Army, serving as a judge advocate in Portugal before becoming Captain of Dragoons.[12] In 1713, he was appointed Deputy Paymaster General to the British Forces in Gibraltar, becoming quite wealthy. Returning to England, his knowledge of financial matters made him an able assistant to Sir Isaac Newton in his work at the Royal Mint – which may explain how John came to meet Catherine.

After a brief romance, the couple applied to the Faculty Office for a licence to marry, Catherine giving her age as thirty-two, although she was thirty-eight. John was twenty-nine; even so, his wife would outlive him. To enhance the bridegroom's credentials in marrying the niece of the legendary Newton, John obtained a grant of arms from the Royal College of Heralds, which was granted on 16 August, just a week before the wedding was supposed to take place on 23 August at his parish church of St Paul's in Covent Garden – according to the licence. Instead, the ceremony took place on 26 August in the parish where Catherine lived with her uncle, at the church of St Martin-in-the-Fields.

The happy couple would live with Newton for a few years until, in 1720, John bought Cranbury Park, a grand house and estate near Winchester in Hampshire, although he continued to spend a great deal of time in London, working at the mint. Unsurprisingly, John was proposed by his new uncle as a Fellow of the Royal Society and was duly elected on 1 December 1718, on the grounds of his interest in antiquities and history.

To ensure he would never be forgotten, in May 1717 Newton presented a portrait of himself by Charles Jervas to the Royal Society, to celebrate the publication of a second English edition of *Opticks,* along with eight new queries. Jervas was an Irish painter and portrayed Sir Isaac wearing – unusually for him – a long, elaborately curled brown wig and a crimson gown: his favourite colour. He was now aged seventy-four.

The year 1719 saw two further significant events in Sir Isaac's life: the publication of a second Latin edition of the *Opticks* and, on the last day of the decade, 31 December, John Flamsteed, the Astronomer Royal, died. Newton must surely have breathed a sigh of relief. His worst detractors and rivals in science – Robert Hooke, Gottfried Wilhelm Leibniz and now John Flamsteed – were all gone. He had outlived his enemies and could have the final word in every argument. As he entered the 1720s, Newton's position was unrivalled and unassailable. In England at least, he truly was the Grand Old Man of Science.

Chapter 10

THE 1720s: THE GRAND OLD MAN OF SCIENCE

Sir Isaac Newton was now famous, well known at the royal court and had standards to maintain in London society. His lifestyle was expensive and he made numerous generous gifts, especially to his relatives, friends and the Royal Society. Such beneficence required money to spare, so a brief look at his finances is worthwhile.

Money Matters
Around 1720, Newton's earnings at the mint were above £2,000 per year, although they fluctuated considerably, depending on the volume of coinage production. Dividends paid on his investments were probably bringing in another £1,500 per year. At the time, a female domestic servant might be paid as little as £2 per year, rising to £15 per annum for an experienced housekeeper.[1] Male wages were always higher: a footman receiving £8 per year and a coachman between £12 and £26, all with food, lodging and clothing supplied by their employer. Non-domestic workers, having to provide all the necessities for themselves and their families, might earn from £15 to £20 per year but this was a low wage and, realistically, an income of £40 was needed to keep a family. The 'middling' sort – gentlemen – required at least £100 per year to live comfortably and someone with an income of £500 was reckoned to be 'rich'. The First Lord of the Treasury had

an income of approximately £4,000, so his receiving of at least £3,500 per year made Newton one of the super rich of his time. Unfortunately, he did not keep detailed financial accounts, so little is known of his expenditure and purchases but his puritanical leanings would suggest that he was usually careful with money. He was familiar with the London financial markets and although he often conducted his business through agents, he also carried out some of his transactions in person.[2]

The Bank of England Archive reveals that Newton began investing in Bank stock in 1709 and two years later this had grown to 1,500 stocks. He continued adding to his investments with the Bank of England until he had 6,000 stocks by October 1715. He then sold 4,000 in December 1716 and the remaining 2,000 in November 1719, making a good profit on each occasion.[3] At the time, Britain's national debt of approximately £50 million at the end of 1719, consisted of about £6.6 million owed to the Bank of England and the East India Company, almost £12 million to the South Sea Company and the rest, about £32 million, directly to the public. Of this £32 million, about half was held in the form of 'irredeemables' administered by the Exchequer. They paid fixed amounts per year until their termination with no return of the principal sum. Most of the capital of the irredeemables that existed in 1720 was in the form of ninety-nine-year annuities issued between 1705 and 1709.

The Bank of England had been set up in 1694 to finance the national debt. The East India Company was almost a century older, having received its royal charter in 1600 with the intention of financing and profiting from mercantile ventures in India and the Far East. The South Sea Company started out as an innovative experiment. Founded in 1711 as a British joint-stock company, this public–private partnership was created in the hope of consolidating and reducing the cost of the national debt. The company was also granted a monopoly to trade with South America and nearby islands. Officially incorporated as 'The Governor and Company of the Merchants of Great Britain, trading to the South Seas and other parts of America, and for the encouragement of Fishing', from the beginning, there was actually no chance that any such trading would happen because Britain was involved in the War of the Spanish Succession and Spain controlled South America. Even so, the company's stock took off as it expanded its operations dealing in government debt. Investing in South Sea stock was more profitable than in Bank of England stock in the 1710s, although not as lucrative as in the East India Company. Newton was an early, if wary, investor in South Sea stock, adding to his holdings gradually and becoming increasingly bold as his gamble proved successful. By 1720, he held at least 12,000 South Sea stocks.

Early in 1720, Newton cashed in most of his South Sea holdings for a profit of about £20,000 but a few weeks later he reinvested all that money, repurchasing the same stock at twice the price. This seems a strange thing to do and he could not have realised the shaky foundations underlying the company's operations. The founders of the scheme were using their advanced knowledge of when the national debt was to be consolidated in order to make large profits from purchasing debt beforehand – insider trading, in other words. Politicians were persuaded with immense bribes to support the various Acts of Parliament necessary for the scheme to function and company money was used to deal in its own shares by lending to individuals, on the condition they used it to purchase shares, driving up their value. All might have been well if the company had actually made substantial profits from trade with South America but since that trade was non-existent, the whole scheme was bound to fail eventually.

In the summer of 1720, the South Sea Bubble burst. Many people were ruined by the share collapse and the country's economy was adversely affected. A parliamentary inquiry was held to discover the causes of the crash. A number of politicians were disgraced and people found to have profited unlawfully from the company had their assets confiscated in proportion to their gains. However, the South Sea Company was restructured and continued to operate for another century but its collapse meant its rival, the Bank of England, confirmed its position as banker to the British government and The Bubble Act of 1720 forbade the creation of any further joint-stock companies without a royal charter to authorise them.

Newton lost a substantial amount of money, in spite of his brilliance and knowledge of the financial markets. Having begun cautiously, making considerable gains early on, he then put all his funds into the South Sea venture at its peak. His optimism was at odds with many of his fellow investors and he even continued to expect an eventually profitable outcome throughout the initial collapse of the Bubble. His mathematical genius did not assist him with sound investment insight. He is supposed to have excused the failure on the grounds that he could not 'calculate ... the madness of people'. But perhaps the 'madness' was his own because another early investor, Thomas Guy, had started cashing in his huge profits before the collapse, just when Newton changed his mind about doing the same and put the money back in. Was Guy more financially prescient than Newton? Another investor who liquidated his assets in the South Sea Company before things went so badly wrong was George Frederic Handel.

The German-born musician and composer arrived in London from Germany in 1710. Handel invested in the South Sea Company, buying stock probably in 1715–16 and sold some time between 1717 and 1719. It is likely that he made a considerable profit, cashing in just before the value reached its peak and a year before its spectacular collapse. Handel continued to make sound financial investments in the future, especially in Bank of England stock. By 24 June 1723, Newton held 10,000 of South Sea stock once again; Handel a more modest 300. Newton also became a stockholder in the Bank of England on 27 January 1724 when he acquired 11,000 stock and an additional 1,000 of Bank stock on three subsequent occasions, bringing the final balance to 14,000, which, when he died, was the largest part of his estate. It is interesting to compare the extent of financial risk taken by a man towards the close of his career with the restrained investments of one at the beginning of his.

A Musical Genius

George Frederic Handel, whose compositions include *The Water Music, Music for the Royal Fireworks* and *The Messiah*, came to the court of Queen Anne at the age of twenty-five. It is possible that Sir Isaac might have met Handel at the royal court although, if they did, the meeting of two geniuses has, sadly, gone unrecorded. Had they held a conversation, they would have discovered much in common from their childhood days. Handel was born in 1685 in Halle upon Saale, then part of Brandenburg-Prussia. His father, Georg Handel, barber-surgeon to the court of Brandenburg, was aged sixty-three when George Frederic was born. All Handel's older siblings followed their father into the medical profession and it seems likely that Georg intended his youngest boy to do the same.

Although Halle was famed for its musicians, Georg, as a strict Lutheran, had no interest in the subject whatsoever. When young George showed an aptitude for music, his father not only forbade any instruments in the house, he banned the boy from visiting any friends who might possess such frivolous items. So, just like Newton, his parent intended him to pursue a career that was not in the youngster's best interests and would be a waste of his supreme talent. Also like Newton, there is sparse information concerning George's early education. Their respective genius was established in their early twenties, both would eventually settle in London – Handel at 25 Brook Street in Mayfair – and neither ever married. But what of music; did Newton have any musical inclination?

According to Brindle, 'music theory has no axiomatic foundation in modern mathematics, yet the basis of musical sound can be described mathematically (in acoustics) and exhibits a remarkable array of number properties'.[4] Therefore, although there is no record of Newton enjoying music for its own sake, the theories behind it may have had an appeal. In an age when music was one of few entertainments available to all, he must have listened to performances at some time and did discuss music in various contexts. There is no mention of him as a lover of music but he was certainly interested in its underlying principles and the idea of harmony throughout the universe. A notebook from early in his career and now in Cambridge University Library (Add. MS4000) reveals his interest in the mathematical division of the musical scale and in the *Principia* he describes the propagation of sound through the air.[5] In doing so, he prepared the way for the mathematical study of music; the science of acoustics. Newton was always intrigued by the number 7 and believed, as mentioned earlier, there was a direct correlation between the colour spectrum – which he perceived as seven distinct colours – and the musical diatonic scale of seven notes, doh to te, the repeated 'doh' making an octave. Headed *Of Musick*, the notebook, dated to the 1660s and well before Robert Hooke wrote on the same idea in 1672, contains a full-length paper on the subject.[6] Newton described music in ways now considered unusual, as having 'sweetness' and 'gratefulness' – hardly scientific terms.

In his *Opticks* (1704), Newton suggested the spectrum was governed by the same ratios that underlay music and although his theory was subsequently discredited, throughout the eighteenth century, both scientists and musicians were keen to explore the idea of a universal law applied to both the natural world and music. The subject could have provided common ground for an intriguing conversation between the Grand Old Man of Science and the young genius of music, although Sir Isaac had this to say of his only known attendance at the opera: 'The first act I heard with pleasure, the second stretched my patience, at the third I ran away.'[7]

Handel would go on to do great things for British music. In the summer of 1727, just a few months after Sir Isaac's death, George I died and was succeeded by his son. Handel composed a number of pieces for the coronation of George II, among them the famous anthem *Zadok the Priest,* a piece which has been played at the coronation of every British monarch ever since.

A New Astronomer Royal

With the passing of John Flamsteed on 31 December 1719, the post of Astronomer Royal at Greenwich Observatory fell vacant. Aware that Flamsteed was unwell, as early 11 December strings were being pulled, suggestions made and people of note being manipulated regarding a replacement. It appears that

Dr Richard Mead, mentioned earlier, had had a few words with his patron, Charles Spencer, the third Earl of Sunderland and First Lord of the Treasury, because on that date a friend wrote to Mead: 'I must heartily congratulate you upon the success you have had in behalf of Dr Halley.' Was Edmund Halley's appointment to the post decided upon at least three weeks prior to Flamsteed's death? If it was, it must be hoped that no one divulged the fact to the man on his deathbed, since his replacement by the younger man he had come to despise would have caused great distress. Yet Flamsteed was intelligent and probably realised that Halley was the best man for the job, even if he could not approve the choice.

By 9 January 1720, it was official: Edmund Halley was the new Astronomer Royal. The Earl of Macclesfield and, most likely, Sir Isaac Newton had also influenced the royal appointment. Halley wasted no time in moving to Greenwich. Flamsteed's widow was told to leave immediately and took all the astronomical instruments with her, claiming they were her husband's personal property. Halley didn't argue: the equipment was old and mostly outdated anyway. He applied to the Crown and was granted £500 by the Board of Ordnance to purchase new instruments, although it was four years before the money actually materialised. By which time, it was a re-imbursement since Halley had equipped the observatory out of his own pocket with better and far more accurate instruments. The only item lacking by 1724 was a huge wall-mounted quadrant known as a mural arc. Using the grant, Halley commissioned a new arc to be constructed by instrument maker Jonathan Sisson, to a design by renowned clockmaker George Graham who adjusted and calibrated it at a cost of more than £200. In addition, the masons were paid £42 17s to fix it to the wall. Surprisingly, with so much state-of-the-art equipment, it is said that Halley still preferred to use a telescope designed and built by Robert Hooke twenty years earlier.[8] This instrument was set up at Greenwich in 1721 and was of such quality that it remained in use until 1774. Hooke would have been delighted; Newton less so, if he knew of it.

Statistics, Longevity and Life Expectancy

During his Grand Tour of Europe in the 1690s, never a man to waste a moment, Edmund Halley had turned his attentions to the statistics of population. He had previously compiled figures comparing the areas and population density of London and Paris but took the opportunity during his tour to look at the figures for Breslau (then in Germany but now Wroclaw in Poland). He believed Breslau had a more stable population, whereas in London and Paris the demographic was distorted by the influx of immigrants. He drew up tables of births and deaths from church registers in Breslau, noting in each case the age at death. From this, he worked out the statistics of life expectancy for its citizens. Back home, his use of statistics to predict the likelihood of age at death was put to use in assessing the relative premiums for life assurance and, since then, similar tables are still used today, albeit with the aid of computer analysis.

However, it was a fact that Newton and Halley lived in a young person's world. In London, perhaps a quarter of the population was of apprenticeship age. No wonder the authorities were anxious whenever the apprentices became inclined to riot – as had happened when Parliament had banned Christmas – if that meant up to 25 per cent of Londoners were up in arms. Apprentice riots continued to be a good citizen's nightmare into the nineteenth century.

As for Sir Isaac Newton, his longevity would have confounded statistical predictions, as would that of his colleagues in the Royal Society: Sir Christopher Wren and Edmund Halley himself. Wren died in 1723 at the grand age of ninety; Halley would live on until 1742, dying peacefully after enjoying a glass of wine and seated in his favourite armchair, aged eighty-five. As Newton's health began to fail, he spent time at Cranbury Park in Hampshire with his niece but must often have returned to London since he continued to preside over a good many of the Royal Society's weekly meetings and regularly oversaw work at the Royal Mint. In 1722, he suffered an attack of 'the stone' in the kidney that caused him great pain.

On 7 March that year, perhaps realising his own mortality, Newton had a considerable discussion with John Conduitt, telling him stories of his earlier life, including the tale of the famous falling apple. As a result, Conduitt became one of the principal sources of information about Sir Isaac's childhood and university years, being the only source for certain events unrecorded elsewhere. Newton also burned boxfuls of manuscripts and what a loss to scientists and historians that may have been – we shall never know. Later in 1722, Newton suffered an inflammation of the lungs, moving to Kensington in south London for a while, where it was hoped the cleaner country air would improve his health.

The respite seems to have proved a success because we know Sir Isaac returned to his home in St Martin's Street but he was forced to slow down. A violent cough and another bout of inflammation of the lungs occurred in 1725 and meant a return to Kensington, but the benefits could not keep him from frequently journeying back to the city. At the end of March 1726, he oversaw the publication of the third edition of the *Principia*. He remained active in his role as President of the Royal Society, attending meetings as regularly as his increasing frailty allowed. On 2 March 1727, he presided for the last time. On the following day he became extremely unwell and suffered a great deal of pain. Although he returned to Kensington once more, hoping to affect a recovery, by 18 March his health had collapsed. His physicians surmised that the kidney stone had been shaken loose 'by the great motion and fatigue of his last journey to London'. Conduitt recalled that although the spasms of pain caused sweat to run down his face, Newton did not cry out but endured stoically and silently. William Stukeley visited his old friend and described 'the bed under him and the very room shook with his agonys' (*sic*). Despite his suffering, when offered the ministrations of a Church of England clergyman and the consolation of the holy sacrament, he refused; this was his first and only open declaration of his Arian beliefs. On 20 March, he died at Kensington in the early hours of the morning: he was aged eighty-four.

No time was wasted. On hearing the news that Sir Isaac was gone, the Government immediately appointed John Conduitt as the new Master of the Mint but, on a more respectful note, arrangements were in hand for a state funeral for the Grand Old

Man of Science. On the day of his demise, there should have been a meeting of the Royal Society but their minute book records 'The Chair being Vacant by the Death of Sir Isaac Newton there was no Meeting this Day'. There was no expression of regret nor acclamation of the departed: just one cryptic sentence without explanation. On 28 March, Newton's body was taken to lie in state in the Jerusalem Chamber in the Palace of Westminster, like a monarch.

On 4 April, he was buried in Westminster Abbey, no matter that his religious beliefs were heretical. His grave by the choir screen bears the Latin inscription *Hic depositum est, quod mortale fuit Isaaci Newtoni;* 'Here lies that which was mortal of Isaac Newton'. As far as the establishment was concerned, that secret went with him, into the grave. This is the account of Sir Isaac Newton's funeral as it appeared in *The London Gazette*, (issue no. 6569):

Whitehall, April 4
On the 28th past the Corpse of Sir Isaac Newton lay in State in the Jerusalem Chamber, and was buried from thence in Westminster-Abbey near the Entry into the Choir. The Pall was supported by the Lord High Chancellour, the Dukes of Montrose and Roxburgh, and the Earls of Pembroke, Sussex and Macclesfield, being Fellows of the Royal Society. The Honourable Sir Michael Newton, Knight of the Bath, was Chief Mourner, and was followed by some other Relations, and several eminent Persons intimately acquainted with the Deceased. The Office was performed by the Bishop of Rochester attended by the Prebends and Choir.

His Majesty has been graciously pleased to grant the Employment of Master and Worker of the Mint, which he enjoyed above 27 years, to his Nephew John Conduitt, Esquire.[9]

Sir Michael Newton, mentioned in the newspaper report as 'Chief Mourner', was said to be Sir Isaac's third cousin once removed. This would mean the two men shared a great-great-grandfather. Michael's great grandfather was Thomas Newton of (variously) Gonerby/Gunnerby/Gunwarley in Lincolnshire; his grandfather was Sir John Newton, 2nd Baronet of Barrs Court in Gloucestershire. To be related as reported, Thomas Newton must have been a brother to Sir Isaac's father, Isaac Newton senior. The family tree of Thomas states simply 'siblings unknown' and the birth dates of Thomas and Isaac senior stretch the possibility of a fraternal relationship. It may be that Sir Michael was not related to the precise degree with Sir Isaac as given in the report but his Lincolnshire ancestry makes a familial connection of some kind quite likely. Perhaps he was simply the most illustrious of the relatives able to attend the state funeral and provided an element of grandeur among the rather homely Newtons that were the great man's closer relations.

Among others of note attending Isaac Newton's funeral may have been the French philosopher, Voltaire. Coming from an autocratic nation, Voltaire was impressed that the English could bury a commoner with all due honour and reverence the French would have reserved for a king or a cardinal. The Frenchman was certainly in London on the occasion and in writing about Newton afterwards in his *Letters on England* declared that he 'was never sensible to any passion, was not subject to the common frailties of mankind, nor had any commerce with women – a circumstance which was assured me by the physician and surgeon who attended him in his last moments'. So, did Newton die a virgin? He was rumoured to have been engaged briefly, according to William Stukeley who wrote on the subject in a letter to Richard Mead soon after Newton's death. Towards the end of the eighteenth century, the mathematician Charles Hutton made a collection of anecdotes and items of oral tradition concerning some of his predecessors in the philosophical community in his *A Mathematical and Philosophical Dictionary* (volume 2, published in 1796). On page 100, referring to Newton, he states:

> There do not appear to be any sufficient reason for his never marrying, if he had an inclination so to do. It is much more likely that he had a constitutional indifference to the state, and even to the sex in general.

He certainly never wed, in which case he treated his niece, Catherine Barton, and her husband, John Conduitt, as his close family, giving all his papers into their hands. Much of his estate had already been shared out among his relatives before his death and this may be why he never drew up a will. Unlike both his parents, Newton chose to die intestate; it was not as if his death came suddenly nor was his mind unsound. Visitors reported that he was rational and lucid right up until he fell into a coma a matter of hours before his death. Why did he not see a need to write a will? Since he did not do so, Woolsthorpe Manor went to his nearest male relative, John Newton, who mortgaged it and had frittered away the house and lands in a few years. Perhaps his original home meant so little to Sir Isaac that he did not care what became of the manor, which is sad because most of his stupendous ideas had evolved there, in the years 1665–66.

Sir Isaac's Legacy

Sir Isaac's failure to make a will does give historians access to an intriguing document that might not otherwise exist: an inventory of his belongings. A 'True and Perfect Inventary (*sic*) of all and Singular the Goods, Chattels and Credits of Sir Isaac Newton' was made in accordance with the legal requirements of the Prerogative Court of Canterbury. Five commissioners were appointed on 18 April 1727, compiled the inventory between 21 and 27 April and handed it in, completed, on 5 May. They were named as Valens Comyn, Thomas Ward, Thomas Money, William Carr and Fletcher Gyles. In the form of a detailed list, the inventory was written on skins of vellum approximately 5 inches wide (12.5 cm) and 30 inches (75.0 cm) long, stitched together to create a length of 17 feet (5.2 metres), and was discovered, buried in the archives, by Lieutenant-Colonel Richard de Villamil. Villamil published it in his book *Newton: The Man* (1932), with a foreword written by Albert Einstein as Professor of Physics at the P. R. Akademie der Wissenschaften.

The inventory concerns Newton's house in St Martin's Street and contains sufficient information that, as Villamil says, 'we could easily re-furnish every room ... as it was at the time of his death.'

From settees to curtains, chocolate pots to cooking equipment, to the sedan chair he used so reluctantly, kept in the stable; these tell the story of a man who, despite his wealth and social position, did not purchase items just for show. Luxurious living seems to have been alien to Newton's puritanical nature and one pair of silver candlesticks is the only thing that might be considered above and beyond the basic necessities. The furniture is sparse and plain in an age when beautiful chests of drawers and elegantly carved tables were all the fashion. In fact, in his bedroom, there is no means of storage for Newton's clothes recorded on the list, although a gilded mirror hung on the chimney breast and there were four pictures. Jugs with matching basins were a frequent bedroom accessory for personal hygiene; there are none listed but 'four pales (*sic*) and washing tubs'.

What is termed 'Mrs Conduitt's' room seems more comfortably furnished with a bedstead, featherbed and mattress, quilts, blankets and pillows. There are two storage chests, a small screen and a chest of drawers, two mirrors, six chairs, a folding table, a close stool (commode) and a clock. However, since other items are described as 'an old sattee (*sic*)', 'two pair of old druggit (coarse woollen cloth) window curtains', 'two old maps and some old china (Chinese) hangings', the room does not suggest any degree of opulence and the contents were valued by the commissioners at £38 18s 6d.

Newton seems to have used two rooms for his work. In the 'fore Garret' he kept mathematical instruments and chemical glassware, an oak chest of drawers, two writing desks and stuff we might describe as 'junk'. His main 'workroom' was up two flights of stairs at the front of the house and its contents are worth listing in full because they provide a picture of Newton's great interest in maps and the form of the world towards the end of his life, as well as the things that surrounded him as he worked:

Item, a walnut tree cabinet and writing desk with drawers, 210 prints, 40 articles in Dutch in 19 sheets, a book of maps and 6 others (?), 3 old weather glasses, a large table with drawers, 6 cases of shelves (presumably, these are the bookcases mentioned below), a pair of steps, a small piece of tapestry and some Irish stitch hangings, 3 globes, a copper plate, a silver watch, a Bath mettle case of instruments, a shagreen case of the same, a small penknife, an embroidered purse, 2 plaistered heads and 2 small pictures... valued at £22 4s.

To explain some of these items, a weather glass was a simple barometer, consisting of a sealed transparent container with an open spout, shaped rather like that of a teapot but calibrated. The glass was partially filled with coloured water that rose up the spout during times of low atmospheric pressure and fell when the pressure rose. Thus, a weather glass was a basic indicator of the weather conditions likely on a given day. Irish stitch hangings were woollen-embroidered linen, sometimes customised to fit the room; 'flame-stitch' designs were especially popular during the seventeenth century. Bath metal is a copper and zinc alloy. Shagreen can be either sharkskin or rough, untanned leather – the former would seem more likely.

Newton appears to have been obsessed by a single colour: crimson. Crimson curtains, bedcovers, wall hangings and a crimson 'sattee' in the dining room. Perhaps, quite simply, crimson was simply his favourite colour. It would certainly have provided an illusion of warmth in the days of coal fires and draughty rooms. There is also a close association of that particular hue with various alchemical processes, although Villamil suggests that living with so much red in an 'atmosphere of crimson', may have been a contributing factor to Newton's irritability in his later years. This is possible because the red dye contained mercury, as mentioned before, and added to the legacy of so many alchemical experiments, low levels of mercury poisoning, evidenced in the modern analysis of his hair snipped off and kept as mementoes after his death, could certainly cause this symptom.

Turning to monetary concerns, the commissioners noted that Newton had £18,130 in Bank of England Stock, £10,200 in South Sea Company Stocks and Annuities and cash which he had given into the care of John Conduitt amounted to £1,711 and 1 penny.

The salary and miscellaneous money owed to him for his work as Master of the Mint totalled £518 3s 9d, plus promissory notes valued at £201 4s and a receipt for 12 guineas paid for books not yet received brought Sir Isaac's estate to an appraised value of £31,821 16s 10d. He was a wealthy man.

Frugal in other matters, Newton's one extravagance – though he considered it a necessity, no doubt – was books. The inventory was concerned with quantities and qualities and records: '362 books in Folio, 477 in Quarto, 1057 in Octavo, duodecimo and 24mo, together with above one hundredweight of pamphlets and wast(e) books'. Waste books were notebooks – the whole weighing 50.8 kilogrammes! The total of 1,896 books were kept in six bookcases and valued at £270. What the inventory did not require was a list of titles, which would have provided a further insight as to Newton's work and interests. However, all was not lost to future historians and biographers. The library was 'pounced on' by one of Newton's neighbours, John Huggins, warden of the Fleet Prison, who paid £300 for it in July 1727. He sent the books to his son, Charles, Rector of Chinnor, a parish near Oxford. Charles pasted his book plate into every volume. Huggins' successor as rector, Dr James Musgrave, paid him £400 for the books. 'Huggins' list' in conjunction with Musgrave's catalogue and what Villamil terms 'a supplementary list' means that the titles of books from Newton's library can be identified with a fair degree of certainty.

There are far too many books to list here but, as examples, there are twenty different titles by Robert Boyle, of whom he approved, yet only one by René Descartes, with whom he disagreed on certain basic principles. There are three books by his old mentor Isaac Barrow and one by John Flamsteed, two books by Robert Hooke published posthumously, one by Leibnitz but nothing by Edmund Halley, which is surprising. Classical works are present, by writers from Sophocles to Tacitus, a Latin dictionary, mathematical treatises by the likes of continental Newtonians Gravesande and l'Hôpital, along with histories and travelogues, George Ripley's alchemical works, plus numerous books concerned with Church history, scriptural interpretation and, of course, copies of every edition of his own publications. Newton's *Chronology of Ancient Kingdoms Amended* (a revised version of that lent to Queen Caroline) published in 1728 after his death, was added to the library by either Huggins or Musgrave to keep the list complete.

Among the hundredweight of papers included in the inventory were a number of tracts concerning the Longitude Problem, written by numerous authors, that Newton probably read before submitting his detailed summary to the Board of Longitude prior to being co-opted onto it. His choice of titles is broad and somewhat eclectic but not a single volume could be construed as 'light reading'; every book served his work and none was purely for pleasure. The library is a reflection of its owner's puritanical ideals.

A Posthumous Reputation
The English poet, Alexander Pope, wrote this famous epitaph to Newton:

> Nature and nature's laws lay hid in night;
> God said 'Let Newton be' and all was light.

The French mathematician, Joseph-Louis Lagrange, once said that Newton was the greatest genius who ever lived and also 'the most fortunate, for we cannot find more than once a system of the world to establish'. Such statements raised Newton to virtual scientific sainthood and, in his own way, he was relatively modest about his achievements. Some of his most famous quotations appear to demonstrate this:

> I do not know what I may appear to the world, but to myself
> I seem to have been only like a boy playing on the sea-shore,
> and diverting myself in now and then finding a smoother
> pebble or a prettier shell than ordinary, whilst the great ocean
> of truth lay all undiscovered before me.

In a letter he wrote to Robert Hooke, Newton said: 'If I have seen further it is by standing on the shoulders of Giants.' Again, this sounds humble but can be taken in two ways. At first reading, it seems as though Newton is being modest about his own achievements, merely extending the work done by his predecessors, the 'Giants' of philosophy and science of earlier times. However, since the unfortunate Hooke was of tiny physical stature, might the unwritten sub-clause 'but not on your shoulders' be inferred? In which case, Newton was insulting Hooke. As Brooks said of this quotation, 'It is largely humbug. Newton was hardly humble, and it would be just as true to say that he achieved greatness by stamping on the shoulders of giants. When others, such as Robert Hooke and Gottfried Leibniz, made breakthroughs in fields he was also researching, Newton fought ferociously to deny them credit for their work.'[10]

One amusingly ironic Newton quotation reads: 'Tact is the knack of making a point without making an enemy.' Did Sir Isaac truly say that? At the time when Newton was determined to have from John Flamsteed, the Astronomer Royal, all the data the latter had collated for the forthcoming catalogue of stars before he was ready to give it, discussions between them became very heated, as Flamsteed told a friend in a letter:

At this he [Newton] fired and called me all the ill names, puppy etc., that he could think of. All I returned was I put him in mind of his passion, desired him to govern it, and keep his temper. This made him rage worse...[11]

Flamsteed also had this to say:

Sly Newton had still more to do, and was ready at coining new excuses and pretences to cover his disingenuous and malicious practices. I had none but very honest and honourable designs in my mind: I met his cunning forecasts with sincere and honest answers, and thereby frustrated not a few of his malicious designs... I have had another contest with the President (Sir Isaac Newton) of the Royal Society, who had formed a plot to make my instruments theirs; and sent for me to a Committee, where only himself and two physicians

(Dr Sloane, and another as little skilful as himself) were present. The President ran himself into a great heat, and very indecent passion.[12]

Newton could be utterly tactless with anyone who thwarted or upset him: diplomacy was never his strong point. He was always determined upon total accuracy in his calculations and yet, in the *Principia,* he was not above massaging the numbers to prove a point. It was fortunate then that, at the time, few could comprehend the figures sufficiently to query the results and, of those who could, none dared.

The French philosopher Voltaire spread the word of Newton's great achievements across Europe. His book, *Eléments de la philosophie de Newton,* was the work in which Voltaire is said to have taken most pride, exaggerating the man's virtues so he seemed more saintly than human:

Sir Isaac, during the long course of years he enjoyed, was never sensible to any passion, was not subject to the common frailties of mankind, nor ever had any commerce with women.[13]

Flamsteed wouldn't have agreed about the lack of passion and common frailties.

However, Sir Isaac also had a softer side and was known for his acts of charity. Less fortunate members of his family received generous handouts, as did total strangers who sent him begging letters. Those who held out an empty hand to him in the street were rarely disappointed; he took his Christian beliefs seriously.

After Newton's death, his niece's husband, John Conduitt, had the unenviable task of sorting through all his papers. His correspondence, notes and manuscripts are estimated to contain 10 million words – about 150 novel-length books.[14] Besides the reams of scientific and mathematical writing, there is much that Conduitt wanted to keep from public scrutiny. Newton's scrupulously detailed analysis of the Bible, his decoding of the prophecies in *The Book of Daniel* and *The Revelation of St John the Divine* – and especially his rejection of the doctrine of the Holy Trinity – were best kept private. Conduitt feared that his hero would become reviled as a heretic. So for 250 years, few knew of this side of Newton's life and it was not until the 1960s that some of the more controversial papers were published.

John Conduitt had attempted to catalogue and edit the papers, intending to write a biography of his wife's uncle. At the time, biographical works were most unusual but Conduitt wanted to be certain the public received the 'corrected' version, revealing the great man's life 'of labour, patience, humility, temperance & piety without any tincture of vice'.[15] Sadly, Conduitt died in 1737, before the biography was begun but his extensive notes made in Newton's last years, referring back to his youth, anecdotes and reminiscences of those who knew him best, provided posterity with most of the familiar stories. Perhaps the most famous is that of the falling apple that supposedly led to his theories on gravity, or Newton's less well known, humble assertion: 'If I have ever made any valuable discoveries, it has been due more to patient attention than to any other talent.'

Conduitt need not have feared; his uncle's reputation was assured. Four years after Newton's burial in a grave in front of the choir screen in Westminster Abbey, a grand monument was erected nearby, north of the entrance to the choir. The monument was designed by the architect William Kent and sculpted in white and grey marble by Michael Rysbrack. It was in place by 1731, although the decorative arch that now encloses the monument was a later addition by Edward Blore when he remodelled the choir screen in 1834.

At the base is a lengthy Latin inscription which supports a sarcophagus upon which a reclining, classically draped figure of Newton rests, his elbow on a pile of books of his works. The figure points at a scroll of calculations held by two cherubs. Behind the figure is a relief panel with cherubs using other Newton-related objects, including a prism, a telescope and items concerned with his work at the Royal Mint. In the background is a pyramid supporting a celestial globe of the heavens with the signs of the Zodiac, the constellations, and with the path marked of the comet of 1680. On top of the globe sits the figure of Astronomy leaning upon a book. Translated from the Latin, the inscription at the base reads:

> Here is buried Isaac Newton, Knight, who by a strength of mind almost divine, and mathematical principles peculiarly his own, explored the course and figures of the planets, the paths of comets, the tides of the sea, the dissimilarities in rays of light, and, what no other scholar has previously imagined, the properties of the colours thus produced. Diligent, sagacious and faithful in his expositions of nature, antiquity and the holy Scriptures, he vindicated by his philosophy the majesty of God mighty and good, and expressed the simplicity of the Gospel in his manners. Mortals rejoice that there has existed such and so great an ornament of the human race! He was born on 25th December 1642, and died on 20th March 1726.[16]

With such an epitaph, though not entirely truthful, Sir Isaac's reputation was unimpeachable. The poet, William Wordsworth, wrote of his thoughts on seeing the monument in 1850:

> And from my pillow, looking forth by light
> Of moon or favouring stars, I could behold
> The antechapel where the statue stood
> Of Newton, with his prism and silent face,
> The marble index of a mind for ever
> Voyaging through strange seas of Thought, alone.[17]

Albert Einstein kept a picture of Isaac Newton on the wall of his study, flanked by pictures of other scientist-mathematicians he particularly admired and found inspiring: the Englishman Michael Faraday and the Scotsman James Clerk Maxwell. And Newton's influence still prevails among today's scientists. In 1999, an opinion poll of 100 leading physicists voted Einstein the 'greatest physicist ever', with Newton the runner-up, while a similar survey of physicists by the website PhysicsWeb gave the top position to Newton. A survey conducted in 2005 by the Royal Society reckoned Newton had the edge over Einstein in having had the greater effect on the history of science and making the larger overall contribution to knowledge.

From 1978 until 1988, an image of Newton designed by Harry Ecclestone appeared on £1 bank notes issued by the Bank of England – the last £1 notes ever issued before being replaced by coins. Newton was shown holding a book and accompanied by a telescope, a prism and a map of the Solar System. (The Bank of England announced in 2019 that the next £50 bank note will show one of Newton's greatest successors in the field of mathematics: Alan Turing, hero of World War II code breaking and recognised as the father of computers; it is expected to be issued by the end of 2021.) In 1995, a huge bronze statue of Newton by Eduardo Paolozzi was constructed and now dominates the square at the entrance to the new British Library, the neighbouring building to St Pancras Station in London. Based on an etching by William Blake, the statue shows a titanic Newton, armed with a pair of compasses, staring at an apple at his feet.

Grantham in Lincolnshire has a grand statue of its local scholar in the centre of town; a bust of their most famous alumnus adorns Trinity College Library and many other scientific institutions and museums. His portraits hang at the Royal Society and the National Portrait Gallery in London. His likeness appears as the frontispiece in numerous scientific school books and more biographies have been written about him than any other scientist.

One thing is certain: the scrawny little Christmas baby, born in a Lincolnshire backwater to a mother who begrudged him any education, went on to amaze and baffle the scientific world of his day and to inspire mankind in its endless quest for knowledge. Sir Isaac Newton, the man, will never be forgotten – but how have his discoveries changed the science of today?

Chapter 11

SCIENCE AFTER ISAAC NEWTON

Early in the seventeenth century, Francis Bacon had stated that the purpose of science was to 'put Nature on the rack' and force her to divulge the answers to mankind's questions. He was foreseeing a new age of knowledge, brought about by vigorous and rigorous scientific thinking, burrowing below what was readily visible on the surface to search out the secrets of Nature. Such methods have changed the way we look at the natural world and think about life itself and they continue to do so. Science has come to dominate our world in ways that Bacon and his contemporaries cannot have imagined. Cause and effect is a crucial feature of science. If Newton had not asked why that apple – apocryphal or not – fell to the ground, the study of gravity might have been left to a later age. As Hermann Bondi said in an article in 1988:

> The landscape [of science since the seventeenth century] has been so totally changed, the ways of thinking have been so deeply affected, that it is very hard to get hold of what it was like before... It is very hard to realize how total a change in outlook he [Newton] has produced. [1]

Despite Voltaire, Gravesande and others promoting Newtonian ideas on the Continent, French scientists were reluctant to abandon some of the theories of their own philosophical hero,

René Descartes. Cartesians claimed the Earth was egg shaped; Newton had said it was oblate, broader at the equator and squashed at the poles. In 1733, the French Académie des Sciences determined to settle the argument, sending expeditions north to Lapland and south to Peru, equipped with telescopes, quadrants and measuring instruments. It took a decade to complete the survey, which was able to confirm Newton's claim as being correct.

Edmund Halley used Newtonian concepts to calculate and predict the path and the return of a particular comet, daring to make his prophesy public. The prediction of the comet's return every seventy-six years proved true and the heavenly body is now known as Halley's Comet.

A Need for God?

While many scientists embraced Newton's ideas, poets often reviled him. In his narrative poem, 'Lamia', published in 1820, John Keats had this to say, referring to Newton's philosophy:

> Do not all charms fly
> At the mere touch of cold philosophy?
> There was an awful rainbow once in heaven:
> We know her woof, her texture; she is given
> In the dull catalogue of common things.
> Philosophy will clip an Angel's wings,
> Conquer all mysteries by rule and line,
> Empty the haunted air, and gnomèd mine –
> Unweave a rainbow, as it erewhile made
> The tender-person'd Lamia melt into a shade.

In Keats's opinion, rational science had turned the beauties and wonders of nature into a soulless system of laws and calculations, reducing the brilliance of the rainbow to a mathematical phenomenon. William Blake, poet and artist, was not a supporter of anything 'Newtonian', so it is ironic that Blake's engraving of Newton was the inspiration for the huge bronze statue outside the British Library. Blake blamed Newton for replacing imagination with reason; mystery with mathematics.[2] Unfortunately for some, this same rationale seemed to remove God from the equations.

Newton's personal reason for wanting to elucidate the mysteries of the universe was in order to better understand the purpose of God as its creator. He never doubted the existence of God, so it is a solemn realisation to discover he achieved the opposite; in some instances, appearing to disprove any need for an Ultimate Creator. Newton never saw the evidence in that way. To him, God had set the divine, cosmic mechanism in motion, to function according to the physical laws Newton had revealed and explained mathematically. But that did not make God redundant: He could still intervene, tweak the machinery, cause a miracle to happen, if He so willed it. God remained a necessity in Newton's universe, ever keeping watch. What was more, Newton was well aware of his own limitations. In a fragment of manuscript headed 'Principles of Philosophy', dated to around 1703, he noted:

> To explain all nature is too difficult a task for any one man or even for any one age. 'Tis much better to do a little with certainty & leave the rest for others that come after you.[3]

Since then, scientists and writers such as Richard Dawkins have disproved the existence of God to their own satisfaction, seeing the cosmos as an intricate system which, ultimately, was created by chance. There was a period in the late nineteenth century when a few physicists thought their discipline was close to completion. The German physicist Max Planck (1858–1947) is said to have related this anecdote from his youth:

> When I began my physical studies in Munich in 1874 and sought advice from my venerable teacher Philipp von Jolly ... he portrayed to me physics as a highly developed, almost fully matured science... Possibly in one or another nook there would perhaps be a dust particle or a small bubble to be examined and classified, but the system as a whole stood there fairly secured, and theoretical physics approached visibly that degree of perfection which, for example, geometry has had already for centuries.

Planck studied physics all the same and discovered energy quanta, which opened up an entire new field: quantum physics. For this revelation, Planck won the Nobel Prize for Physics in 1918 and the Royal Society's Copley Medal. His name remains at the forefront of the discipline because he formulated the Planck Constant, the Planck Postulate, Planck's Law, the Third Law of Thermodynamics, etc. Although, like Jolly, Lord Kelvin had similar thoughts on the completion of physics in 1900, Planck proved them wrong, believing the mysteries of the physical world would never be explained fully:

> Science cannot solve the ultimate mystery of nature. And that is because, in the last analysis, we ourselves are a part of the mystery that we are trying to solve. [1932]

As long ago as Ancient Greece, the philosopher Anaxagorus (*c.*500–*c.*430 BC) had begun the search for a simple explanation of the physical world involving logic alone, without recourse to gods, magic or superstition. Unsurprisingly, he did not find one. Albert Einstein (1878–1955) revealed that physics was far from having all the answers when he developed his Special and General Theories of Relativity, opening up the concepts of space and time to scientific research. Einstein had also hoped to find a unifying theory to explain the structure and function of the universe in a single equation. But he never achieved this, having to concede, like Newton, that the work must be left to others. Professor Stephen Hawking (1942–2018), who held Newton's post as Lucasian Professor of Mathematics at Cambridge from 1979 to 2009, and others introduced the idea of string theory; the possibility of the existence of multiple universes to bring the conflicting quantum and relativity theories together in a unified field theory – M-theory. In 2010, Hawking made this statement in his lecture on 'The Grand Design':

> M-theory is the unified theory Einstein was hoping to find... If the theory is confirmed by observation, it will be the successful conclusion of a search going back more than 3,000 years. We will have found the grand design.[4]

The Grand Unifying Theory may yet be some way off but, while searching for it, Einstein kept the images of his scientific heroes before him as inspiration: Isaac Newton and the ingenious experimenter and inventor, Englishman Michael Faraday (1791–1867), as well as James Clerk Maxwell (discussed below). If Newton was the ultimate proponent of mathematical theory, Faraday excelled at the practical elements of science. Faraday made incredible discoveries in the fields of electromagnetism and electrochemistry – some refer to him as the father of electricity. His inventions ultimately changed the world and led to many technologies used today. He discovered electromagnetic induction and found a way to convert magnetic force into electrical force. As a prolific chemist and physicist, he invented or developed many items and methods, including electrolysis, the electric motor, the transformer, the generator, the dynamo, the Faraday cage and many other achievements. The two scientists must have been the perfect inspiration for Einstein who had begun his career in a patent office for new inventions and taught himself mathematics.

In 1934, Einstein had this to say about Newton's invention of fluxions:

> In order to put his system into mathematical form at all, Newton had to devise the concept of differential quotients and propound the laws of motion in the form of total differential equations – perhaps the greatest advance in thought that a single individual was ever privileged to make.[5]

To the Moon and Beyond

The science of physics appears to have advanced significantly since Newton wrote his *Principia* so long ago. Yet his work remains not only vital and relevant to physicists today but was sufficiently advanced to provide all the mathematics required for the NASA Moon landings of the late 1960s and 1970s. The work of Einstein, Hawking and others will be necessary if space travel ever advances beyond the inner planets of the Solar System, but for man's first tentative steps beyond the Earth, Newton's work of more than 300 years ago still sufficed – just. The fact that Apollo 11's module *Eagle* landed a little off target was no fault of Newtonian mathematics but due to the supercomputers of the day being so rudimentary; today's home PC or laptop is more sophisticated, faster and more capable than those NASA had available sixty years ago and a mobile phone has more computing capacity than the orbiting space module of 1969. What an incredible achievement for an illiterate farmer's son who could hardly have envisaged space exploration beyond the pages of science fiction.[6]

In Book III of the *Principia*, Newton calculates the speed at which a projectile must travel in order to escape the Earth's gravitation pull – in other words, a space craft's escape velocity. Newton also provided the calculations necessary to determine the craft's trajectory for a successful Moon landing, its safe return to Earth orbit and the reduction of speed and angle of re-entry into the atmosphere required to avoid burning up before splashdown.[7]

Today, Newton's fluxions – calculus – are taught in schools' mathematics classes. His Laws of Motion underpin some of the most basic physics lessons. Everyone has seen the intriguing phenomenon of the so-called Newton's cradle, consisting of four or five identical metal balls suspended in line, just touching, from a framework. If two balls are swung so they collide with the three remaining, just two from the far end will swing away, leaving the central ball unmoving, although the energy required to move the two has been transferred through it. The device was invented in 1967 by the English actor Simon Prebble as an amusing toy, which he named in Newton's honour since it shows his Laws of Motion in operation. The first Law of Motion states that every object will remain at rest or in uniform motion in a straight line unless compelled to change its state by the action of an external force. The second law states that the rate of change of momentum of a body is directly proportional to the force applied and takes place in the direction of the applied force. The third law states that for every action (or force) in Nature there is an equal and opposite reaction.

Newton's laws are, apparently, best experienced by astronauts during a spacewalk or EVA (extra-vehicular activity). Without weight, friction or air resistance, the least push against the space module or space station could send them floating into oblivion, if they were not tethered. One female astronaut described how she moved a payload from a supply ship to the orbiting space station single-handed. On Earth, the payload weighed 800 kilogrammes but, in orbit, she simply nudged it into place, according to a BBC documentary to celebrate the fiftieth anniversary of the first Moon landing (*Stargazing – Moon Landing Special,* 15 July 2019).

The Marvels of Electromagnetic Radiation

In science classes, children can play with prisms, mirrors and lenses to instil their fascination with light and colours. All the glassware is ready made; grinding lenses and polishing mirrors – things young Newton had to do for himself – are no longer requirements. As John Conduitt noted after a discussion with his wife's uncle concerning the reflecting telescope he had first sent to the Royal Society in 1671:

> I asked him where he had it made, he said he made it himself & when I asked him where he got his tools, he said he made them himself & laughing added if I had staid [waited] for other people to make my tools and things for me, I had never made anything.[8]

Newton's discoveries in exploring and explaining the components of white light were ground-breaking in themselves but have been further developed, revealing wavelengths far beyond the narrow, visible colour spectrum he could see. Since then, other forms of 'invisible light' have been revealed, from radio waves, microwaves and infrared with longer wavelengths and lower frequencies, to ultraviolet, x-rays and gamma rays with shorter wavelengths and greater frequency. Frequency can be interpreted as the energy level of that light, hence the penetrating power of x-rays and gamma rays.[9] But who discovered these different kinds of light, if they are invisible?

James Clerk Maxwell (1831–79) was a Scottish physicist. He realised that electricity and magnetism – previously thought to be entirely different things – were connected. By a series of equations, he set science on the path to a new field of study, to better understand how light – now described by the new term: electromagnetic radiation – worked and how it could be utilised. However, William Herschel (1738–1822), a German-British astronomer, discoverer of the planet Uranus and music composer, first discovered infrared radiation while investigating how much heat was given off by each of the seven colours of the rainbow. In 1800, he used a prism to split sunlight into its visible components, as Newton had done, and used the improved thermometers of the day to measure their temperatures. He found that red light was the hottest and violet the coolest. However, he left the experiment in place for a while and, as the Sun moved so did the colours of the spectrum.

To his surprise, as the red light shifted away from the thermometer, instead of the temperature falling in the dark region beyond the colour, it rose higher. Although there was no visible light, there was greater heat. This was the first clue that there was more to light than the human eye can see.

The following year, a young German scientist, Johann Ritter (1776–1810), following Herschel's experiment, turned his attention to the effect of the seven colours on the compound silver chloride. It was known that silver chloride darkens when exposed to sunlight but Ritter used a prism and measured its reaction to the separate colours. The compound reacted considerably more at the violet end of the spectrum but most strongly of all just beyond the visible violet. Ritter called his discovery 'chemical rays' but we know them as 'ultraviolet'. The spectrum of light had been further expanded beyond what was visible to the naked eye.

In 1895, another German scientist, Wilhelm Rontgen (1845–1923), made an accidental discovery while experimenting with beams of electrons, passing them through a gas-filled tube. He noticed that a fluorescent screen, in the room but quite unconnected with the experiment, glowed whenever the tube was turned on. He did not know what was causing the glow and called it x-radiation; 'x' standing for an unknown. Later, instead of the screen, he used photographic plates and was shocked to see an image appear of the bones in his hand with only a faint outline of the flesh around them. It must have been a scary experience. Marie Curie (1867–1934) took the work on x-rays much further, developing mobile x-ray units that saved the lives of hundreds of troops during the First World War by locating shrapnel and bullets within their bodies.

However, the ill effects of exposure to this high-energy form of light on humans were not fully understood and Marie and other investigators paid the price, dying of cancers related to their work with radiation. Even in the 1950s, the effects of long-term exposure to x-rays were not fully appreciated. The British scientist, Rosalind Franklin (1920–58) used x-ray crystallography as a means of studying the structure of complex molecules. Her work revealed the mysteries of the double helix of DNA, the code for all life on Earth. She might have shared the Nobel Prize for the discovery of DNA with James Watson and Francis Crick, if she had not died of ovarian cancer – most probably caused by her continuous exposure to x-rays. Unfortunately, the Nobel Prize is never awarded posthumously.

But x-rays were not the ultimate in high energy rays. New Zealander Ernest Rutherford (1871– 1937) discovered gamma rays, the even more penetrating by-product of radioactive decay. A pioneer of both nuclear physics and chemistry – winning the Nobel Prize for Chemistry in 1908 – he proved in 1914 that gamma rays were yet another form of light with even shorter wavelengths than x-rays. They are also far more destructive of living tissue. Mankind's only natural experience of gamma rays is a nanosecond of emission during a lightning strike. However, gamma rays are used today in medical procedures with appropriate extensive safety measures.

Returning to the opposite end of the spectrum, Heinrich Hertz (1857–94) was a German physicist who conclusively proved the presence there, beyond infrared light, of radio waves. The unit of frequency (one cycle of waves from peak to peak per second) was named the 'Hertz' in his honour. Radio waves were already believed to exist, according to James Clerk Maxwell's electromagnetic theory of light, formulated in 1865, which suggested wavelengths greater than those of infrared light should be possible. In his short career, Hertz proved that radio waves not only existed but, since they travelled at the same speed as visible light, they must indeed be simply another kind of invisible light. He also discovered that pulses of radio waves could be sent out or 'broadcast', a characteristic which was soon put to use in the later nineteenth century with the invention of the telegraph. Ultimately, the wireless capabilities of radio waves led to the invention of radio receivers, television and all the modern technologies of today, by overlaying information, voices or music onto the moving waves. Another important feature of radio waves is their ability to pass, unchanged, through other media, such as air, water, even brick, glass and concrete and to remain unaffected by the electromagnetic waves of most other forms of light.

The universe can also be explored using radio waves. Radio telescopes can 'see' into space, whether the sky is dark, bright or obscured by cloud, making equipment like that at Jodrell Bank Observatory in Cheshire perfectly usable even in rainy, misty English weather. Many phenomena across the universe emit radio waves of different frequencies: gas and dust clouds, galaxies, stars, planets and comets, enabling radio maps and images to be created, making invisible objects 'visible' for study. Black holes (*see* below) can give off great bursts of radio waves every so often, as if the particles and electromagnetic radiation that has been swallowed up has to be excreted in these huge jets of energy. At the centre of our galaxy, the Milky Way, lies a black hole, discovered by radio telescopes as a source of radio waves and, towards the other end of the electro-magnetic spectrum, x-rays too.[10]

In between radio waves and infrared light on the electromagnetic spectrum lie the microwaves. Their wavelengths are shorter, their frequencies higher than radio waves. Whereas radio waves have a wide field of broadcast, microwaves are more readily focussed into narrower beams. This makes them more useful for person-to-person communication, such as in mobile phones, rather than broadcasting TV programmes to large audiences. Microwaves of even shorter wavelengths and higher frequency, tending closer towards infrared, are great for cooking a single meal rather than heating a room. These shorter wavelength microwaves energise and react with water molecules, heating all the food at once, not just the outside to begin with, nor the plastic or glass dish. But this also means they are absorbed by the atmosphere, reacting with both water and oxygen molecules, hence they are less efficient at communicating information across distances.

Laser beams, once at the heart of science fiction but now used in everything from scanning barcodes to keyhole surgery, make use of a technology that was first discovered in 1953 at Columbia University by Charles Townes and others. Originally, the team was working on 'masers' – microwave amplification by stimulated emission of radiation. Masers are used today as the timekeeping devices in atomic clocks, as low-noise microwave amplifiers in radio telescopes and in spacecraft communication ground stations. Since those early technologies, masers have now been designed to generate electromagnetic beams at radio and infrared frequencies, as well as microwave frequencies, and Townes suggested replacing 'microwave' with the word 'molecular' as the first word in the acronym maser.

'Lasers' were invented by Theodore Maiman in 1960, although, at first, he called them 'optical masers'. They were simply masers that used wavelengths of visible light and the word 'light' replaced the word 'microwave'. When atoms are energised, the electrons in the atoms become more active but as they slow to their original state, they give off that extra burst of energy as a photon of visible light. This light is then amplified and concentrated into a beam. Astronomers can use these powerful beams to see things in the night sky which are otherwise blurred by the effects of the Earth's atmosphere; where ordinary light is diffused, lasers can penetrate.

Lasers truly are a marvel of electromagnetic radiation. In the early days of laser technology, it may well have come as a surprise that these tools of light could be used in medicine, to heal or otherwise improve patients' physical well-being. But doctors and medical researchers quickly began to see the possibilities and the number of uses for medical lasers has multiplied over the years. Among other applications, these include cutting into tissue in surgical procedures, using laser 'scalpels'. Some surgical operations are difficult to perform with a conventional scalpel and it was realised that a laser beam might be used instead. Initial trials proved that a finely focussed beam from a carbon dioxide gas laser could cut through human tissue swiftly and precisely, directed from any angle by use of a mirror. The incision made was always of a consistent depth: a difficulty for human hands, however skilled, and therefore healed more evenly.

Another advantage was that the heat of the laser beam cauterized the smaller blood vessels as it went, although larger blood vessels still had to be closed off using the more conventional methods of clamping and suturing. A third major advantage was that human cell tissue, being a poor conductor of heat, whether skin or brain or any other organ, areas close to the laser incision remained unaffected by the beam. This was a considerable advantage when only a minute area required surgical intervention but was surrounded by otherwise healthy tissue or organs.[11]

Lasers are now used in numerous surgical procedures, including the removal of cataracts in the eye or reshaping the cornea of the eye to improve sight. They can clear blocked arteries by targeting the fatty deposits of plaque which have built up, reducing blood flow. Deep-seated cancerous tumours can be burned away in positions otherwise impossible for traditional surgery to reach, without destroying healthy tissue, such as within the brain. More recent applications in brain surgery reduce the worst of the tremors caused by Parkinson's decease. This is done by using a laser to neutralise the over-activity of the particular nerve centre in the brain causing the tremor.

In cosmetic surgery, lasers are used to burn away teeth cavities and to whiten the enamel. They can remove unwanted hair for good by destroying the hair follicles. Unsightly port-wine birthmarks can be erased using a green light laser. The birthmark consists of thousands of minute blood vessels that show up as a deep reddish purple stain. The fact that it appears this colour is because the blood capillaries are absorbing green light, so the application of a green light laser will only heat and burn away these numerous tiny malformed blood vessels, leaving the normal coloured skin untouched. The superficial burns will still have to heal but the birthmark is gone. A similar procedure may be used to remove tattoos. On a more drastic level, lasers are also employed in plastic surgery, when the bones of the face require reshaping, such as in rhinoplasty procedures to change the shape of the nose.

Spectrophotometers analyse the elemental make-up of chemical compounds using the colour absorption capabilities of different molecules. Much the same can now be done for distant galaxies and stars, using special telescopes to analyse the electromagnetic radiation they emit, revealing their component elements. Spectrophotometry is a means of measuring how much light a chemical substance absorbs by detecting the change in intensity of a beam of light as it passes through a sample solution. The basic idea is that each compound absorbs, reflects or transmits light over a certain range of wavelengths, according to its elemental composition.

Spectrophotometry is widely used for analysis in various fields: chemistry, physics, biology, biochemistry, material and chemical engineering, clinical applications and industrial applications. In biochemistry, for example, it is used to determine enzyme-catalysed reactions or in clinical applications, to examine blood or tissues for clinical diagnosis. There are also several variations of spectrophotometry, such as atomic absorption spectrophotometry and atomic emission spectrophotometry, which use wavelengths other than visible light.

In visible light spectrophotometry, the absorption or the transmission of a certain substance is determined by the observed colour. For instance, a solution sample that absorbs light across all visible ranges (i.e. the sample transmits no light of visible wavelengths) appears black. If all visible wavelengths are transmitted (i.e. the sample absorbs nothing), it appears white. If a sample absorbs red light, it appears green because green is the complementary colour of red. Visible light spectrophotometers use a prism to produce light of a particular colour and wavelength, filtering out other wavelengths so that a beam of, say, red light only is passed through a solution sample. Newton's discoveries are still at work today.

Beyond the Everyday

In-depth study of the way light behaved in space under the influence of gravity led to the discovery of black holes. A black hole is a region of space with a gravitational pull so strong that nothing – no particles or even electromagnetic radiation such as light – can escape from it. The Theory of General Relativity predicts that a sufficiently compact mass, such as a collapsing star, can deform spacetime to form a black hole.

While their enigmatic name – 'black' because all light is absorbed into them and none is reflected, making them invisible – was first coined in 1967, by American astronomer John Wheeler, the idea of objects whose gravity is so intense not even light can escape them is far older. In 1783, an English cleric and amateur scientist, John Michell, showed that Newton's Law of Gravity suggested such objects could exist. But Michell went further, suggesting that, despite being invisible, such objects might reveal themselves if they happened to have a star in orbit around them.

Michell was proved to be incredibly prescient on both accounts. During the 1930s, using Einstein's more sophisticated Theory of Gravity, advanced in 1916 and known as General Relativity, theorists showed that sufficiently massive stars could collapse under their own gravity at the end of their life and become black holes. Ironically, Einstein himself never accepted that such objects could really exist. Michell's second claim was confirmed in the early 1970s. British astronomers Louise Webster and Paul Murdin at the Royal Greenwich Observatory and Thomas Bolton, a student at the University of Toronto, independently announced the discovery of a massive but invisible object in orbit around a blue star more than 6,000 light years away. The object, an intense x-ray source codenamed Cygnus X-1, is now regarded as the first black hole to be identified. There are now reckoned to be three types of these phenomena: stellar black holes, supermassive black holes and intermediate black holes.[12]

If mankind ever ventures into such distant realms of the universe, it will probably be a virtual voyage, rather than an actual one. The distances are so vast that unless that science fiction anomaly, the 'worm hole', can be utilised to shrink time itself, the eons required to travel so far would probably see our species and our home planet go extinct before any specific destination was achieved. Some kind of artificial intelligence – AI – could be a possibility and already advanced and sophisticated probes have visited every planet in the Solar System. Incredibly, Newtonian mathematics are basic to the development of AI. Machine learning requires the mathematic principles of both differential and integral calculus, alongside linear algebra, probability, statistics and optimisation.

Machine learning enables computer systems to perform a specific task without relying on explicit instructions. Algorithms and statistical models provide the system with sufficient information and likely patterns which it uses to enact appropriate behaviour. In other words, the system can 'learn' what to do when a situation arises that has not been precisely experienced before. A simple example is the android Echo device (developed by Amazon.com as 'Alexa') which uses speech recognition to perform a wide range of tasks on command. If the device is greeted 'Hello, Alexa, my name's Dave', it will respond 'Hello, Dave', statistical probability modelling suggesting that this particular speech pattern is likely to end with a name. The greeting: 'Hello, Alexa, my name is Pobble No-Toes' would result in the response 'Hello, Pobble No-Toes', even though the device has never heard the name before, simply because the pattern of sentence structure is recognised. Probability modelling makes use of integral calculus (integration).

Alternatively, differential calculus (differentiation) is used in finding optimal solutions to problems. As an example, 'smart' floor-cleaning robots employ navigation algorithms involving differential calculus and, over time, 'learn' their way around a floor space, finding optimal solutions to the problem of avoiding obstacles, improving their efficiency and reducing the time taken to complete the task. Similar algorithms are used in planning delivery and pick up services on the road which have time constraints, determining the best 'fit' for each vehicle to achieve maximum efficiency, taking into account legally required rest stops for drivers, if not traffic jams and road closures that may be difficulties needing human ingenuity and intervention. No doubt, the day will soon come when the vehicles themselves are driverless, operated by AI.

However, mankind has already made an effort to contact any intelligent life forms out there in deep space – that is the vastness of the universe beyond the Sun's magnetic field which marks out the full extent of the Solar System. Two copies of a gold-plated disc were sent with Voyagers I and II, launched by NASA in 1977, showing Earth as a very minor body in the universe – how the view of our world has changed since Newton's day. The discs are time capsules of life on Earth in analogue form, constructed like vinyl 78 rpm phonograph records but meant to play at 16 rpm. Although neither spacecraft is heading in the direction of any particular star, in 40,000 years, Voyager I will pass within 1.6 light year's distance of the star Gliese 445, in the constellation of Camelopardalis. We can but hope some alien intelligence finds the disc and is able to interpret it.

The Golden Disc, as it is known, contains greetings in fifty-five different languages, ancient and modern, music of many kinds, from J. S. Bach to Chuck Berry and from various eras and cultures. Other human sounds, such as laughter and footsteps and even a message in Morse code: *Per aspera ad astra* (Latin for 'through difficulty to the stars') are there as well as the 'song' of humpbacked whales and bird song. There are messages from the then President of the United States, Jimmy Carter, and from the United Nations Secretary-General at the time, Kurt Waldheim.

The disc also holds a collection of images in black and white and colour. Those of a scientific nature include human anatomy and reproduction – quite controversial when the disc was designed – the structure of DNA, the Solar System and its planets. Others of the 115 images show animals, insects, plants, landscapes, food, architecture, humans in portraits and going about their everyday lives. Some pictures are annotated to indicate scales of time, size or mass; others include their chemical composition. All measurements used are defined in the first few images using physical references that are probably consistent throughout the universe. As a more intimate connection to humankind, an hour-long recording of Ann Druyan's brainwaves is also on the disc. As the recording was being made, she thought about Earth's history, its civilizations and the problems they face. She even considered what it meant to fall in love – something Isaac Newton may never have experienced.

In Conclusion

Brilliant as he was, Sir Isaac Newton, travelling in his sedan chair, can never have foreseen such marvellous eventualities being derived from the use of his 'fluxions'. Neither can he have had any idea that his analysis of the visible spectrum through his prism would one day be extended to include all the other forms of electromagnetic radiation, from radio waves to gamma waves. His legacy remains – the wonders of physics and mathematics that he strived to consolidate into a coherent, measurable form. Ultimately, Newton did, in a way, set up a perpetual motion machine in that his successors in the field have never ceased to advance his discoveries.

Android phones, online games, satellite navigation and cancer surgery are further progress along the path where Newton took those first steps towards modern science and mathematics. In his world, his contemporaries recognised him as a great philosopher but today, with the benefit of hindsight, he was so much more than that, the instigator of a whole new world of technology – our world.

Yet the incredible things he achieved, alone in his study, are now everyday things; 'accepted knowledge' taken for granted. Perhaps the last word should be left to Albert Einstein who wrote in his foreword to Newton's *Opticks,* the 1952 edition by Dover Publications:

> Newton's age has long since passed through the sieve of oblivion, the doubtful striving and suffering of his generation has vanished from our ken; the works of some few great thinkers and artists have remained, to delight and ennoble those who come after us. Newton's discoveries have passed into the stock of accepted knowledge.

The debt we owe to one man's thought processes is more than he or anyone else could ever have imagined more than three centuries ago. The world that Isaac Newton knew has changed beyond all recognition: how much of that change is down to him alone?

NOTES

Chapter 1: 1540–1640 *Life and Science before Newton*

1. For photograph see https://www.nasa.gov/content/blue-marble-image-of-the-earth-from-apollo-17 (accessed 1.3.18)
2. https://answersingenesis.org/astronomy/the-universe-confirms-the-bible/ (accessed 1.3.18)
3. https://creation.com/isaiah-40-22-circle-sphere (accessed 1.3.18)
4. British Library, Harley MS 7182, ff. 58v–59.
5. Map Courtesy of Library of Congress, Geography and Map Division (use permitted for educational purposes)
6. http://www.history.com/this-day-in-history/drake-claims-california-for-england (accessed 2.3.18)
7. *The Science of Shakespeare,* Dan Falk, (Thomas Dunne Books, New York, 2014), p.59.
8. *The Science of Shakespeare,* Dan Falk, p.48.
9. *Before Galileo,* John Freely, (Overlook Duckworth, London, 2012), p249.
10. *Before Galileo,* John Freely, pp.242–43.
11. *The Science of Shakespeare,* Dan Falk, (Thomas Dunne Books, New York, 2014), p.53.
12. http://www.mhs.ox.ac.uk/staff/saj/thesis/digges.htm from Stephen Johnston, 'Making mathematical practice: gentlemen, practitioners and artisans in Elizabethan England' (Ph.D. Cambridge, 1994).
13. *The Science of Shakespeare,* Dan Falk, p.103.
14. https://www.britannica.com/biography/Richard-Hakluyt
15. *The King James Bible,* Psalm 107, v.23–24.
16. For the text go to http://www.gutenberg.org/ebooks/7476
17. *Local Heroes,* Adam Hart-Davis, BBC Publications, 1997, pp.12–13.

18. https://www.tandfonline.com/doi/abs/10.1080/00033790310001642812

19. *The Science of Shakespeare*, Dan Falk, p.202.

20. *Circulation – William Harvey's Revolutionary Idea,* Thomas Wright (Vintage Books, London, 2013), pp.160–61.

21. http://scienceworld.wolfram.com/biography/Descartes.html (accessed 24.8.18)

Chapter 2: The 1640s A Genius is Born

1. With thanks to the staff at Lincolnshire Archives LN2 5AB for hunting down the will of Isaac Newton senior, misfiled for over a century, ref. LCC_1642_446.

2. With thanks to the staff at Lincolnshire Archives LN2 5AB for the inventory ref. INV_151_066.

3. Wright, Thomas, *Circulation,* p.214.

4. http://bcw-project.org/military/english-civil-war/midlands-and-east/lincolnshire-1643 (accessed 12.9.18)

5. Hughes, Ann (editor), *Seventeenth-century England – A Changing Culture, volume I: Primary Sources,* (The Open University with Ward Lock Educational, 1980), pp.63–67.

6. Hughes, pp.80–81.

7. https://www.thelancet.com/journals/lancet/article/PIIS0140-6736(11)60590-4/fulltext (accessed 15.9.18)

8. Thomas, Ian (editor), *Culpeper's Book of Birth,* (London, Grange Books, 1985), p.54.

9. Thomas, p.68.

10. Thomas, pp68–75.

11. Ackroyd, Peter, *Isaac Newton,* (London, Chatto & Windus, 2006), pp1–2.

12. With thanks to Simon Jowitt, Churchwarden at St John the Baptist's Church at Colsterworth for a most instructive and enjoyable tour of the church, January 2018.

13. White, Michael, *Isaac Newton – The Last Sorcerer,* pp.14–15.

14. https://archive.org/stream/cu31924082458229/_djvu.txt (accessed 1.10.18)

15. Pride's Purge was an event that took place on 6 December 1648, when troops of the New Model Army under the command of Colonel Thomas Pride forcibly removed from the Long Parliament all those who were not supporters of Oliver Cromwell and the Generals (known as the Grandees) in the Army.

16. For more on this subject *see*: Borman, Tracy, *Witchcraft – James I and the English Witch Hunts,* (London, Jonathan Cape, 2013).

17. Newton, Russell, *Woolsthorpe manor house – the story of a story,* (sponsored by the Heritage Lottery Fund, 2014 https://www.newtontreeparty.co.uk/, (accessed 24.9.18)

Chapter 3: The 1650s The Reluctant Farmer

1. Baird, K. A. 'Some influences upon the young Isaac Newton' in *Notes & Records of the Royal Society of London,* vol. 41, pp.169–179 (1987), p.173.

2. http://www.newtonproject.ox.ac.uk/view/texts/normalized/ALCH00069 (accessed 12 October 2018.)

3. A blue plaque was put up to mark Newton's lodging at William Clarke's Apothecary Shop in Grantham in 2012; it was a 'Pizza Express' in September 2018.

4. White, Michael, *Coffee with Isaac Newton,* (London, Duncan Baird Publishers, 2008), pp.102 & 110.

5. White, Michael, *Isaac Newton – The Last Sorcerer,* (London, Fourth Estate Ltd, 1997), p.20.

6. Reconstruction of model at Science Discovery Centre, Woolsthorpe Manor, Lincolnshire, visited January 2018.

7. Crook, R., 'William Clarke – The Man' in Manterfield, John B., ed., *Newton's Grantham,* (Grantham Civic Society, 2014), pp.42–43.

8. Crook, Ruth, *Arthur Storer's World – Family, Medicine and Astronomy in Seventeenth-Century Lincolnshire and Maryland,* (Grantham Civic Society, 2014), pp.9–10. Author's notes and explanations added in square brackets.

9. From the Author's collection of historic recipes.

10. Foster Watson, M. A. *The English Grammar Schools to 1660 – their Curriculum and Practice,* (Cambridge University Press, 1908) available at https://archive.org/stream/cu31924082458229/_djvu.txt (accessed 1 October 2018.)

11. King's College Library, Cambridge, MS 136, p.18.

12. http://www.discoverstwulframs.org.uk/the-trigge-library.aspx (accessed 16 October 2018). Also https://en.wikipedia.org/wiki/Francis_Trigge_Chained_Library which includes a list of books.

13. Aldersey-Williams, Hugh, *In Search of Sir Thomas Browne,* (London & New York, W. Norton & Co., 2015), pp.97–99.

14. The Bible mentions unicorns and/or their horns in Numbers ch.23, v.22 and ch.24, v.8, Deuteronomy ch.33, v.17, Job ch.39, vs. 9 and 10 and Psalms ch.22, v.21 and ch.92, v.10.

15. Crook, Ruth, *Arthur Storer's World – Family, Medicine and Astronomy in Seventeenth-Century Lincolnshire and Maryland,* (Grantham Civic Society, 2014), p.27.

16. Foster Watson, M. A. *The English Grammar Schools to 1660 – their Curriculum and Practice,* (Cambridge University Press, 1908) available at https://archive.org/stream/cu31924082458229/_djvu.txt accessed 1 October 2018

17. Crook, Ruth, *Arthur Storer's World,* (2014), p.73.

18. Lynch, Michael, *The Interregnum 1649–60,* (Hodder & Stoughton, London, 2004), p.78.

Chapter 4: The 1660s: The Student of Light

1. White, Michael, *Isaac Newton – The Last Sorcerer,* (London, Fourth Estate Ltd, 1997), pp.46–47.
2. O'Connor, J. J. & Robertson, E. F., *Isaac Barrow,* http://www-groups.dcs.st-and.ac.uk/history/Biographies/Barrow.html (accessed 16 November 2018).
3. P. H. Osmond, *Isaac Barrow His Life and Times* (London, 1944), (accessed 19 November 2018).
4. Ackroyd, Peter, *Brief Lives: Newton,* (Chatto & Windus, London, 2006), p.16.
5. Westfall, Richard S., *Never at Rest – A Biography of Isaac Newton,* (Cambridge U.P., 2008 ed.), p.89.
6. Gaskell, P. & Robson R., *The Library of Trinity College, Cambridge: A Short History* (Cambridge, 1971), p.8.
7. Gaskell, p.60.
8. Gaskell, plate 2.
9. Vickers, Brian, (editor), *English Science: Bacon to Newton,* (Cambridge University Press, 1987), p.96.
10. This would have been 24 March 1662 by our reckoning. Since medieval times, 25 March, known as the Feast of the Annunciation or Lady Day, was the first quarter day of the new financial year, rather than the calendar New Year of 1 January. This resulted in dates from 1 January to 24 March often being given as 1298/99 or 1475/76 or 1661/62, as in this case. The other quarter days were 24 June (the feast of St John the Baptist, better known as Midsummer Day), 29 September (the Feast of St Michael and All Angels, better known as Michaelmas) and 25 December (Christmas Day). On these days, quarterly rents were due to be paid and contracts were often dated to begin or end on a quarter day. Dating methods changed in 1752, when Britain aligned her calendar with the Gregorian calendar that had been in use on the Continent since the sixteenth century. To the great consternation of many Englishmen – who feared their lives were being shortened – the old Julian calendar had to leap forward by eleven days so Wednesday 2 September 1752 was followed by Thursday 14 September 1752, making that year only 355 days long. But one institution refused to be 'robbed' of eleven days of financial income, so in 1753, the Exchequer ended its financial year on 5 April, instead of on the day before Lady Day. And it remains so today, the UK financial year still begins on the seemingly arbitrary date of 6 April.

Chapter 5: The 1670s: The Professor of Mathematics

1. Ellis, Markman, *The Coffee House – A Cultural History,* (London, Weidenfeld & Nicolson, 2004), pp.86–87.
2. Ellis, pp.95–99.

3. In all my historical research, I have found only one similar dispensation granted prior to Newton's. This was at Cambridge in the 1450s, when William Hobbes, a trained surgeon, wished to study medicine, to become a physician. As graduates, physicians had to take minor holy orders and, as clerics, were then forbidden from 'spilling blood', so they could not carry out surgical procedures. Hobbes had already 'spilt blood' as a surgeon – surgeons did apprenticeships – so could not take holy orders or, theoretically, be granted his doctorate. Yet he achieved his degree and lectured at the university. His patron was the Duke of York which must have helped him get his dispensation. At the time, before the Reformation, it would have been granted by the pope, rather than the king.

4. Ackroyd, Peter, *Brief Lives: Newton,* (London, Chatto & Windus, 2006), p.57.

5. Aldersey-Williams, Hugh, *In Search of Sir Thomas Browne – The Life and Afterlife of the Seventeenth Century's Most Inquiring Mind,* (London & New York, W. Norton & Co., 2015), p.98.

6. Arians, not to be confused with Aryans – white supremacists.

7. Ackroyd, Peter, *Brief Lives: Newton,* (London, Chatto & Windus, 2006), p.53.

8. O'Connor, J. J. & Robertson, E. F., *Isaac Barrow,* http://www-groups.dcs. st-and.ac.uk/history/Biographies/Barrow.html (accessed 16 November 2018).

9. Ackroyd, Peter, *Brief Lives: Newton,* (London, Chatto & Windus, 2006), pp.61–62.

10. Visit to St John's Church, Colsterworth, our thanks to the Church Warden Simon Jowitt, 26–28 January 2018.

Chapter 6: The 1680s: The Published Philosopher

1. For example, Mars is 1.52 times as far from the sun as the Earth is and its year is 1.88 Earth years: $1.52^2 = 3.53 = 1.88^3$ (example taken from Rooney, Anne, *The Story of Physics,* (Arcturus Publishing Ltd, London, 2015, p.159).

2. Jordan, Don, *The King's City,* (Little, Brown Book Group, London, 2017), pp.338–39.

3. All above information is taken from the website of the Royal Meteorological Society, https://doi.org/10.1002/wea.789 (accessed 5 Jan 2019).

4. Brewer, Clifford, *The Death of Kings,* (Abson Books, London, 2000), pp.178–80.

5. Ackroyd, Peter, *Brief Lives: Newton,* (London, Chatto & Windus, 2006), p.82.

Chapter 7: The 1690s: The Alchemist and Crime Investigator

1. White, Michael, *Isaac Newton – The Last Sorcerer*, (London, Fourth Estate Ltd, 1997), p.213.

2. Westfall, Richard S., *Never at Rest – A Biography of Isaac Newton*, (Cambridge U.P., 2008 ed.), p.286, footnote 17.

3. Roberts, Gareth, *The Mirror of Alchemy*, (The British Library, London, 1994), p.55.

4. The University of Indiana at Bloomington has an excellent website, detailing the recreation of this and other experiments following the instructions in Newton's notebooks. It can be viewed at http://webapp1.dlib.indiana.edu/newton/reference/chemProd.do (accessed 22 Jan 2019)

5. Martin, Sean, *Alchemy & Alchemists*, (Pocket Essentials, Hertfordshire, 2006), p.138.

6. Emsley, John, *Elements of Murder – A History of Poison*, (Oxford University Press, 2005), p.14.

7. Emsley, p.13.

8. Westfall, Richard, *Never at Rest – A Biography of Isaac Newton*, (Cambridge University Press, 2008 ed.), p.287.

9. Emsley, p.35.

10. White, Michael, *The Last Sorcerer*, (Fourth Estate Ltd, London, 1997), p.223.

11. Newton Correspondence, vol.4, p.349.

12. Levenson, Thomas, *Newton and the Counterfeiter*, (Faber and Faber, London, 2009), pp.69–71.

13. Levenson, p.166.

Chapter 8: The 1700s: The Master and President

1. The society remained an all-male fellowship until 22 March 1945 when Marjory Stephenson, a biochemist, and Kathleen Lonsdale, a crystallographer, were finally elected Fellows. However, Hertha Ayrton had read a paper to the society in 1904 and won the society's Hughes Medal for discoveries in the physical sciences in 1906, but was still denied membership. Tinniswood, Adrian, *The Royal Society*, (Head of Zeus Ltd, London, 2019), pp.155–56.

2. Tinniswood, Adrian, *The Royal Society*, (Head of Zeus Ltd, London, 2019), pp.37–38.

3. Brewer, Clifford, *The Death of Kings*, (Abson Books, London, 2000), p.204.

4. Can be viewed at the National Portrait Gallery, London.

5. His ideas may have developed from some of the Royal Society's earliest enquiries. In 1662, a list of 48 queries had been sent to Iceland, including: what substances came out of volcanoes; did mercury congeal in the cold;

how did whales breathe; were there such things as 'spirits' and what did they say and do? (This last question to a country where elves and trolls are still deemed probable.) Tinniswood, Adrian, *The Royal Society,* (Head of Zeus Ltd, London, 2019), p.56.

6. Driver, Christopher, (ed.), John Evelyn, *Acetaria – A Discourse of Sallets, 1699,* (Prospect Books, Devon, 1996), pp.58–59.

7. Driver, p.65.

8. Berridale-Johnson, Michelle, *The British Museum Cookbook,* (British Museum Publications, London, 1987), p.122.

9. Both recipes can be found in full in Ayrton, Elisabeth, *Royal Favourites – Recipes from Palace Kitchens,* (The Folio Society, London, 1971), pp.48–55.

10. Richard Bradley's recipes are taken from Berriedale-Johnson, Michelle, *The British Museum Cookbook,* (British Museum Publications, London, 1987), pp.128–31.

11. https://sipsmith.com/gin-and-london-the-origin/ (accessed 5 May 2019)

12. https://www.tate.org.uk/art/artists/william-hogarth-265 (accessed 5 May 2019)

Chapter 9: The 1710s: The Famous Philosopher

1. Iliffe, Rob, *Priest of Nature – The Religious Worlds of Isaac Newton,* (Oxford University Press, 2017), p.200.

2. In *Observations upon the Prophecies of Daniel, and the Apocalypse of St John* https://publicdomainreview.org/collections/sir-isaac-newtons-daniel-and-the-apocalypse-1733/ (accessed 14 Feb 2019.)

3. White, Michael, *Isaac Newton – The Last Sorcerer,* (Fourth Estate Ltd, London, 1997), p.309.

4. Bardi, Jason, *The Calculus Wars – Newton, Leibniz and the Greatest Mathematical Clash of All Time,* (High Stakes Publishing, London, 2006), p.35.

5. Since this is not a mathematical text book, for readers who want further explanation of calculus, I recommend Ross, G. MacDonald, *Leibniz,* (Oxford University Press, 1984), pp.31–32.

6. White, Michael, *Rivals – Conflict as the Fuel of Science,* (Secker & Warburg, London, 2001), pp.42–43.

7. From de Duillier's *A Two-fold Geometrical Investigation of the Line of Briefest Descent,* published in London, 1699.

8. Sobel, Dava, *Longitude,* (Fourth Estate Ltd, London, 1995), p.45.

9. Sobel, p.60.

10. Brewer, Clifford, *The Death of Kings,* (Abson Books, London, 2000), p.206.

11. Cook, Alan, *Edmond Halley – Charting the Heavens and the Seas,* (Clarendon Press, Oxford, 1998), p.351.

12. Dry, Sarah, *The Newton Papers,* (Oxford University Press, 2014), p.10.

Chapter 10: The 1720s: The Grand Old Man of Science

1. https://www.oldbaileyonline.org/static/Coinage.jsp (accessed 19 March 2019)
2. The subsequent financial information is taken from Andrew Odlyzko 'Newton's financial misadventures with the South Sea Bubble', https://royalsocietypublishing.org/doi/full/10.1098/rsnr.2018.0018 (accessed 19 March 2019)
3. Bank of England Archives, ledger pages AC27/418:1442, AC27/422:3182, AC27/425:4777, AC27/436:7140 and AC27/444:1105.
4. Smith Brindle, Reginald, *The New Music*, (Oxford University Press, 1987), pp 42–43.
5. https://www.whipplelib.hps.cam.ac.uk/special/exhibitions-and-displays/exhibitions-archive/universal-harmony/newton (accessed 29 March 2019).
6. Pesic, Peter, 'Isaac Newton and the mystery of the major sixth: a transcription of his manuscript "Of Musick" with commentary' in *Journal of Interdisciplinary Science Reviews,* Volume 31, (2006 – Issue 4: The Sound of Science, published online: 18 Jul 2013), pp.291–306. https://doi.org/10.1179/030801806X143268 (accessed 19 March 2019)
7. Ackroyd, Peter, *Brief Lives: Newton,* (London, Chatto & Windus, 2006). p.119.
8. Cook, Alan, *Edmond Halley – Charting the Heavens and the Seas,* (Oxford University Press, 1998), p.393.
9. From The Newton Project (from http://www.newtonproject.ox.ac.uk/view/texts/normalized/OTHE00002), (accessed 12 March 2019).
10. Brooks, Michael, *Free Radicals: The Secret Anarchy of Science* (London, Profile Books Ltd, 2013), accessed online 17 May 2019.
11. Clark, David H. & Clark, Stephen P. H., *Newton's Tyranny,* (New York, W. H. Freeman and Company, 2000), p.109.
12. Clark & Clark, p.115.
13. Hanley, William, *Voltaire, Newton and the Law* (from https://academic.oup.com/library/article-abstract/s6-13/1/48/974029?redirectedFrom=PDF), (accessed 17 May 2019).
14. https://www.wired.com/2014/05/newton-papers-q-and-a/ (accessed 20 May 2019).
15. Dry, Sarah, *The Newton Papers,* (Oxford UP, 2014), p.17.
16. https://www.westminster-abbey.org/abbey-commemorations/commemorations/sir-isaac-newton (accessed 20 May 2019) The date of death is given in the old style when the new year of 1727 would have commenced on 25 March.
17. Wordsworth, William, *The Prelude* (1850), Book 3, lines 58–63.

Chapter 11: Science after Isaac Newton

1. Bondi, Hermann, 'Newton and the Twentieth Century – A Personal View' in *Let Newton Be! A New Perspective on his Life and Works* (1988) R. Flood, J. Fauvel, M. Shortland, R. Wilson, p. 241.
2. Gleick, James, *Isaac Newton,* (London, Fourth Estate, 2003), p.186.
3. British Library Add MS 39703.
4. Rooney, Anne, *The Story of Physics,* (London, Arcturus Publishing Ltd, 2015), p.203.
5. Einstein, Albert, 'Clerk Maxwell's Influence on the Evolution of the Idea of Physical Reality' in *Essays in Science* (1934).
6. Francis Godwin had published the wildly popular science fiction novel, *The Man in the Moone,* in 1638 and the novel was still in print in 1768 – not that Newton would ever have read anything so frivolous but the idea of space travel was out there.
7. From https://www.open.edu/openlearn/history-the-arts/history/history-science-technology-and-medicine/history-science/newton-the-expert-view (accessed 25 May 2019)
8. John Conduitt, *Memorandum,* 31 August 1726.
9. Arcand, Kimberly & Watzke, Megan, *Light,* (New York, Black Dog & Leventhal Publishers, 2015), pp.14–15.
10. Arcand & Watzke, *Light,* (New York, Black Dog & Leventhal Publishers, 2015), p.39.
11. From http://www.scienceclarified.com/scitech/Lasers/Medical-Uses-of-Lasers.html#ixzz5pshSdPsX (accessed 4 June 2019)
12. From https://www.sciencefocus.com/space/who-really-discovered-black-holes/ (accessed 27 May 2019)

Appendix

TRANSCRIPTION OF THE WILL OF ISAAC NEWTON SENIOR

In the name of God Amen. The first day of October Anno dom. 1642 / Izacke Newton of Wolsthorpe in the parrish of Coulsterworth
in the County of Lincoln yeoman sicke of body but of good and perfect memorie god be praysed doo make and ordaine this my last will and Testament in maner & forme followinge that is to say first I com[m]end my soule into the handes ^{of god} my maker
hopinge assueredly through the ^{onely} merrits of Jesus ^{Christe} my Saviour
to be made partaker of life everlastinge and I Commend my body to the earth where it was made and for my temporall estate as followeth .... I give unto Elizabeth
Cristian dowghter to Tho. Cristian of Shillington five poundes of Corrant English money ^{to be paide within} three monethis after
my decease It[e]m I give to Issabell Coake Dowghter to John Coke of Shillington five poundes of like lawfull English money to be paid as afore said It[e]m I give unto the Rest of John Cookes Childrell [sic] fower poundes to be equally
devided amoungst them and to be paid as afore said It[e]m

I give unto Ann Newton dowghter to my brother Richard
Newton seaven pounds of Corrant English money to be
paid as afore said It[e]m I give unto my Uncle Richard
Newton Twenty shillings to be paid as afore said It[e]m
I give unto the poore of the parrish Fortie shillinges to
be payd at my decease It[e]m I give ten shillinges to repaire
the Bridge betwixt Coulsterworth and Woolsthorpe and
all the Rest of my goodes moveable and unmoveable
I give unto my loveinge wife whom I make full +
executrix of this my last will and Testament desire-
inge ^Mr James Ascough my Father and my brother in ^law
William Ascough parson of Borton to be Supervisers
of this my will in witnes heare of I have heareto
set my hand and seale the day and yeare above
written

Sealed and   Izacke Newton
deliv[er]ed in the   his .... marke
presence of

James Ascough
William Venton?
Edward Foster   6th Oct 1642 ......

BIBLIOGRAPHY

Books

Ackroyd, Peter, *Brief Lives: Newton,* (London, Chatto & Windus, 2006).

Aldersey-Williams, Hugh, *In Search of Sir Thomas Browne – The Life and Afterlife of the Seventeenth Century's Most Inquiring Mind,* (London & New York, W. Norton & Co., 2015).

Arcand, Kimberly & Watzke, Megan, *Light,* (New York, Black Dog & Leventhal Publishers, 2015).

Ayrton, Elisabeth, *Royal Favourites – Recipes from Palace Kitchens,* (London, The Folio Society, 1971).

Bardi, Jason, *The Calculus Wars – Newton, Leibniz and the Greatest Mathematical Clash of All Time,* (London, High Stakes Publishing, 2006).

Berriedale-Johnson, Michelle, *The British Museum Cookbook,* (London, British Museum Publications, 1987).

Brewer, Clifford, *The Death of Kings,* (London, Abson Books, 2000).

Bryson, Bill, ed., *Seeing Further,* (London, Royal Society, 2010).

Clark, David H. & Clark, Stephen P. H., *Newton's Tyranny,* (New York, W. H. Freeman and Company, 2000).

Cook, Alan, *Edmond Halley – Charting the Heavens and the Seas,* (Oxford University Press, 1998).

Crook, Ruth, *Arthur Storer's World – Family, Medicine and Astronomy in Seventeenth-Century Lincolnshire and Maryland,* (Grantham Civic Society, 2014).

Crook, Ruth & Manterfield, John B., eds, *Newton's Grantham,* (Grantham Civic Society, 2014).

De Villamil, Lieut-Col Richard, *Newton: The Man,* (London, Gordon D. Knox, 1932).

Bibliography

Driver, Christopher, (ed.), John Evelyn, *Acetaria – A Discourse of Sallets, 1699,* (Devon, Prospect Books, 1996).

Dry, Sarah, *The Newton Papers,* (Oxford & New York, Oxford UP, 2014).

Ellis, Markman, *The Coffee House – A Cultural History,* (London, Weidenfeld & Nicolson, 2004).

Emsley, John, *Elements of Murder – A History of Poison,* (Oxford University Press, 2005).

Falk, Dan, *The Science of Shakespeare,* (New York, Thomas Dunne Books, 2014).

Freely, John, *Before Galileo,* (London & New York, Overlook Duckworth, 2012).

Gaskell, P & Robson R., *The Library of Trinity College, Cambridge: A Short History* (Cambridge, 1971).

Gleick, James, *Isaac Newton,* (London, Fourth Estate, 2003).

Hannam, James, *The Genesis of Science,* (London & Washington, Icon Books, 2011).

Hughes, Ann. ed., *Seventeenth-century England – A Changing Culture, volume I: Primary Sources,* (The Open University with Ward Lock Educational, 1980).

Iliffe, Rob, *Priest of Nature,* (Oxford & New York, Oxford UP, 2017).

Jordan, Don, *The King's City,* (London, Little, Brown Book Group, 2017).

Kennedy, Alexander, *Newton – Secrets of the Universe,* (Amazon, USA, 2016).

King, Tom, *Isaac Newton,* (Amazon, UK, 2017).

Levenson, Thomas, *Newton and the Counterfeiter,* (London, Faber and Faber, 2009).

Lynch, Michael, *The Interregnum 1649–60,* (London, Hodder & Stoughton, 2004 ed.).

Martin, Sean, *Alchemy & Alchemists,* (Pocket Essentials, Hertfordshire, 2006).

Roberts, Gareth, *The Mirror of Alchemy,* (London, The British Library, 1994).

Rooney, Anne, *The Story of Physics,* (London, Arcturus Publishing Ltd, 2015).

Snyder, Laura J., *Eye of the Beholder,* (London, Head of Zeus, 2015).

Sobel, Dava, *Longitude,* (London, Fourth Estate Ltd, 1995).

Thomas, Ian, ed., *Culpeper's Book of Birth,* (London, Grange Books, 1985).

Tinniswood, Adrian, *The Royal Society & The Invention of Modern Science,* (London, Head of Zeus, 2019).

Westfall, Richard S., *Never at Rest – A Biography of Isaac Newton,* (Cambridge University Press, 2008 ed.).

White, Michael, *Isaac Newton – The Last Sorcerer,* (London, Fourth Estate Ltd, 1997).

White, Michael, *Rivals – Conflict as the Fuel of Science,* (London, Secker & Warburg, 2001).

White, Michael, *Coffee with Isaac Newton,* (London, Duncan Baird Publishers, 2008).

Wright, Thomas, *Circulation – William Harvey's Revolutionary Idea,* (London, Vintage Books, 2013).

Websites and information accessed online

Black holes: https://www.sciencefocus.com/space/who-really-discovered-black-holes/ (accessed 27 May 2019).

Experiments recreated from Newton's notebooks: http://webapp1.dlib.indiana.edu/newton/reference/chemProd.do (accessed 22 Jan 2019)

Foster Watson, M. A. *The English Grammar Schools to 1660 – their Curriculum and Practice,* (Cambridge University Press, 1908) available at: https://archive.org/stream/cu31924082458229/_djvu.txt (accessed 1 October 2018).

Imagined portrait of Isaac Newton as a child: https://www.npg.org.uk/collections/search/portrait/mw198678/Imaginary-portrait-of-Sir-Isaac-Newton-as-a-child

Laser surgery: http://www.scienceclarified.com/scitech/Lasers/Medical-Uses-of-Lasers.html#ixzz5pshSdPsX (accessed 4 June 2019).

Moon landing information: https://www.open.edu/openlearn/history-the-arts/history/history-science-technology-and-medicine/history-science/newton-the-expert-view (accessed 25 May 2019).

Peter Pesic on Newton's 'On Musick': https://doi.org/10.1179/030801806X143268 (accessed 19 March 2019).

The Prophesies of Daniel: https://publicdomainreview.org/collections/sir-isaac-newtons-daniel-and-the-apocalypse-1733/ (accessed 14 Feb 2019).

The Royal Meteorological Society: https://doi.org/10.1002/wea.789 (accessed 5 Jan 2019).

LIST OF ILLUSTRATIONS

(*See* half title page) Sir Isaac Newton in his role as President of the Royal Society. Wood engraving by J. Quartley after (J.M.L.R.), 1883. (Creative Commons Public Domain)

(*See* title page) '*Worthies of Britain*' (*Sir Isaac Newton; Edmond Halley; Nicholas Saunderson; John Flamsteed*), by John Bowles (died 1784), given to the National Portrait Gallery, London in 1916. (NPG/Public Domain)

1. Martin Waldseemuller's map of 1507/8. (Public Domain)
2. Thomas Digges's diagram of the heliocentric universe from *A Prognostication Everlasting,* published in 1576.
3. The will of Isaac Newton senior. (Courtesy of Lincolnshire Archives)
4. The inventory of Isaac Newton senior. (Courtesy of Lincolnshire Archives)
5. The record of Isaac Newton junior's baptism; held at Grantham Library. (Photograph by Glenn Mount, permission granted for publication in this book, hereafter GM)
6. Woolsthorpe Manor, Colsterworth, Lincolnshire. (GM)
7. Isaac Newton's bedroom at Woolsthorpe Manor, Colsterworth, Lincolnshire. (GM)
8. The apple tree at Woolsthorpe Manor, Colsterworth, Lincolnshire. (GM)
9. Isaac Newton's sundial at St John the Baptist Church Colsterworth, Lincolnshire. (GM)
10. Site of William Clarke's Apothecary Shop, Grantham. (GM)
11. Grantham Grammar School, external view. (GM)
12. Grantham Grammar School, internal view, courtesy of King's School. (GM)
13. St Wulfram's Church, Grantham. (GM)

14. Plaque in the High Street, Oxford, marking the site of the house occupied by Robert Boyle and Robert Hooke. (GM)
15. Trinity Great Court Cambridge. (Courtesy of Trinity College Library Cambridge)
16. Trinity College Cambridge and apple tree. (GM)
17. Newton's Note Book. (Courtesy of Trinity College Library Cambridge)
18. Newton's diagram of his 'crucial experiment', 1672. (Royal Society Publishing under Creative Commons)
19. Newton's telescope. Photograph © Andrew Dunn, 5 November 2004. (Creative Commons/Public Domain)
20. Newton's astrolabe at Woolsthorpe Manor. (GM)
21. Isaac Barrow, the first Lucasian Professor of Mathematics at Cambridge University. (Wiki Commons)
22. Gresham College. (Welcome Collection, Creative Commons)
23. Sir Christopher Wren by Sir Godfrey Kneller, 1711 © National Portrait Gallery. (Getty Images/The Bridgeman Art Library)
24. Front cover of Hooke's Micrographia. (Courtesy of British Library)
25. Thames Frost Fair by Thomas Wyke 1683–84. (Museum of London/Public Domain)
26. Edmund Halley by Thomas Murray *c.*1690. (Wiki Commons/Royal Society Collection/Public Domain)
27. Front cover of Newton's *Principia Mathematica*. (Courtesy of Trinity College Cambs)
28. Isaac Newton by Sir Godfrey Kneller. Institute for Mathematical Sciences, University of Cambridge. (Wiki Commons)
29. St Martin's Street, London. (GM)
30. The Royal Society at Crane Court. Wood engraving after (W.H.), 1877. (Creative Commons Wellcome Collection image V0013121)
31. Charles Montagu 1st Earl of Halifax by Sir Godfrey Kneller.
32. Front cover of Newton's *Opticks*. (Wiki Commons/Public Domain)
33. A copy of Newton's *Opticks* at Woolsthorpe Manor. (GM)
    35. The modern electromagnetic spectrum. (Public Domain)
34. The Golden Record cover sent into outer space on the Voyager missions. (Public Domain)
35. The Earth taken from the Moon taken during the Apollo 11 mission. (NASSA/Public Domain)
36. Newton statue in Grantham, Lincolnshire. (GM)
37. Newton bust at Trinity College, Cambridge. (Courtesy of Trinity College)

INDEX